Brief

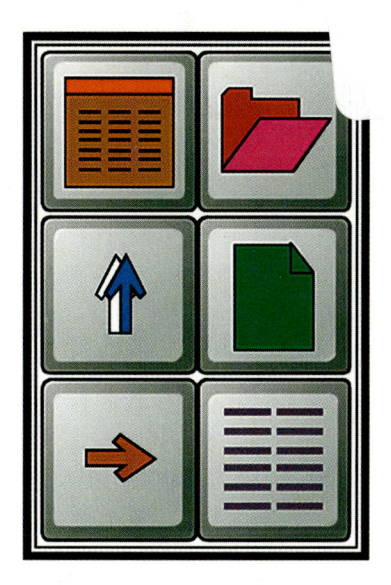

Microsoft®
Windows® 3.1 and DOS

JUNE JAMRICH PARSONS
University of the Virgin Islands

MICHAEL HALVORSON

A Susan Solomon Book

CTI

A DIVISION OF COURSE TECHNOLOGY
ONE MAIN STREET, CAMBRIDGE, MA 02142

an International Thomson Publishing company I(T)P

Cambridge • Albany • Bonn • Boston • Cincinnati • London • Madrid • Melbourne • Mexico City
New York • Paris • San Francisco • Singapore • Tokyo • Toronto • Washington

Brief Microsoft Windows 3.1 and DOS is published by Course Technology, Inc.

Editorial Director	Joseph B. Dougherty
Series Consulting Editor	Susan Solomon
Managing Editor	Marjorie Schlaikjer
Product Manager	David Crocco
Director of Production	Myrna D'Addario
Production Editor	Christine Spillett
Desktop Publishing Supervisor	Debbie Masi
Desktop Publishers	Tom Atwood
	Andrea Greitzer
	Debbie Masi
Copyeditor	Joan Wilcox
Proofreader	Erin C. Bridgeford
Indexer	Sherri S. Dietrich
Product Testing and Support Supervisor	Jeff Goding
Technical Reviewers	Erin C. Bridgeford
	Mark Vodnik
	Jane Dougherty
Manufacturing Manager	Elizabeth Martinez
Text Designer	Sally Steele
Illustrations	Andrew Giammarco
	illustrious, inc.
Cover Designer	John Gamache

Brief Microsoft Windows 3.1 and DOS © 1994 Course Technology, Inc.

All rights reserved. This publication is protected by federal copyright law. No part of this publication may be reproduced, stored in a retrieval system, or transmitted in any form or by any means, electronic, mechanical, photocopying, recording, or otherwise, or be used to make derivative work (such as translation or adaptation), without prior permission in writing from Course Technology, Inc.

Trademarks

Course Technology and the open book logo are registered trademarks of Course Technology, Inc.

Windows is a trademark of Microsoft Corporation.

Some of the product names and company names used in this book have been used for identification purposes only and may be trademarks or registered trademarks of their respective manufacturers and sellers.

Disclaimer

Course Technology, Inc. reserves the right to revise this publication and make changes from time to time in its content without notice.

ISBN 1-7600-4583-6

Printed in the United States of America

10 9 8 7 6 5 4 3 2 1

Preface

Course Technology, Inc. is proud to present this new book in its *Windows Series*. *Brief Microsoft Windows 3.1 and DOS* is designed to introduce students to the basic commands of DOS and Windows 3.1. This book capitalizes on the energy and enthusiasm students naturally have for Windows-based applications and clearly teaches students how to take full advantage of both DOS and Windows.

Organization and Coverage

Brief Microsoft Windows 3.1 and DOS begins with a chapter entitled "Essential Computer Concepts". This chapter includes concepts students need to know before they go into the lab. This is followed by a DOS module which introduces students to the most important DOS commands. This module is followed by two hands on tutorials on Microsoft Windows 3.1. Topics covered include menus, dialog boxes, using Help and file management.

Approach

Brief Microsoft Windows 3.1 and DOS distinguishes itself from other Windows textbooks because of its unique two-pronged approach. First, it motivates students by demonstrating *why* they need to learn the concepts and skills. This book teaches DOS and Windows using a task-driven, rather than a feature-driven approach. By working through the tutorials, students learn how to use DOS and Windows in situations they are likely to encounter in the workplace, rather than learn a laundry list of features one-by-one out of context. Second, the content, organization, and pedagogy of this book exploit the experimental nature of the Windows environment.

Features

Brief Microsoft Windows 3.1 and DOS is an exceptional textbook also because it includes the following features:

- **"Read This Before You Begin" Page** This page is consistent with Course Technology, Inc.'s unequaled commitment to helping instructors introduce technology into the classroom. Technical considerations and assumptions about hardware, software, and default settings are listed in one place to help instructors save time and eliminate unnecessary aggravation.
- **Tutorial Case** Each Windows tutorial begins with a business-related problem that students could reasonably encounter. Thus, the process of solving the problem will be meaningful to students. These cases touch on multicultural, international, and ethical issues—so important to today's business curriculum.
- **TROUBLE?** TROUBLE? paragraphs anticipate the mistakes that students are likely to make and help them recover from these mistakes. This feature facilitates independent learning and frees the instructor to focus on substantive conceptual issues rather than common procedural errors.

- **Task Reference** The Task Reference appears at the end of the book and summarizes how to accomplish tasks using the mouse, the menus, and the keyboard.
- **Questions, and Tutorial Assignments** Each tutorial concludes with meaningful, conceptual Questions that test students' understanding of what they learned in the tutorial. The Questions are followed by Tutorial Assignments, which provide students with additional hands-on practice of the skills they learned in the Tutorial.
- **Exploration Exercises** The Windows environment allows students to learn by exploring and discovering what they can do. The Exploration Exercises are Questions, or Tutorial Assignments designated by an **E** that encourage students to explore the capabilities of the computing environment they are using and to extend their knowledge using the Windows on-line Help facility and other reference materials.

The CTI WinApps Setup Disk

The CTI WinApps Setup Disk, bundled with the Instructor's copy of this book, contains an innovative Student Disk generating program that is designed to save instructors time. Once this software is installed on a network or a standalone workstation, students can double click the "Make *Win 3.1* Student Disk" icon in the CTI WinApps icon group. Double clicking this icon transfers all the data files students need to complete the tutorials, and Tutorial Assignments, to a high-density disk in drive A or B. These files free students from tedious keystroking and allow them to concentrate on mastering the concept or task at hand.

Adopters of this text are granted the right to install the CTI WinApps icon group on any standalone computer or network used by students who have purchased this text.

For more information on the CTI WinApps Setup Disk, see the page in this book called *Read This Before You Begin*.

Supplements

- **Instructor's Manual** The Instructor's Manual is written by the author *(or authors)* and is quality assurance tested. It includes:
  - Answers and solutions to all of the Questions, and Tutorial Assignments. Suggested solutions are also included for the Exploration Exercises
  - A disk (3.5-inch) containing solutions to all of the Questions, and Tutorial Assignments
  - Tutorial Notes, which contain background information from the authors about the Tutorial Case and the instructional progression of the tutorial
  - Technical Notes, which indclude troubleshooting tips as well as information on how to customize the students' screens to closely emulate the screen shots in the book
  - Transparency Masters of key concepts

Acknowledgments

The author(s) would like to thank the following individuals for their support on this very exciting project: Gary Armstrong, Shippensburg University; Warren Boe, University of Iowa; Sue Cox, Suffolk Community College; Judy Sunayama Foster, Diablo Valley College; Charles Hommel, University of Puget Sound; and Joseph Limmer, Saint Louis Community College at Meramec and Anheuser-Busch, Inc.

Also special thanks to Christine Spillett, Erin Bridgeford, Andrea Greitzer and Tom Atwood for their production expertise; Dan Oja for his excellent software engineering; and Susan Solomon, David Crocco and Joe Dougherty for their editorial vision.

Contents

Preface	iv

Essential Computer Concepts — EC 3

What is a Computer?	EC 5
Types of Computers	EC 7
Computer Hardware	EC 10
Data Communications	EC 22
Computer Software	EC 27
Index	EC 37

Introduction to DOS Tutorials — DOS 1

Introduction to DOS

Using the DOS Operating System and Essential DOS Commands	DOS 3
Getting Started with DOS	DOS 3
Starting Your Computer	DOS 4
The DOS Prompt	DOS 4
Checking the DOS Version	DOS 5
Setting the Time and Date	DOS 5
Getting Help from DOS	DOS 6
Viewing Your Disk Using the DIR Command	DOS 7
Creating a File Using the EDIT Utility	DOS 9
Viewing a File Using the TYPE Command	DOS 12
Renaming a File Using the RENAME Command	DOS 13
Duplicating a File Using the COPY Command	DOS 14
Deleting a File Using the DEL Command	DOS 14
Creating Subdirectories	DOS 15
Understanding Floppy Disks	DOS 17

	Working with Floppy Disks	DOS 19
	Questions	DOS 21
	Tutorial Assignments	DOS 22

DOS Index   DOS 23

Microsoft Windows 3.1 Tutorials   WIN 1

	Read This Before You Begin	WIN 2

TUTORIAL 1   Essential Windows Skills

Using the Program Manager, the CTI Keyboard Tutorial, the CTI Mouse Practice, CTI WinApps and Windows Menus, Dialog Boxes, Toolbar and Help	WIN 3
Using the Windows Tutorials Effectively	**WIN 4**
Starting Your Computer and Launching Windows	WIN 4
Basic Windows Controls and Concepts	**WIN 5**
Organizing Application Windows on the Desktop	WIN 11
Using Windows to Specify Tasks	**WIN 19**
Using Paintbrush to Develop Your Windows Technique	WIN 26
Questions	**WIN 33**
Tutorial Assignments	**WIN 35**

TUTORIAL 2   Effective File Management

Using the File Manager   WIN 37

Files and the File Manager	WIN 38
Formatting a Disk	WIN 41
Preparing Your Student Disk	WIN 43
Finding Out What's On Your Disks	WIN 44
Changing the Current Drive	WIN 45
The File Manager Window	WIN 46
The Directory Tree	WIN 47
Organizing Your Files	WIN 48
Expanding and Collapsing Directories	WIN 50
The Contents List	WIN 50
Filenames and Extensions	WIN 51
Moving Files	WIN 52
Renaming Files	WIN 55
Deleting Files	WIN 56
Data Backup	WIN 56
The Copy Command	WIN 57
Copying Files Using a Single Disk Drive	WIN 58
Making a Disk Backup	WIN 60
Questions	WIN 62
Tutorial Assignments	WIN 63

Windows Tutorials Index   WIN 65

Windows Task Reference   WIN 69

Photography Credits

Figure		Credit	Page
1	PC	Courtesy of International Business Machines	EC 4
	printer	Photo courtesy of Hewlett-Packard Company	EC 4
2		Courtesy of International Business Machines	EC 5
4		Courtesy of International Business Machines	EC 7
5		Reprinted with permission of Compaq Computer Corporation All rights reserved	EC 8
6		Courtesy of Toshiba America Information Systems, Inc.	EC 8
7		Courtesy of International Business Machines	EC 8
8		Courtesy of International Business Machines	EC 9
9		Photo by Paul Shambroom, courtesy of Cray Research, Inc.	EC 9
12		Courtesy of Microsoft Corporation	EC 11
13		Courtesy of Intel Corporation	EC 12
18		Courtesy of NEC Technologies, Inc.	EC 16
20		Courtesy of Panasonic Communications Systems Company	EC 16
22		Photo courtesy of Hewlett-Packard Company	EC 17
23		Photo courtesy of Hewlett-Packard Company	EC 17
26		Richard Morgenstein	EC 19
27		Richard Morgenstein	EC 20
28		Photo courtesy of Seagate Technology, Inc.	EC 20
32		Toshiba's XM-3301 Series CD-ROM disc drive	EC 24
35		Courtesy of Microsoft Corporation	EC 29
36		Courtesy of Microsoft Corporation	EC 30
37		Used with permission of Borland International, Inc.	EC 30
1-4	3-button mouse	Photo courtesy of Logitech, Inc.	WIN 7
	2-button mouse	Courtesy of International Business Machines	WIN 7

Essential Computer Concepts

What is a Computer?

Types of Computers

Computer Hardware

Data Communications

Computer Software

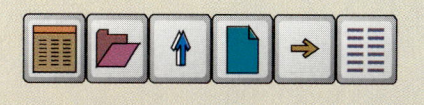

Essential Computer Concepts

OBJECTIVES

In this chapter you will learn:

- The major components of a computer system
- The terms used to specify the capacity and the speed of computer memory, processors, and storage
- How data are represented by the binary number system and the ASCII code
- The common types of network cards and network software
- How peripheral devices are connected to a computer system
- The basic concepts of data communications
- The difference between systems software and applications software

CASE **PR #516859** It is Tenzing Lu's first day in the purchasing department of International ComAir. Her main responsibility is to review purchase requisitions, the paperwork that departmental managers submit to purchase equipment and supplies. Tenzing must find the vendor with the best price and then fill out a purchase order form, which will be sent to the vendor as the official order.

The first purchase requisition, PR #516859, is for a computer system and has a computer ad stapled to it (Figure 1). Tenzing studies the ad for a few minutes and then asks her boss, Pat Kenslea, what the usual procedure is for computer purchases. Pat explains that since prices change so rapidly in the computer industry, it is important to get price quotes from several vendors. She also warns Tenzing that the prices must be for a system with the correct configuration and technical specifications for International ComAir's needs.

ESSENTIAL COMPUTER CONCEPTS

After considering this procedure, Tenzing confesses that she doesn't have much technical background in computers and asks if there is some way to pick up the basics quickly. Pat appreciates Tenzing's initiative and pulls out some reference materials and recent computer magazines from her bookshelf. Pat suggests that Tenzing read through the reference materials and then browse through the magazines to get an idea of current prices and features.

If you were a purchasing agent for International ComAir, what would you buy? Does the ad in Figure 1 represent a viable system configuration? How much do you think the system should cost? The information in this chapter will help you answer these questions by developing your understanding of computer technology and terminology.

Computer Daily   July, 1996   page 78

System includes:
- 66 MHz 486 processor
- 8 MB RAM expandable to 32 MB
- Novell compatible
- 1.44 MB 3.5" and 1.2 MB 5.25" floppy drives
- 245 MB 12 ms hard disk drive
- Super VGA 1024 x 768 .28 dot pitch 14" monitor
- 2 serial ports
- 1 parallel port
- 8 expansion slots
- 101 keyboard
- Microsoft DOS 6.2
- Microsoft compatible mouse
- 9600 baud modem (Hayes compatible)
- 8 ppm laser printer with cable

All for the low price of $

NEW

INTERNATIONAL COMAIR — PURCHASE REQUISITION

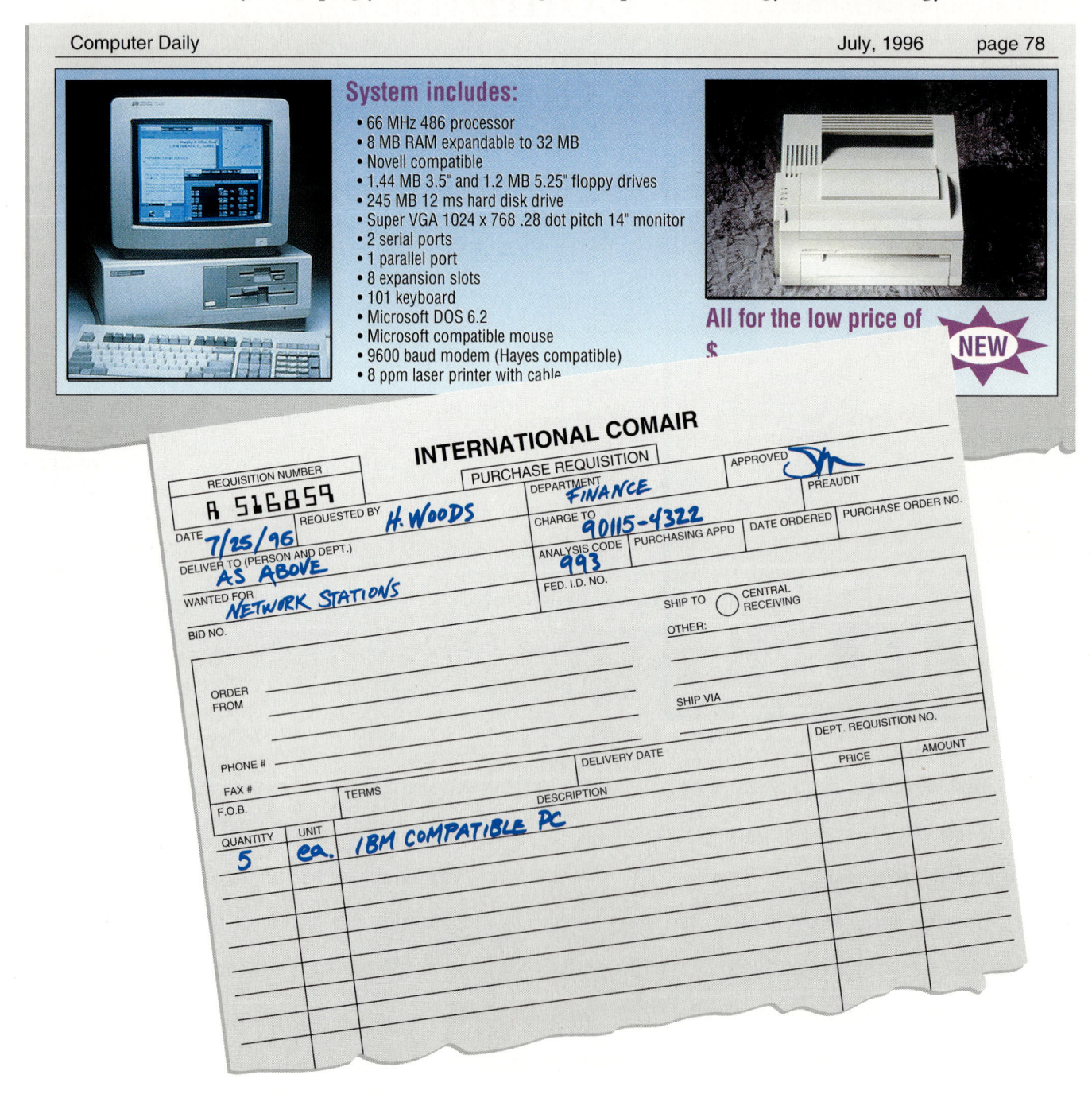

REQUISITION NUMBER: A 516859
REQUESTED BY: H. WOODS
DEPARTMENT: FINANCE
APPROVED: [signature]
DATE: 7/25/96
CHARGE TO: 90115-4322
ANALYSIS CODE: 993
DELIVER TO: AS ABOVE
WANTED FOR: NETWORK STATIONS

QUANTITY: 5   UNIT: ea.   DESCRIPTION: IBM COMPATIBLE PC

Figure 1: Purchase requisition #516859 and attached computer ad

Figure 2:
Office workers at their computers

What Is a Computer?

Computers have become essential tools in almost every type of activity in virtually every type of business (Figure 2). A **computer** can be defined as an electronic device that accepts information, performs arithmetic and logical operations using that information, and then produces the required results. It is a versatile tool with the potential to perform many different tasks.

A **computer system** is composed of a computer and additional devices such as a printer. A computer system can manage financial information, create and manipulate graphs, record day-to-day business transactions, help managers make critical business decisions, maintain inventories, and perform many other tasks to help business personnel be more efficient and productive.

The components of a computer system that you can see and touch are referred to as **hardware**. Keyboards, screens, disk drives, printers, and circuit boards are all examples of hardware. The selection of components that make up a particular computer system is referred to as the **configuration**. The technical details about the speed, the capacity, or the size of each component are called **specifications**. So, a computer system might be *configured* to include a printer, and a *specification* for that printer might be a print speed of eight pages per minute.

Software refers to the components of a computer system, particularly the **programs**, or lists of instructions, that are needed to make the computer perform a specific task. Software is the key to a computer's versatility. When your computer is using word processing software, for example, the Microsoft Word program, you can type memos, letters, and reports. When your computer is using accounting software, such as the DacEasy accounts receivable program, you can maintain information about what your customers owe you.

The hardware and the software of a computer system work together to process **data**—the words, figures, and graphics that describe people, events, things, and ideas.

EC 6   ESSENTIAL COMPUTER CONCEPTS

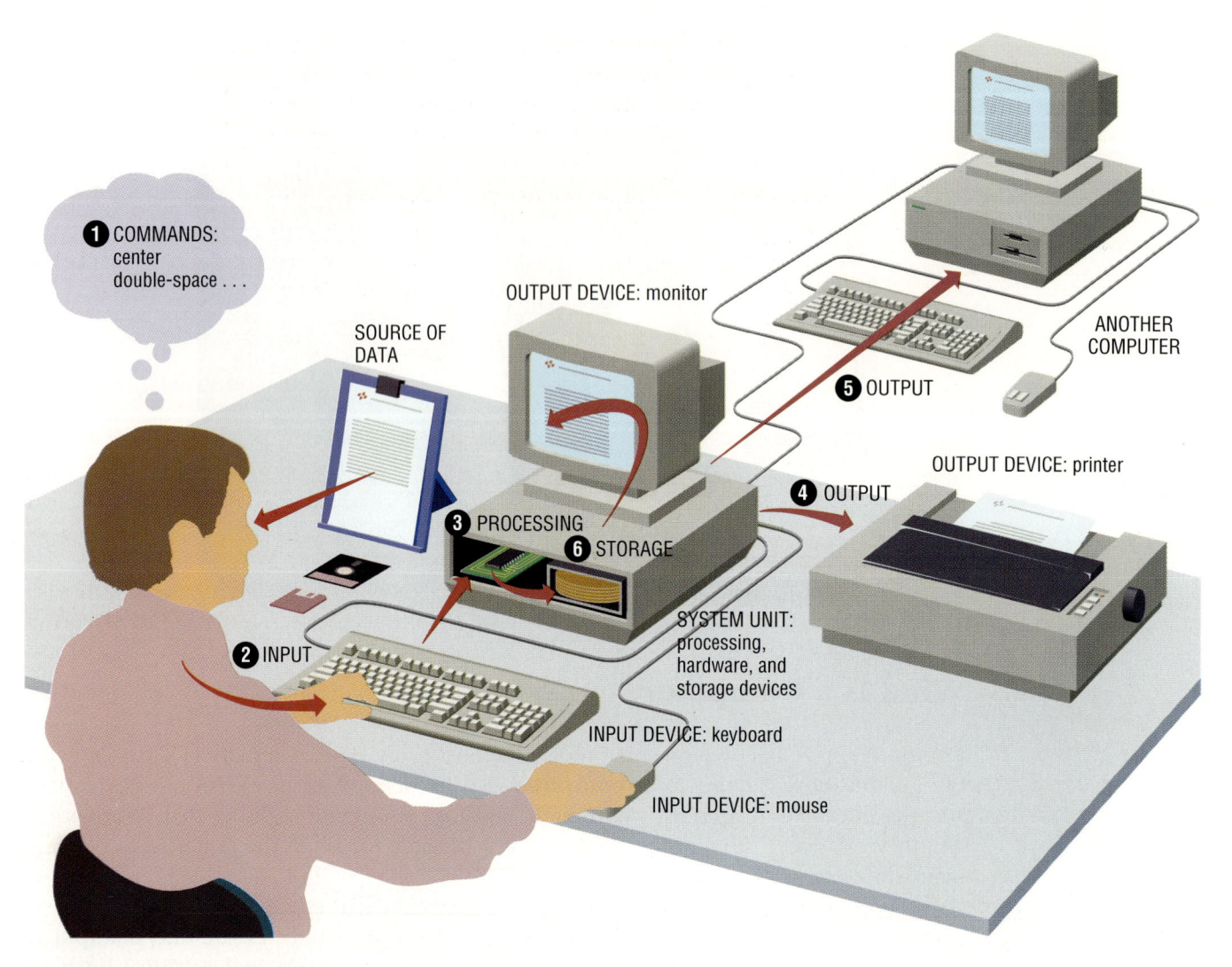

Figure 3: Data are input, processed, stored, and output

Figure 3 shows how you, the computer, the data, and the software interact to get work done. Let's say you want to write a report. First, you would instruct the computer to use the word processing program (1). Once the word processing program has been activated, you would begin to type the text of your report (2). What you type into the computer is called **input**. You might also need to issue commands that tell the computer exactly how to process your input—maybe you want the title to be centered and the text to be double-spaced. You use an **input device**, such as a keyboard or a mouse, to input data and issue commands.

The computer would process the report according to your commands and the instructions contained in the software—the title would be centered and all the text double-spaced. **Processing** changes the data that you have input (3), for example, by moving text, sorting lists, or performing calculations. The processing takes place on the **main circuit board** of the computer, also referred to as the **main board** or the **mother board**, which contains the computer's major electronic components. The electronic components of the main circuit board are referred to as **processing hardware**.

After you have written your report, you might want to print it out (4). The results of computer processing are called **output**. The printers and screens that display output are called **output devices**. Or, instead of dealing with printed output, you might want to send the report electronically (5) so that it gets to a co-worker almost immediately. Sending data from one computer to another is referred to as **data communications**. To send your report to another computer you use a **communications device**.

When you have finished working, you would use a **storage device** (6), such as a disk drive, to save your report on some sort of **storage medium**, such as a disk. The text of your report would be stored on the disk as a **file** under the filename of your choice.

Types of Computers

Computers often are classified by their size, speed, and cost. **Microcomputers**, also called **personal computers (PCs)**, are inexpensive—$500 to $15,000—and small enough to fit on an office desk. Two typical desktop configurations are shown in Figure 4 and Figure 5 (on the following page). Figure 4 shows a standard horizontal system unit. The vertical system unit in Figure 5 is referred to as a **tower case**.

Desktop computers receive their power from a wall outlet, which makes them basically stationary. Notebook microcomputers, such as the one in Figure 6 (on the following page), are transportable. They are smaller and lighter than desktop microcomputers and use rechargeable batteries.

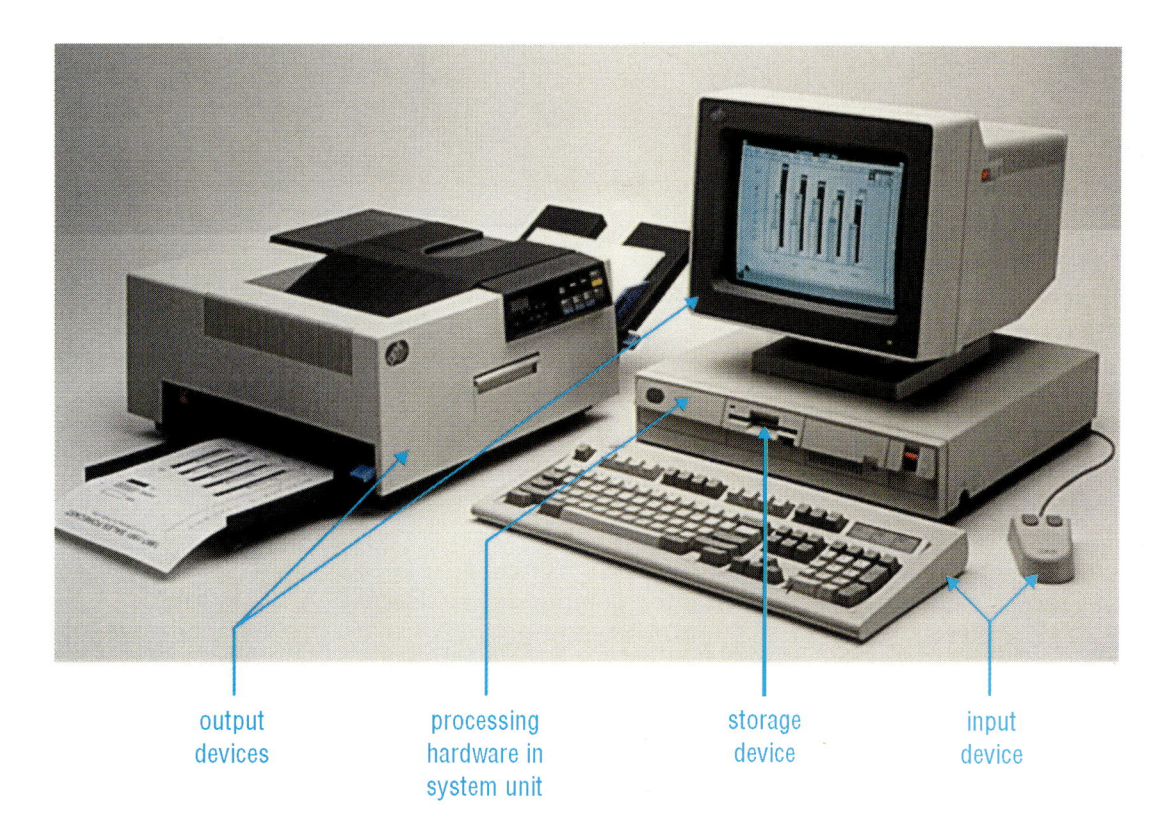

Figure 4: Standard desktop microcomputer system

EC 8   ESSENTIAL COMPUTER CONCEPTS

storage devices | processing hardware in tower system unit | input device | output devices

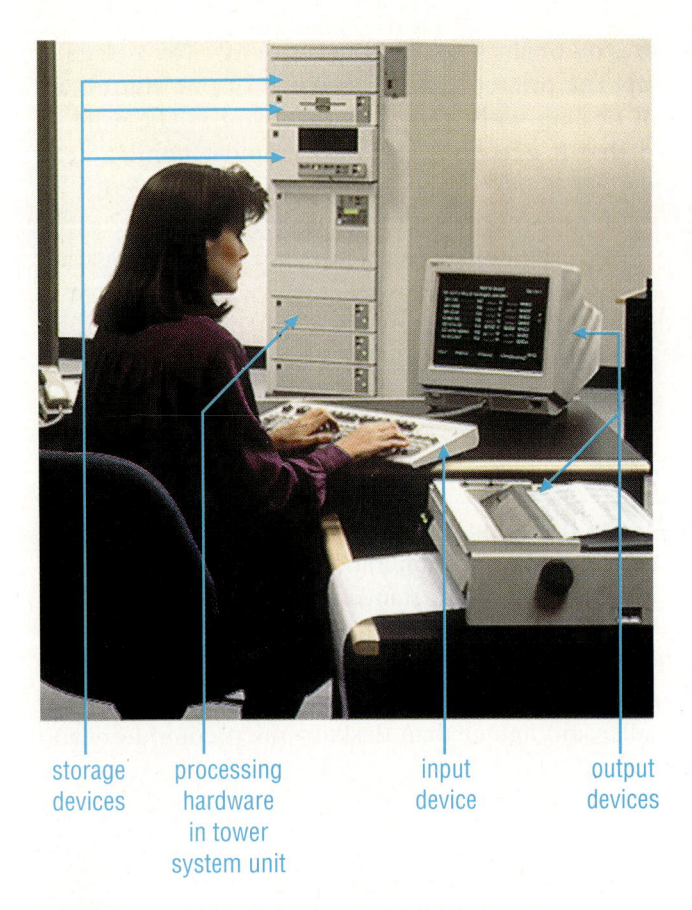

Figure 5: Desktop microcomputer with tower system unit

processing hardware | input device | input device | storage device | output device

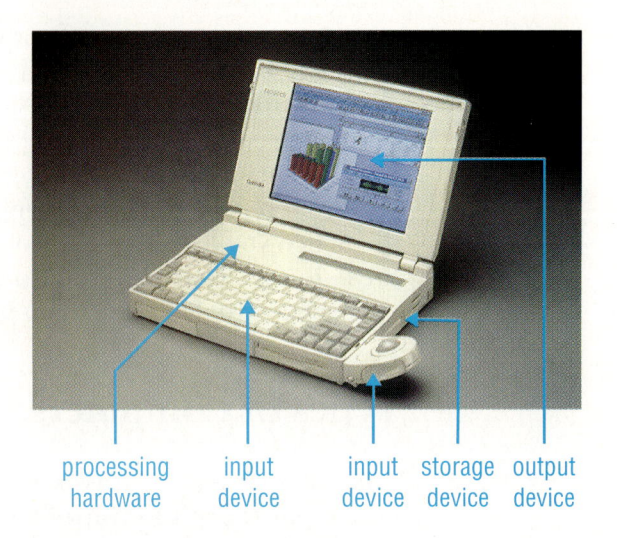

Figure 6: A notebook computer

output device | input device | processing hardware | storage devices

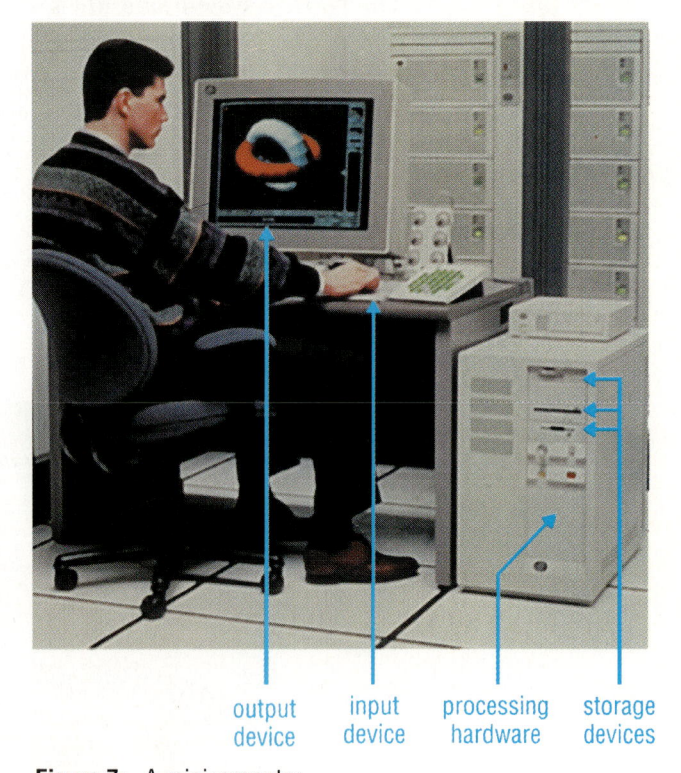

Figure 7: A minicomputer

Though smaller in size, a notebook computer generally costs more than a desktop computer with equivalent specifications.

Microcomputers are used extensively in small and large businesses. But some businesses, government agencies, and other institutions also use larger and faster types of computers: minicomputers, mainframes, and supercomputers.

Minicomputers, such as the one in Figure 7, are too large and too heavy for desktops. They operate three to 25 times faster than microcomputers and cost anywhere from $15,000 to $500,000. **Mainframe computers**, like the one shown in Figure 8, are larger and more powerful than minicomputers. Mainframes have large capacities for storing and manipulating data, operate 10 to 100 times faster than microcomputers, and cost between $100,000 and $2 million.

Types of Computers **EC 9**

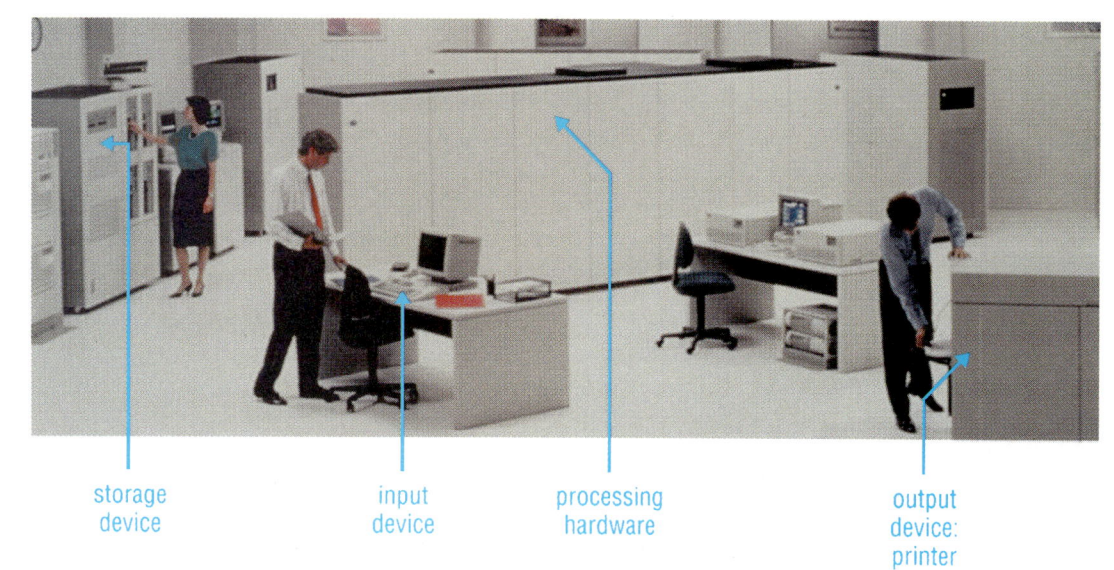

Figure 8:
A mainframe computer

storage device · input device · processing hardware · output device: printer

The largest and fastest computers, called **supercomputers**, are so expensive that only the largest companies, government agencies, and universities can afford them. Supercomputers, such as the one shown in Figure 9, operate 50 to 10,000 times faster than microcomputers.

processing hardware

With the accelerated development of newer and better computers, the guidelines for classifying types of computers have become fuzzy. For example, some recently developed microcomputers operate at higher speeds than some minicomputers.

Now consider the ad attached to PR #516859, the purchase requisition at the beginning of this chapter. How would Tenzing classify the computer in that ad? If your answer is "a desktop microcomputer," you are correct. The computer in that ad fits on a desktop, is not portable, and probably costs $1,000 to $2,000.

The remainder of this chapter will focus on microcomputer hardware and software concepts. These concepts will help you to use successfully the software featured in the tutorial chapters.

Figure 9: A Cray supercomputer

Computer Hardware

As you've already learned, computer hardware can be defined as the components of a computer that you can see and touch. Let's now look at the hardware you might use in a typical microcomputer system.

Input Devices

As you have already seen, you can input data and commands by using an input device such as a keyboard or a mouse. The computer can also receive input from a storage device. This section takes a closer look at the input devices you might use. Storage devices are covered in a later section.

Figure 10 shows an 83-key IBM PC-style keyboard; Figure 11 shows an enhanced 101-key IBM PS/2-style keyboard. Both keyboards consist of three major parts: the main keyboard, the numeric keypad, and the function keys. The major difference between the two keyboards is that the enhanced keyboard contains a separate editing keypad. In general these keyboards can do the same things, but the enhanced keyboard makes it easier to do some editing and input tasks. Ask your instructor which keyboard you'll be using.

Your computer also should be equipped with a pointing device such as a **mouse** (Figure 12). As you push or pull the mouse on the surface of your desk, a **pointer** moves on the screen. Using the mouse, you can position the pointer anywhere on the screen,

Figure 10: Standard 83-key keyboard

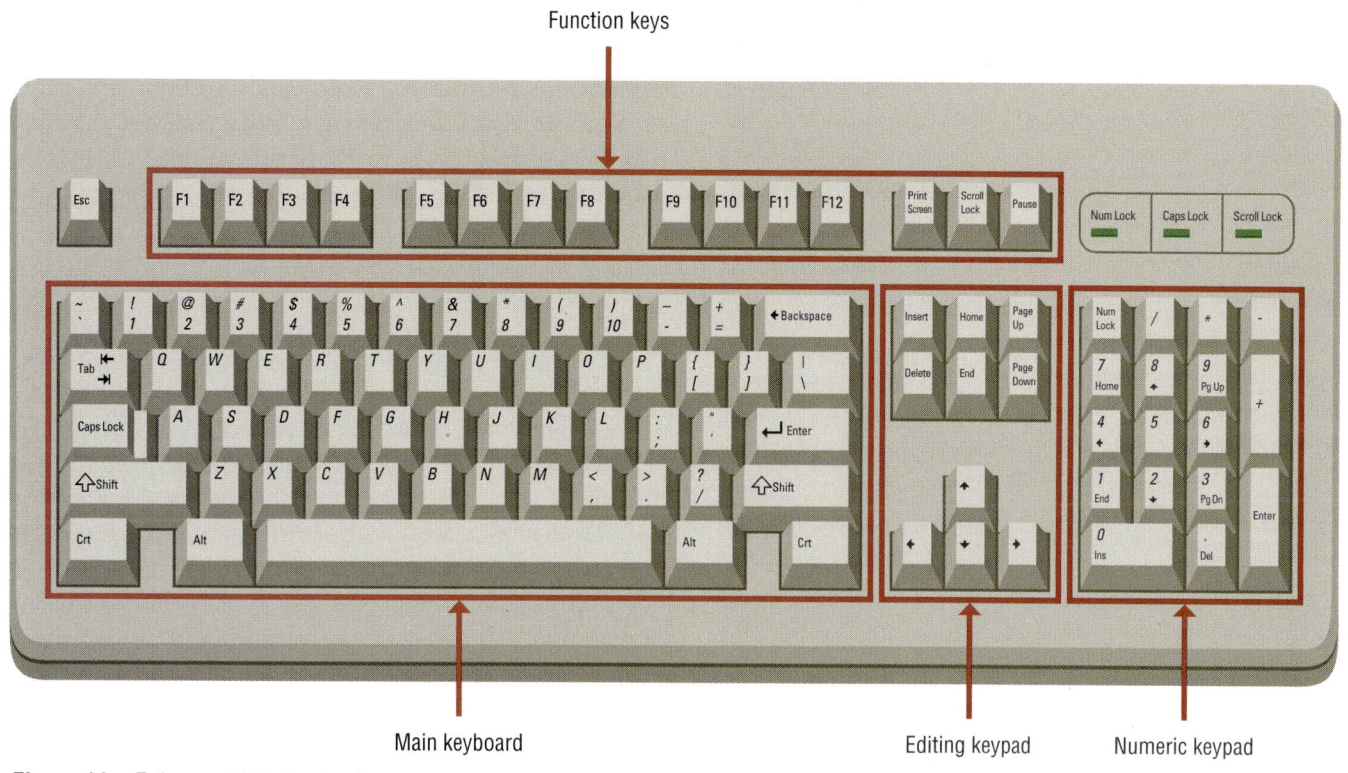

Figure 11: Enhanced 101-key keyboard

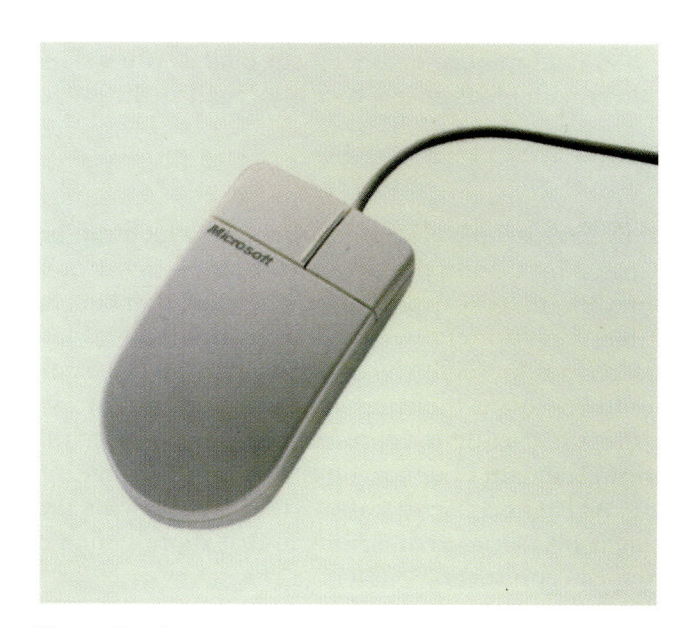

Figure 12: A mouse

manipulate pictorial objects on the screen, and select commands.

Some computer programs, such as Microsoft Windows, are specifically designed to be used with a mouse. If a mouse is not included with your computer system, you can generally add one.

Now that you have read about input devices, refer back to the ad attached to PR #516859 at the beginning of the chapter. Can you list the input devices included with the advertised system? If you said that the system comes with two input devices, a mouse and a keyboard, you are right. You also might have noted that the keyboard is an enhanced 101-key keyboard with a separate editing keypad.

Processing Hardware

The two most important components of microcomputer hardware are the **microprocessor**, sometimes called the **central processing unit (CPU)**, and the **memory**, which stores instructions and data. You should know what type microprocessor is in your computer, and you should know its memory capacity. These factors directly affect the price of a computer and the efficiency of its performance.

Figure 13: An Intel 80486 microprocessor, found in many IBM-compatible computers

THE MICROPROCESSOR

The microprocessor is an **integrated circuit**—an electronic component often called a "chip"—on the main circuit board of the computer. The most popular microprocessors in IBM-compatible computers are the Intel 8088, 8086, 80286, 80386, 80486, and Pentium (Figure 13). The numbers are simply model numbers designated by the manufacturer. Models of more recent processors often are abbreviated 286, 386, and 486. Generally speaking, the higher the model number, the more powerful the microprocessor; this means that the microprocessor can handle larger chunks of data and can process data faster.

The speed of a microprocessor is determined by its clock rate. The computer clock is part of a group of circuits associated with the microprocessor. Think of the **clock rate** as the heartbeat or the pulse of the computer. The higher the clock rate, the faster the computer. Clock rate is measured in millions of cycles per second, or **megahertz (MHz)**. The Intel 8088 microprocessor on the first IBM PC models operated at only 4.77 MHz. The newer Intel Pentium microprocessor typically operates at 90 MHz.

Let's take another look at the ad attached to PR #516859. What is the type and the speed of the microprocessor? Your answer should be that it is an 80486 microprocessor, that can operate at 66 MHz. Since the 486 microprocessor is a recent model, you would expect it to be more costly than computers with older microprocessors such as the 8088, 80286, and 80386.

DATA REPRESENTATION

Within a computer, data is represented by microscopic electronic switches, which can be either off or on. The off switch is designated by a 0 and the on switch by a 1. Each 1 or 0 is called a **binary digit,** or **bit**, for short. Bits are very handy for representing numbers in the binary number system. A series of bits can also represent character data, such as letters and punctuation marks. Each character is represented by a pattern of 1s and 0s, similar to using patterns of dots and dashes to represent the letters of the alphabet in Morse code. Microcomputers commonly use the **ASCII code** to represent character data. ASCII (pronounced "ask-ee") stands for American Standard Code for Information Interchange.

A string of eight bits is called a **byte**. As Figure 14 shows, the byte that represents the integer value 0 is 00000000, with all eight bits set to zero. The byte that represents the integer value 1 is 0000001, and the byte that represents 255 is 11111111.

Each byte can also represent a character such as the letter A or the symbol $. For example, Figure 15 shows that in ASCII code the letter A is represented by the byte 01000001, the letter B by 01000010, and the letter C by 01000011. The symbol $ is represented by 00100100. The phrase "Thank you!" is represented by 10 bytes—each of the eight letters requires one byte, and the space and the exclamation point also require one byte each. To find out how many *bits* are needed to represent the phrase "Thank You!", multiply the number of bytes by eight, since there are eight bits in each byte.

Number	Binary Representation
0	00000000
1	00000001
2	00000010
3	00000011
4	00000100
5	00000101
6	00000110
7	00000111
8	00001000
⋮	⋮
14	00001110
15	00001111
16	00010000
17	00010001
⋮	⋮
253	11111101
254	11111110
255	11111111

Figure 14: Binary representation of the numbers 0 through 255

Character	ASCII
A	01000001
B	01000010
C	01000011
D	01000100
E	01000101
F	01000110
G	01000111
H	01001000
I	01001001
J	01001010
K	01001011
L	01001100
M	01001101
N	01001110
O	01001111
P	01010000
Q	01010001
R	01010010
S	01010011
T	01010100
U	01010101
V	01010110
W	01010111
X	01011000
Y	01011001
Z	01011010
#	00100011
$	00100100
%	00100101
&	00100110

Figure 15: ASCII code representing the letters A to Z and the symbols # $ % &

Byte values can represent not only integers and characters but also other types of data or program instructions. A computer can determine the difference between the various types of data or instructions based on the context of the byte value, just as you can tell, based on context, the difference between the two meanings of the word *hit* in the sentences "He hit me in the arm" and "The movie was a big hit."

As a computer user you don't have to know the binary representations of numbers, characters, and instructions, because the computer handles all the necessary conversions internally. However, because the amount of memory in a computer and the storage capacity of disks are expressed in bytes, you should be aware of how data is represented so you will understand the capacity and the limitations of your computer.

MEMORY

Computer **memory** is a set of storage locations on the main circuit board. Your computer has two types of memory: read-only memory and random-access memory.

Read-only memory (ROM) is the part of memory reserved for a special set of commands that are required for the internal workings of the computer. The microprocessor can read these commands but cannot erase or change them. When you turn off your computer, the commands in ROM remain intact and ready for use when you turn the computer on again.

Random-access memory (RAM) temporarily stores data and program instructions. RAM is measured in kilobytes (K or KB) and megabytes (MB). The prefix *kilo* (pronounced "kee-lo") means one thousand, but for historical and technical reasons a **kilobyte** is actually 1024 bytes. The prefix *mega* usually means one million, but a **megabyte** is precisely 1,024 × 1,024—or 1,048,576—bytes. As shown in Figure 16, each RAM storage location can hold one character of data. Most IBM-compatible microcomputers have a minimum of 640K of RAM. A 640K computer can hold the equivalent of 655,360 (640 × 1,024) characters in RAM.

RAM is one of the most critical elements of a computer system. To use an analogy, we could say that RAM is the major traffic hub of the micro world, where data and instructions wait until it is time to travel elsewhere to be processed or stored. Figure 17 illustrates the flow of data in and out of RAM. When you first switch on your computer, operating system instructions are loaded into an area of RAM, where they remain until you turn the computer off (1). The **operating system** controls many essential internal activities of the computer system. When you want to use an application program, such as a word processor, all or part of the application program is loaded into RAM (2). When you input data from a device such as the keyboard, the data is temporarily stored in RAM (3).

Operating system instructions and program instructions are sent from RAM to the microprocessor for processing (4). Any data needed for the processing indicated by these instructions is fetched from RAM (5). After the data has been processed, the results are sent back into RAM (6). If you want a permanent record of the results, the data is stored (7) or output (8). When you have finished using an application, RAM is freed up for the next program you want to use. When you turn your computer off, all the data in RAM disappears.

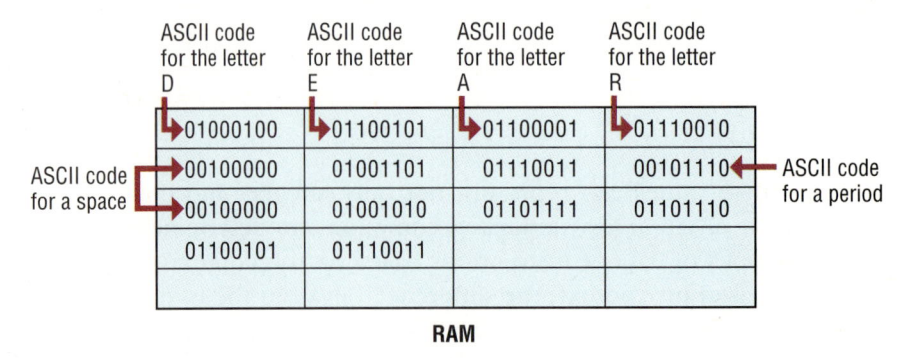

	ASCII code for the letter D	ASCII code for the letter E	ASCII code for the letter A	ASCII code for the letter R	
	01000100	01100101	01100001	01110010	
ASCII code for a space	00100000	01001101	01110011	00101110	ASCII code for a period
	00100000	01001010	01101111	01101110	
	01100101	01110011			

RAM

Figure 16: A conceptual model of how data (DEAR[space] MS. [space] JONES) is stored in RAM in ASCII code

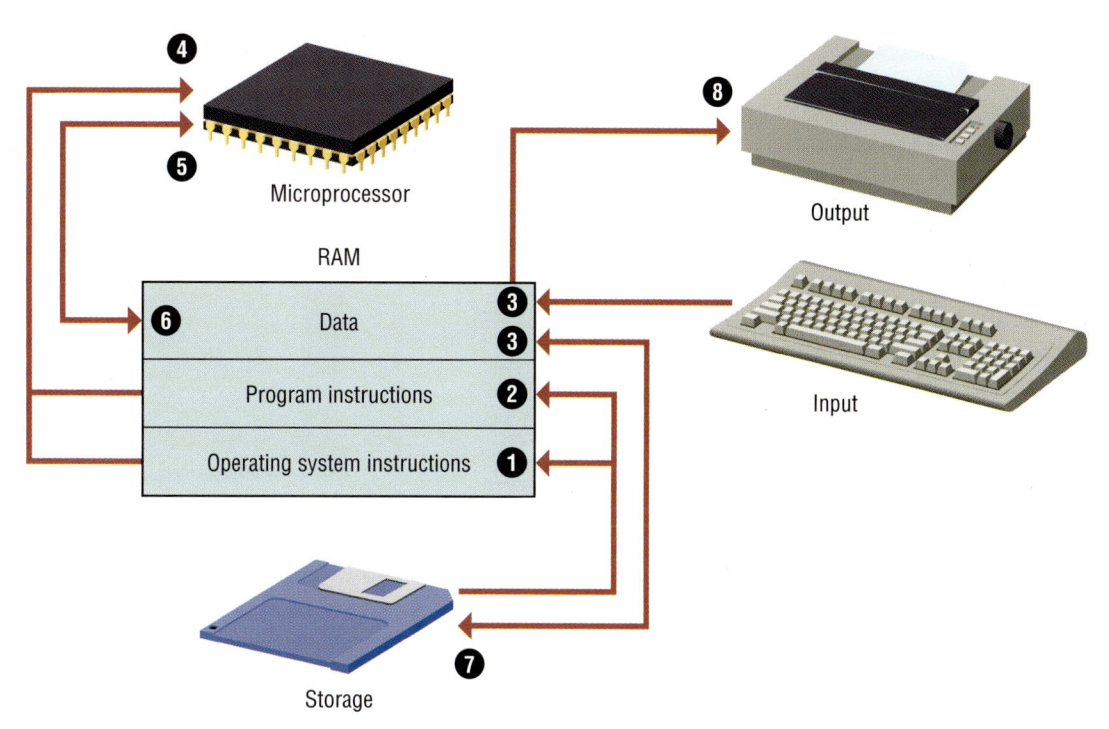

Figure 17: RAM is a temporary storage area for data, programs, and the operating system

Large programs generally require large amounts of RAM. The amount of RAM required for an application program usually is specified on the package or in the program documentation. Computers configured with more RAM typically cost more than those with smaller amounts of RAM. It is usually possible to expand the amount of RAM in a computer up to a specified limit.

Take another look at the ad attached to PR #516859. How much RAM is included with the computer? What is the maximum amount of RAM that can be installed? You are correct if you said that 8MB of RAM are included and that the RAM can be expanded to a maximum of 32MB.

Output Devices

Output is the result of processing data; **output devices** show you those results. The most commonly used output devices are monitors and printers.

A **monitor** is the TV-like video screen that displays the output from a computer (Figure 18 on the following page). Most desktop computer monitors use **cathode ray tube (CRT)** technology, while notebook computers use a flat-panel display technology such as a **liquid crystal display (LCD)**.

Figure 19 (on the following page) shows how text and graphics displayed on computer monitors are created with little dots of light called **pixels**, short for "picture elements." The entire monitor screen is a grid of pixels that combine to create the illusion of a continuous image. A **color graphics adapter (CGA)** monitor has a grid that is 320 pixels across and 200 pixels high. A **video graphics array (VGA)** monitor has a 640 × 480 grid, and a super VGA monitor has a maximum grid size of 800 × 600 or 1024 × 768. As the number of pixels in the grid increases, the **resolution** of the monitor increases. Monitors with higher resolution have displays that are clearer, sharper, and easier to read.

A **display card**—also called a **display adapter**, **video controller**, or **graphics adapter**—connects the monitor to the main circuit board of the computer. The display card must match the monitor. For example, suppose you have purchased a super VGA monitor to add to your current computer system. You need to check the specification sheet that accompanied your old display card to see if it will work with the new monitor. If the specification sheet indicates that the original display card is not compatible with your new monitor, you will need to purchase a new display card.

Figure 18: A color monitor

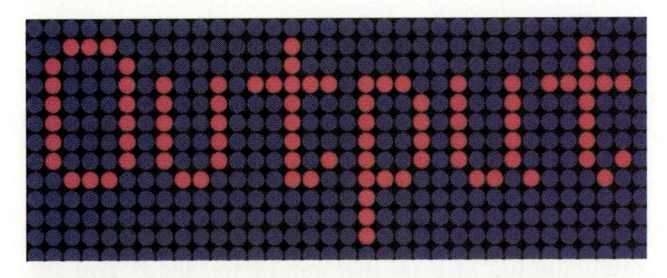

Figure 19: Pixels combining to form the word "output"

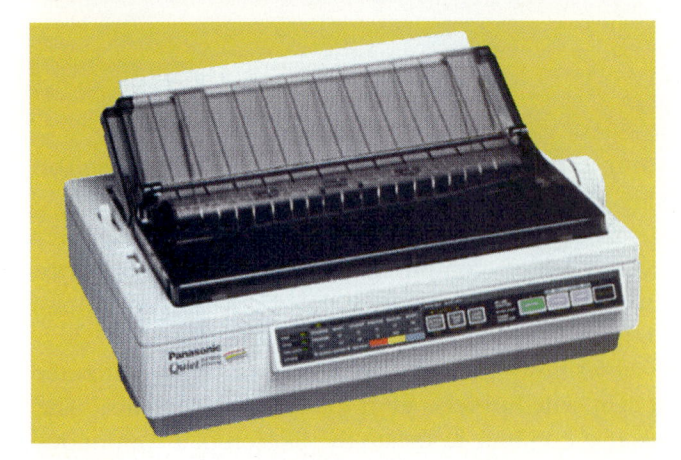

Figure 20: A dot-matrix printer

A **printer** produces a paper copy of the text or graphics processed by the computer. A paper copy of computer output is called **hard copy**, because it is more tangible than the electronic or magnetic copies found on a disk, in the computer memory, or on the monitor.

The three most popular types of printers are dot-matrix, ink-jet, and laser printers. **Dot-matrix printers**, like the one shown in Figure 20, form text and graphic images by producing tiny dots of ink on the printer paper. The dots are formed when pins strike an inked ribbon. Less expensive dot-matrix printers have nine pins. More expensive models have 24 pins and produce higher-quality output. Figure 21 shows text that was output in two different modes: draft mode and near-letter-quality mode. **Draft mode** prints very quickly but produces relatively low-quality print, while **near-letter-quality (NLQ) mode** prints more slowly but produces higher-quality print. The speed of a dot-matrix printer usually is measured in characters per second (cps).

Ink-jet printers, like the one in Figure 22, spray tiny dots of ink onto the paper to form text and graphics. Ink-jet printers are quieter than dot-matrix printers and produce graphics of reasonable quality and text of high quality. The speed of an ink-jet printer is comparable to that of a dot-matrix printer.

Computer Hardware   EC 17

Figure 21: Sample output from a dot-matrix printer

Figure 22: An inkjet printer

Laser printers, such as the model in Figure 23, use laser beams to bond a black powdery substance, called **toner**, to the paper. The technology is similar to that used in copy machines. The speed of a laser printer is usually indicated in pages per minute (ppm). Laser printers are quiet and fast and produce the highest-quality printing of any type of printer. For those reasons laser printers are becoming the standard type of printer in the business world.

Figure 23: A laser printer

Return to the beginning of the chapter and list the output device(s) included with the computer system in PR #516859. If you listed a monitor and a laser printer, you are correct.

Storage Devices and Media

Because RAM retains data only while the power is on, your computer must have a more permanent storage option. As Figure 24 shows, a **storage device** receives data from RAM and writes it on a storage medium, such as a disk. Later the data can be read and sent back to RAM. So a storage device is used not only to store data but also for data input and output.

There are a variety of microcomputer storage devices, each using a particular storage medium (Figure 25). Hard disk drives store data on hard disks and floppy disk drives store data on floppy disks; tape drives store data on tape cartridges or cassettes; and CD-ROM drives store data on compact discs.

Floppy disks, sometimes called diskettes, are flat circles of oxide-coated plastic enclosed in a square case called a **disk jacket**. The most common sizes of disks for microcomputers are 5.25" and 3.5" (Figure 26). The 5.25" disks have flexible disk jackets and are usually stored in paper sleeves for protection. The 3.5" disks have hard plastic cases and don't require sleeves.

The most common types of disks are double-sided, double-density (DS/DD) and double-sided, high-density (DS/HD). The 5.25" DS/DD disks have a capacity of 360K, and the 3.5" DS/DD disks have a capacity of 720K. The 5.25" DS/HD disks have a capacity of 1.2MB, and the 3.5" DS/HD disks have a capacity of 1.44MB.

Disk drives are also available in double-density and high-density models. A high-density drive can read from both high-density and double-density disks. A double-density drive, on

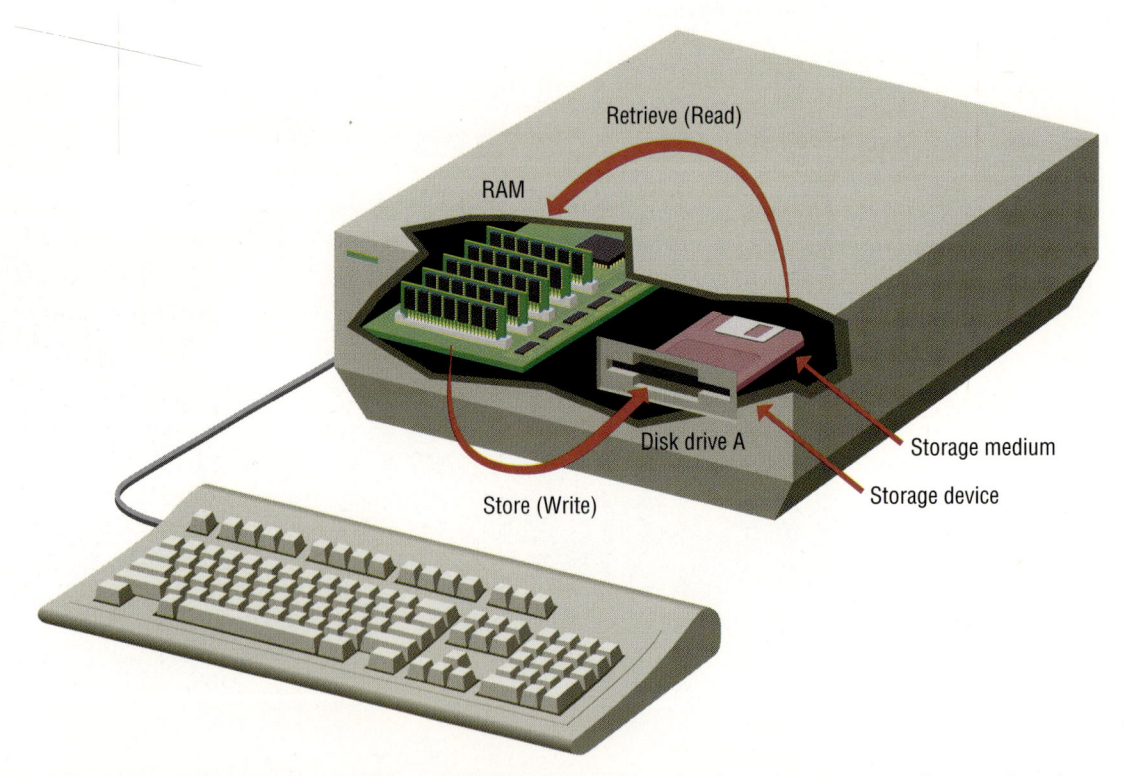

Figure 24: A storage device receives information from RAM, writes it on the storage medium, and reads and sends it back to RAM

Computer Hardware **EC 19**

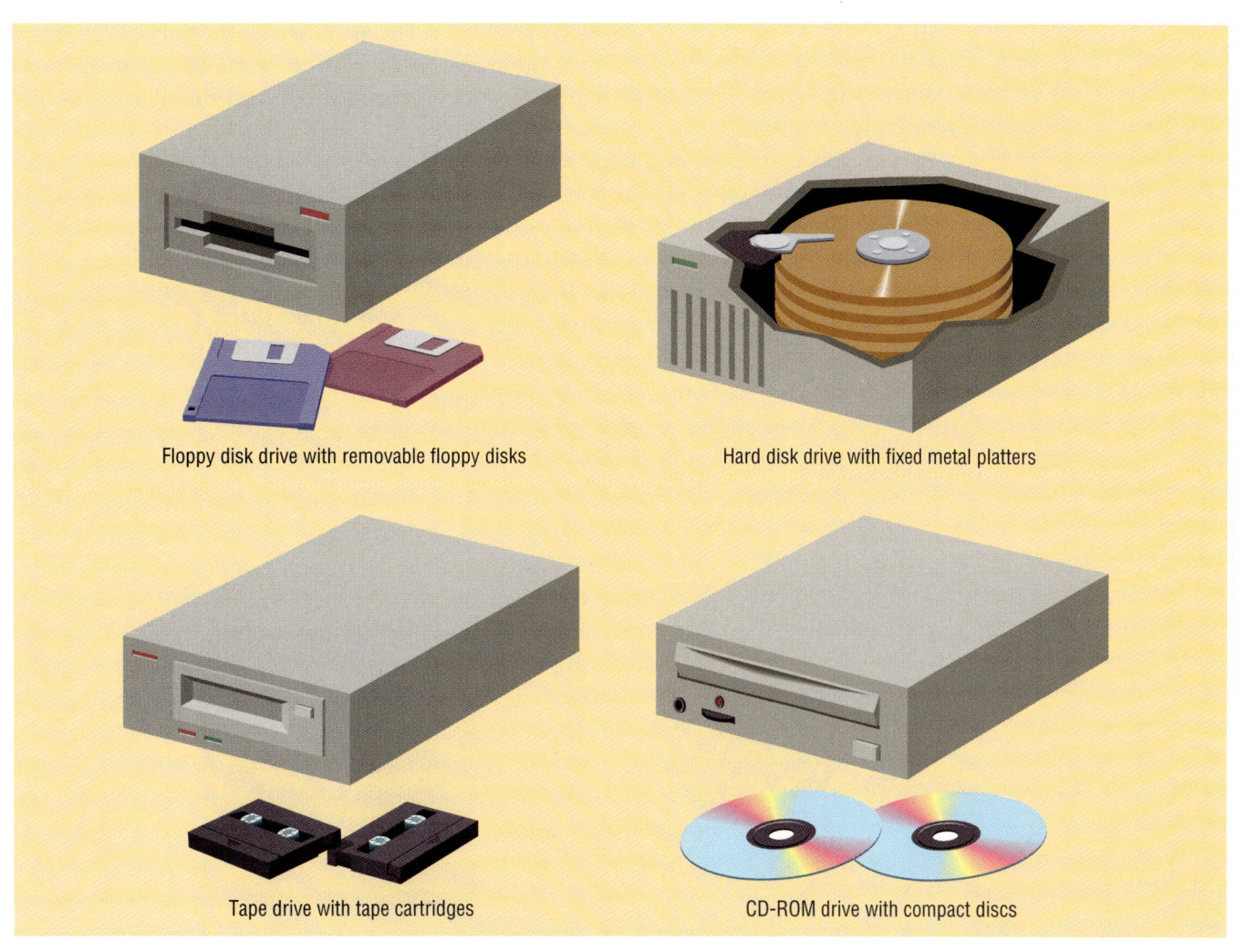

Figure 25: Storage devices and their associated media

Figure 26: 3.5" disk (*left*) and 5.25" disk (*right*)

the other hand, can read only double-density disks. This is important to know before you purchase disks. Make sure the disks you purchase are the correct size and density for your disk drive. For example, if you have a 3.5" low-density disk drive, you should buy and use only 3.5" low-density disks.

Usually you cannot distinguish between double-density and high-density disks just by looking at them. Sometimes, however, high-density 3.5" disks have HD written on their cases and generally have a second square hole in addition to the write-protect window.

You can write protect a disk to prevent any changes to the data on it. **Write protection** prevents additional data from being stored on the disk, and any data from being erased from the disk. To write protect a 5.25" disk, you would place a sticker over the write-protect notch. To write protect a 3.5" disk, you would open the write-protect window, as shown in Figure 27.

Hard disks, also called **fixed disks**, are oxide-covered metal platters that are usually sealed inside a hard disk drive (Figure 28). Hard disk storage has two advantages over floppy disks: speed and capacity.

Figure 27:
Write-protected
3.5" disk (*left*)
and 5.25" disk (*right*)

Figure 28:
A hard disk drive,
opened to illustrate
internal components

Computer Hardware   EC 21

The speed of a disk drive is measured by its **access time**, the time required to read or write one record of data. Access time is measured in **milliseconds (ms)**, one-thousandths of a second. A hard disk drive typically has an access time in the range of 10 to 80 ms, the 10-ms access time being the fastest. Floppy disk drives typically have slower access times.

The capacity of microcomputer hard disks is between 20 and 400MB. A small hard disk with a capacity of 20MB can store the equivalent of about 6,500 pages of single-spaced text, compared to only 110 pages on a 360K 5.25" floppy disk. Large hard-disk storage capacity is becoming increasingly important for the new graphics-based computing environments. For example, to install the Microsoft Windows program, you must have a minimum of 6MB of free disk space. The WordPerfect for Windows word processing program needs a minimum of 6MB of disk space.

Optical storage devices use laser technology to read and write data on compact discs (CDs) or laser discs. The advantages of optical storage include reliability and capacity. Unlike data stored on magnetic media, such as floppy disks and hard disks, data stored on optical discs are less susceptible to environmental problems such as dirt, dust, and magnetic fields. Typical storage capacities for optical drives begin at 128MB and can exceed 1 gigabyte (1,000 megabytes). CD-ROM drives are the most common type of optical storage for microcomputers.

Tape drives provide inexpensive archival storage for large quantities of data. Tape storage is much too slow to be used for day-to-day computer tasks; tapes are used to make backup copies of data stored on hard disks. If a hard disk fails, data from the backup tape can be re-loaded on a new hard disk with minimal interruption of operations.

You generally will have a number of storage devices on your computer, each labeled with a letter. Your diskette drive usually will be drive A, and your hard disk drive usually will be drive C. Figure 29 shows some common configurations of storage devices.

Look back at the ad Tenzing is using with PR #516859; how many storage devices are included? How would you describe the type and capacity of each? Your answer should be that the computer comes with three drives: a hard disk drive with 245MB capacity, a 5.25" disk drive with 1.2MB capacity, and a 3.5" disk drive with 1.44 MB capacity.

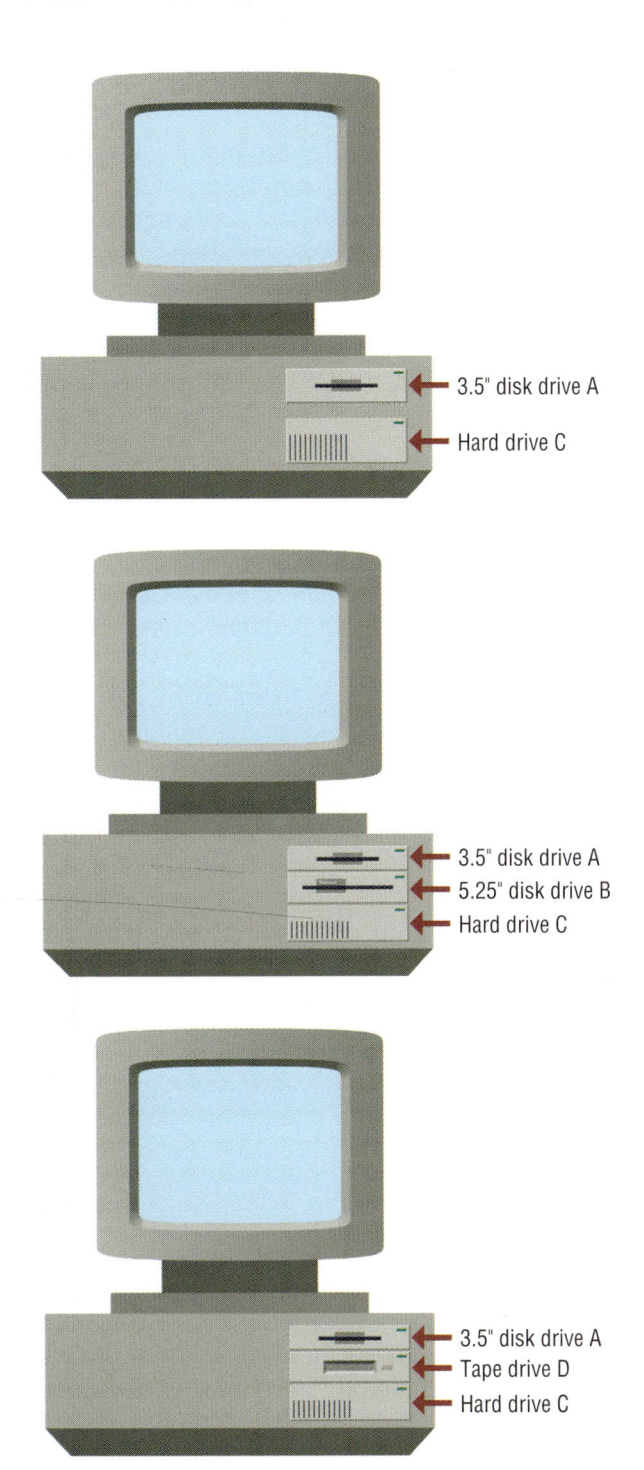

Figure 29: Some common microcomputer storage configurations

Data Communications

The transmission of text, numeric, voice, or video data from one machine to another is called **data communications**. This broad-based definition encompasses many critical business activities, such as sending a fax, sending electronic mail, and accessing an information service such as the Dow Jones News/Retrieval. Data communications also refers to the process of sending data between two devices in your computer system, for example, between the computer and the printer.

The four essential components of data communications are a sender, a receiver, a channel, and a protocol. The machine that originates the message is the **sender**. The message is sent over some type of **channel**, such as a twisted-pair phone cable, a coaxial cable, microwaves, or optical fibers. The machine that is designated as the destination for the message is called the **receiver**.

The rules that establish an orderly transfer of data between the sender and the receiver are called **protocols**. For example, when you are talking on the phone, you and the person with whom you are communicating generally have an implied agreement that while one of you is speaking, the other one is listening. This agreement could be called a protocol, because it assists in the orderly exchange of information between you and the person at the other end of the line. Data communication protocols are handled by hardware devices and by software. Usually this means that for two machines to communicate each machine requires a communication device and appropriate communication software.

Peripheral Interfaces

Input and output devices sometimes are referred to as **peripherals**. Communication between your computer and its peripherals is essential. Without it you would not be able to print or to use your mouse. This communication between the computer and its peripheral devices is sometimes referred to as **interfacing**. If you are going to set up a computer, move it, or add peripheral devices, you should have some understanding of interfacing.

Figure 30 shows the components of a device interface. A cable connects the peripheral, in this case, a printer, to the computer. The cable plugs into a connector called a **port**, which usually is located in the back of the system unit. The port is connected to circuitry that controls the transmission of data to the device. This circuitry either is part of the main computer circuit board or is on a **controller card**. Controller cards are also referred to as **interface cards** or **expansion cards.** These cards plug into electrical connectors on the main board called slots or **expansion slots**. The transmission protocol is handled by a **device driver**, a computer program that can establish communication because it contains information about the characteristics of your computer and of the device.

Microcomputers can have several types of ports, including keyboard, video, serial, parallel, MIDI, and SCSI (Figure 31). A **serial port** sends one bit of data at a time. Typically a mouse, a laser printer, a modem, and speech hardware require a serial port. Serial ports are designated COM1, COM2, COM3, and COM4.

A **parallel port** sends more than one bit at a time. Most dot-matrix printers use a parallel port. Parallel ports are designated LPT1 and LPT2.

A **SCSI port** is a variation of the parallel port. **SCSI** (pronounced "scuzzy") stands for small computer system interface. First popularized for Apple Macintosh computers, SCSI has also become established in the IBM-compatible market. Some tape devices, hard disk drives, and CD-ROM drives use a SCSI port. One of the advantages of the SCSI port is that

Data Communications   EC 23

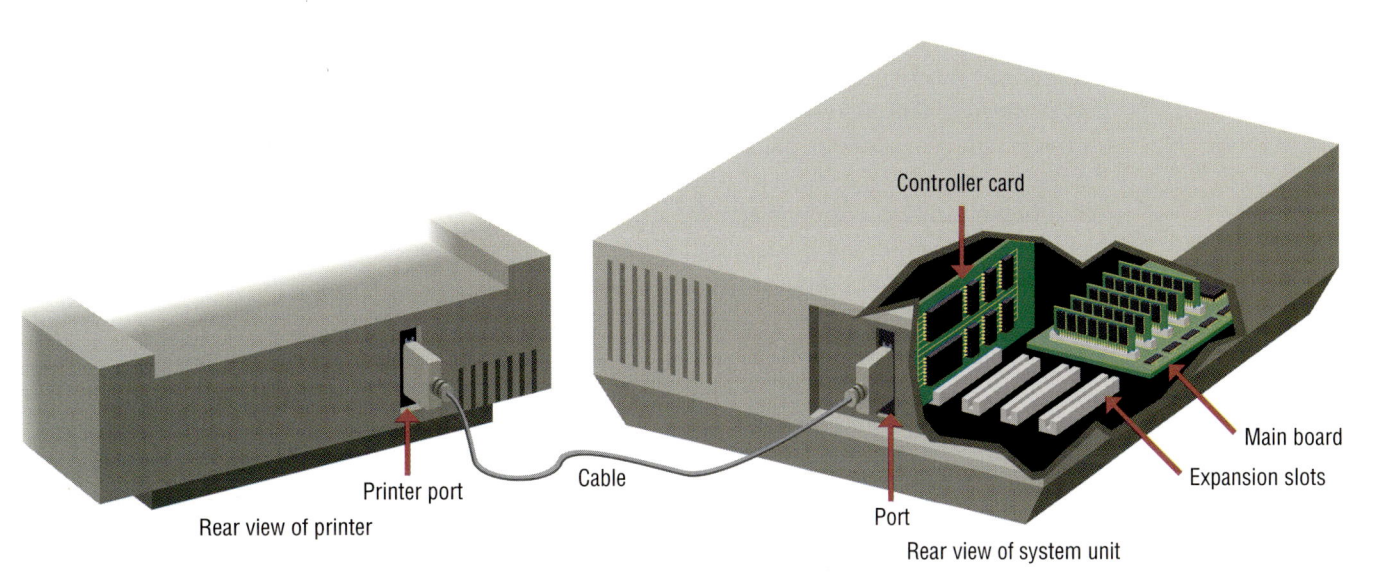

Figure 30: The components necessary to connect a printer to a computer

it has the potential to provide a connection for more than one peripheral device at a time, unlike standard parallel or serial ports, which can provide a connection for only one device at a time.

MIDI ports were originally used in the music industry to send data efficiently between devices that create and play electronic music. MIDI (pronounced "middy") stands for musical instrument digital interface. Now MIDI ports are used to connect computers to electronic instruments and recording devices.

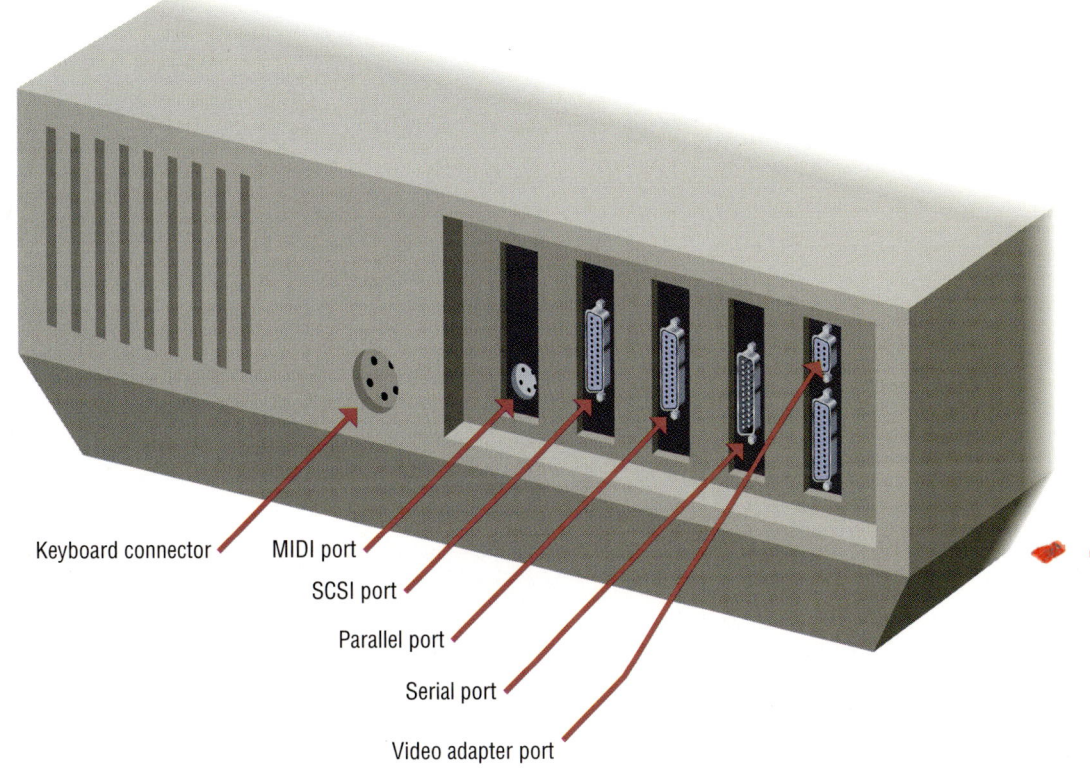

Figure 31: Ports in the back of the system unit

Suppose you want to install a CD-ROM drive, such as the one in Figure 32, so you can use CD-ROM encyclopedias and other reference resources. You need four things: the CD-ROM device, the correct type of cable, the correct port or controller card, and the device driver. Often a device is packaged with all the necessary components. If yours is not, you need to find out what type of port and cable the CD-ROM requires. Usually the packaging or documentation contains this information. If you do not have the correct type of port on your computer or if the port is already in use, you should be able to purchase an expansion card that contains the appropriate port.

This discussion of ports and interfacing may seem a bit technical, but it pertains to an important aspect of computing—expandability. New innovations in computing appear every day, and you probably will want to use some of the new technology without having to purchase a new computer system. Expansion slots make this possible. All other factors being equal, computers with many expansion slots are a better investment than those with only a few.

Now refer back to the ad attached to PR #516859. What types of ports are included with the computer system described in the ad? Is this computer system expandable? How? Your answer is correct if you said that there are two serial ports and one parallel port. The system also appears to have an adequate number of expansion slots. The ad says there are eight but does not indicate if all of them are free. It is likely that some of the slots already are filled with expansion cards for devices such as the modem, the disk drive controller, and the video controller. Tenzing should find out how many of the expansion slots are empty.

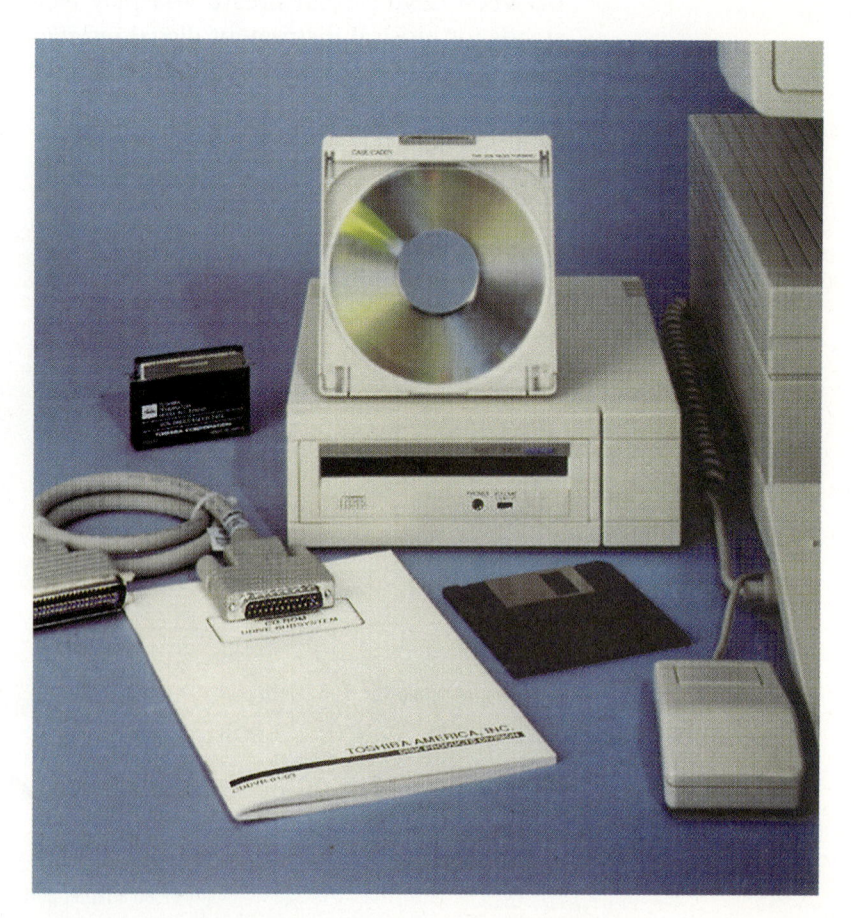

Figure 32:
CD-ROM drive ready for installation

Network Communication

In the business world you usually don't work alone but rather as part of a team. As a team member you'll probably use a computer that is part of a network. A **network** connects your computer to the computers of other team members. It enables you to share data and peripheral devices, such as printers, modems, and fax machines.

There are a variety of networks, too many to discuss thoroughly here. We will focus our discussion on some of the basic concepts pertaining to a local-area network, one of the network types commonly found in businesses.

In a **local-area network (LAN)** computers and peripheral devices are located relatively close to each other, generally in the same building. If you are using a network, it is useful to know three things: the location of the data, the type of network card in your computer, and the software that manages the communications protocols and other network functions.

Many networks have a **file server** (Figure 33), which is a computer that acts as the

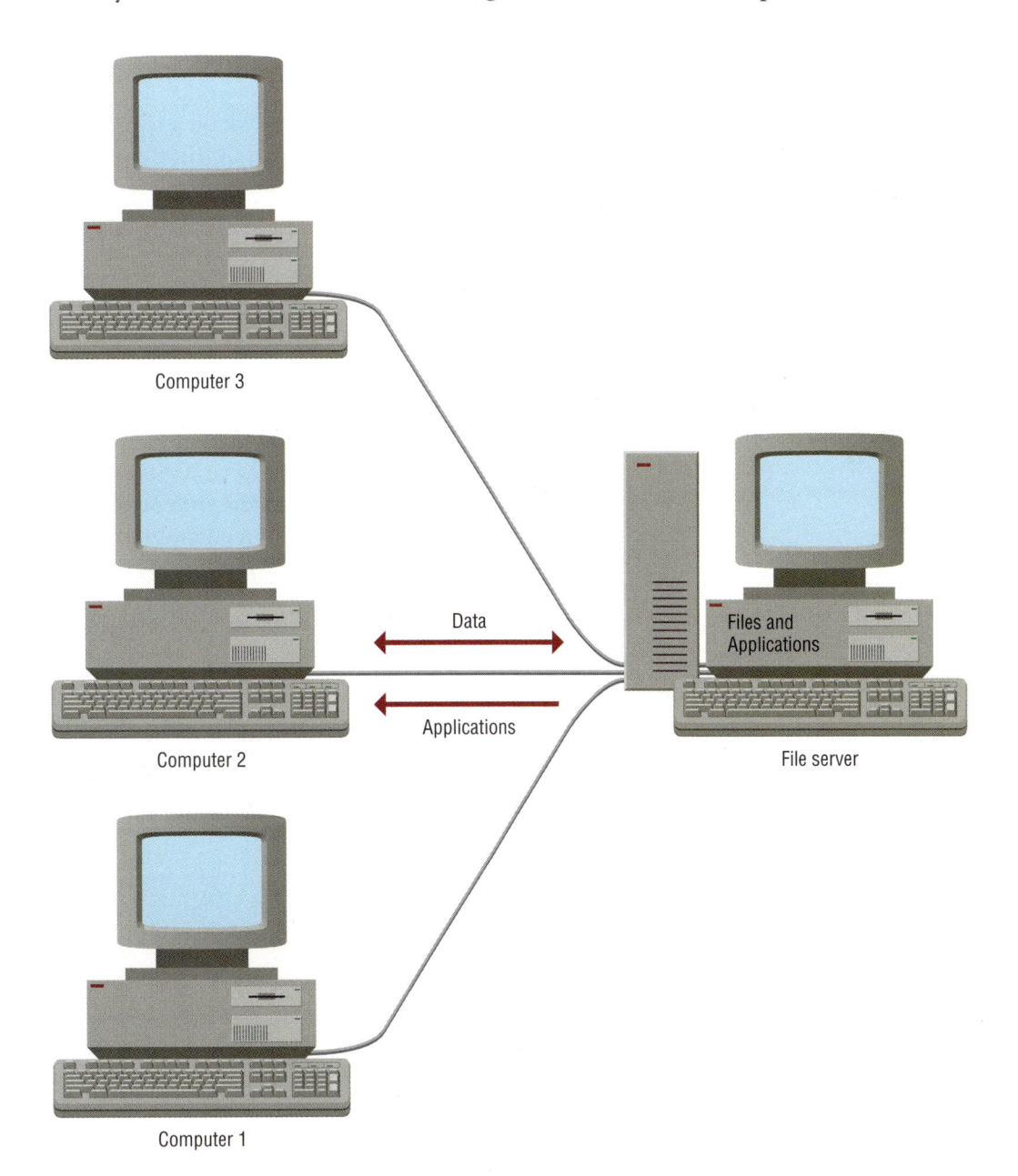

Figure 33:
A file server is the central repository for data and applications programs

central repository for application programs and provides mass storage for most of the data used on the network. A network with a file server is sometimes referred to as a **hierarchical network**. This type of network is dependent on the file server because the file server contains most of the data and software. When a network does not have a file server, all the computers essentially are equal, and the task of storing files and programs is distributed among them. This is called a **peer-to-peer network**.

The type of network card that you have in your computer affects the transmission speed of your data. The network card generally is plugged into one of the expansion slots in your computer. The most common network cards are **Ethernet**, **Arcnet**, and **Token-Ring**.

Network software establishes the communications protocol for the network. Your network software resides on a disk in drive A or on your hard disk drive. Additional network software might be stored on the file server. The most common microcomputer networking software packages include Novell NetWare, Banyan Vines, and Microsoft Windows for Workgroups. Why is it important to know the type of network software you are using? Some software is designed to be used on specific types of networks. If you have a network, before you purchase software, read the packaging or documentation to determine whether the software is designed to work with your network. In addition, some hardware is tested specifically for compatibility with particular networks. The term "Novell compatible," for example, indicates that the hardware should work on a Novell network.

Turn once again to the ad at the beginning of the chapter and think about these questions: Is this computer networked? Can it be networked? Why or why not? Your answer should be that the computer is not currently part of a network and is not shipped with a network card. However, it should be possible to connect this computer to a Novell network with the appropriate network card and software, which would have to be purchased separately.

Telecommunications

Telecommunications means communicating over a long distance. Telecommunications enables you to send data over the phone lines to another computer and to access data stored on computers located in another city, state, or country.

The telecommunications process requires a communications device called a **modem**, which connects your computer to a standard phone jack and converts the **digital** signals your computer uses into **analog** signals, which can traverse the phone lines. An external modem connects to the serial port in the back of the computer, while an internal modem plugs into one of the expansion slots on the computer's main board.

Figure 34 shows the telecommunications process, in which a modem converts digital signals to analog signals at the transmitting site and a second modem converts the analog signals back to digital signals at the receiving site.

To use a modem for telecommunications, you also must have **communications software** to handle the transmission protocols. When you initiate a telecommunications call, you are required to provide specifications about your modem and the destination computer. To do this, you need to know the **baud rate** (speed) of your modem and the port it uses (COM1 or COM2). You also need to know how the destination computer's modem is expecting to receive data: the number of data bits, the number of stop bits, and the parity. To obtain this information, you often need to call the technical support group for the destination computer.

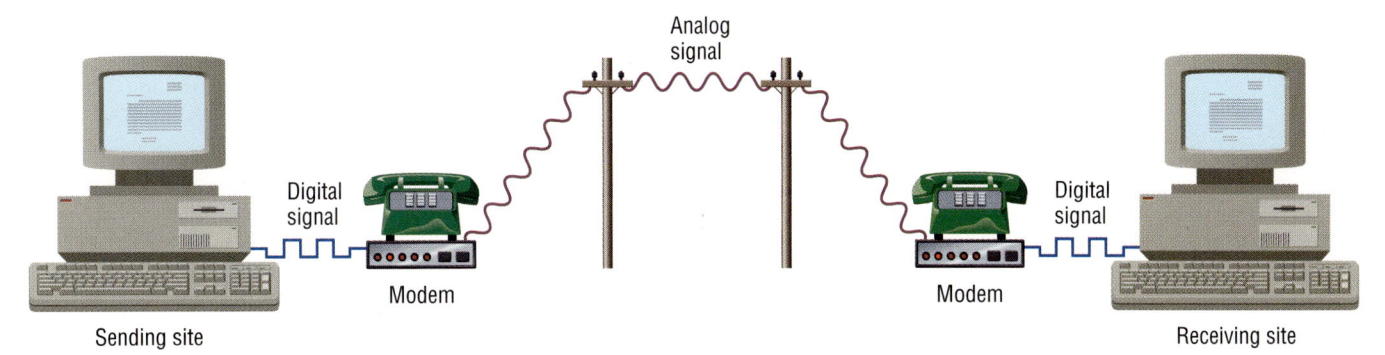

Figure 34: Using modems to send and receive a memo

What about the computer in the ad attached to PR #516859? What do the specifications tell you about its telecommunications capabilities? Your answer should be that the computer system comes with a 9600-baud modem. This is the hardware necessary to connect the computer to the telephone line. However, the ad does not mention communications software, so this may be an additional cost.

Computer Software

Just as a tape recorder or a compact-disc player is worthless without tapes or compact discs, computer hardware is useless without computer software. The types of software that you use determine what you can do with your computer. For example, word processing software enables you to use a computer to prepare documents; graphics software lets you to use a computer to create graphs and illustrations. Software can be divided into two general types: systems software and applications software.

Systems Software

Systems software includes the programs that run the fundamental operations in your computer, such as loading programs and data into memory, executing programs, saving data on a disk, displaying information on the screen, and sending information through a port to a peripheral.

A special type of systems software is the **operating system**, which works like an air-traffic controller to coordinate the activities within the computer. The most popular operating system for IBM-compatible microcomputers is usually referred to as the **disk operating system** or **DOS** (rhymes with "boss"). DOS has been sold under the trade names PC-DOS and MS-DOS. Both systems were developed primarily by Microsoft Corporation, so they are essentially the same.

DOS has gone through several revisions since its introduction in 1981. The original version, numbered 1.0, has been followed by versions 2.0, 3.0, 3.1, 3.3, 4.0, 4.1, 5.0, 6.0, and 6.2. Early versions of DOS lack some of the capabilities of later versions. Consequently, some newer software will not run on computers that use older versions of DOS. You can install newer versions of DOS on your computer if the computer meets certain memory, processor, and storage requirements.

As an operating system, DOS has several drawbacks. It was originally designed for computers with limited amounts of memory and small storage capacities that performed only one task at a time and serviced only one user. Another drawback of DOS is the complexity of commands that you must use to specify tasks. To use most versions of DOS, you must memorize a list of command words and understand the punctuation and spacing rules for constructing valid command "sentences." DOS users often complain that they forget the command words and that typing mistakes or punctuation errors in commands sometimes produce unexpected results.

In response to user complaints, several companies have designed easy-to-use **operating environments**—software that provides a sort of protective layer between the user and DOS. The goal of operating environments such as Microsoft's Windows and Digital Research's GEM is to provide an easier way for users to issue DOS commands. Once the operating environment is installed, you basically can forget that DOS was there.

Microsoft has expanded on the concept of operating environments. With Windows versions 2.0, 3.0, and 3.1 it has tried to make an environment that simplifies the use of any program and provides users with some of the features they need for the newer, more powerful computers.

The first versions of Microsoft Windows were operating environments that supplemented the DOS operating system. More recent versions of Windows, Windows NT and Windows 95, are complete operating systems that do not require DOS. However, these operating systems do allow you to use software written for DOS as well as software written for Windows.

As an alternative to DOS and Windows, IBM has developed an operating system called **OS/2**, which is specifically designed for today's more powerful microcomputer systems with large amounts of RAM and very large disk capacities. To take advantage of the capabilities of OS/2, you must use applications software specifically written to operate in this environment. Since OS/2 is a relative newcomer to the market, the selection of OS/2 applications software is somewhat limited. You can use many of the programs designed for DOS and Windows, but they will function in essentially the same way as on a computer that uses DOS for the operating system.

Applications Software

A wide variety of software exists to help you accomplish many different tasks using your computer. This type of software is called **applications software** because it enables you to apply your computer to accomplish specific goals. Four major types of applications software are word processing, spreadsheet, database management, and graphics.

Word processing software enables you to electronically create, edit, format, and print documents. The advantages of a word processor over a typewriter are numerous. With a word processor you can move paragraphs, check spelling, create tables and columns, modify margins, correct typos, and view how a document will appear before you print it. A wide selection of word processing software is available for the Windows environment, including Microsoft Word for Windows, WordPerfect for Windows, and Lotus Development Corporation's Ami Pro. An example of a screen from a word processing program is shown in Figure 35.

An **electronic spreadsheet** enables you to perform calculations with numbers arranged in a grid of rows and columns on the computer screen. You type numbers into

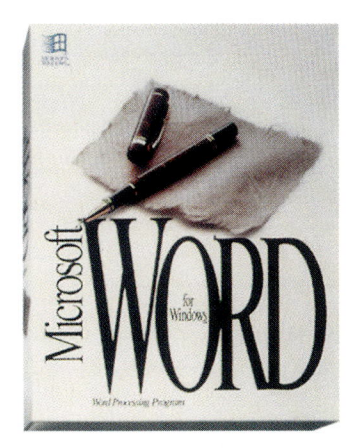

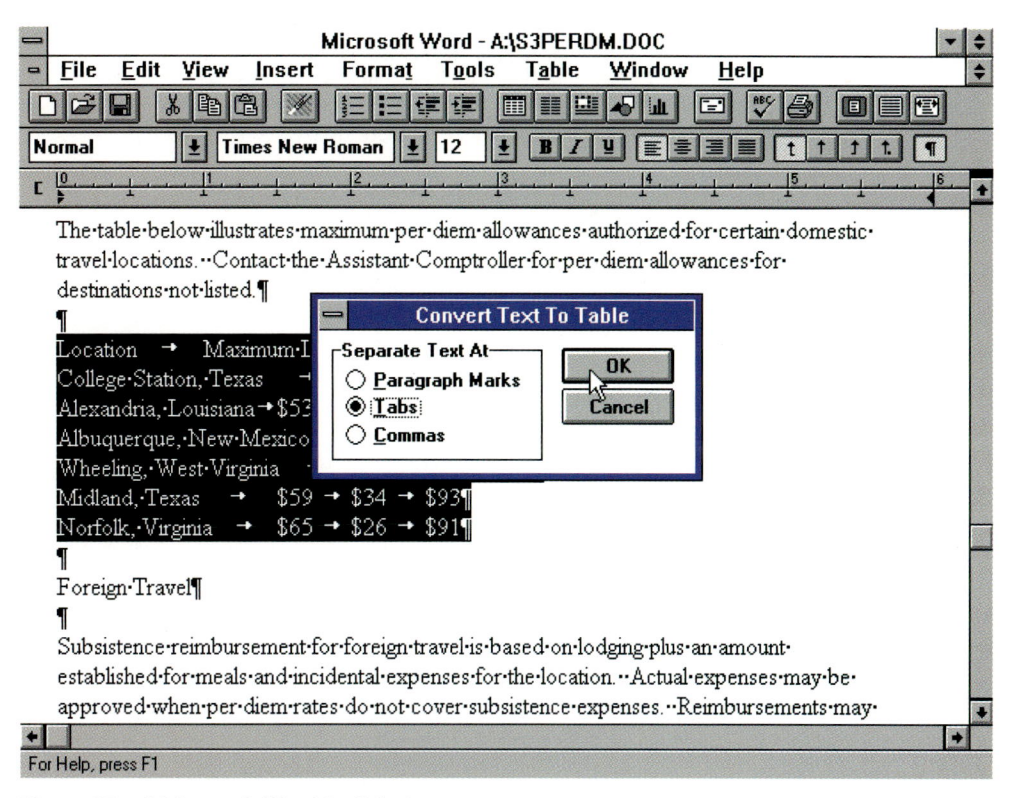

Figure 35: A Microsoft Word for Windows screen

the grid, then create formulas that perform calculations using those numbers. In many ways a spreadsheet is the ultimate calculator—once your numbers are on the screen, you don't have to reenter them when you want to redo a calculation with revised or corrected numbers. As an additional benefit, spreadsheet software provides you with excellent printouts of the raw data or of graphs created from the data.

With the appropriate data and formulas, you can use an electronic spreadsheet to prepare financial reports, analyze investment portfolios, calculate amortization tables, examine alternative bid proposals, and project income, as well as perform many other tasks involved in making informed business decisions. Three of the top-selling spreadsheets for Windows are Microsoft Excel, Borland's Quattro Pro for Windows, and Lotus Development's Lotus 1-2-3 for Windows. An example of a spreadsheet screen is shown in Figure 36 (on the following page).

Database software helps you manage and manipulate information that you previously might have stored in file cabinets or on rolodex cards or index cards. Information about employees, clients, schedules, supplies, and inventory can be managed effectively with a database. Database software lets you easily search, sort, select, delete, and update your file of information. Versatile reporting capabilities also are offered. Borland International's Paradox, Oracle's Card, and Microsoft Corporation's Access are examples of database management software available for the Windows environment. An example of a database screen is shown in Figure 37 (on the following page).

Graphics software makes it possible for you to create illustrations, diagrams, graphs, and charts. Most graphics software provides you with tools to draw lines, boxes, and circles; to fill in or erase areas of your drawing; to enlarge, shrink, or scale a drawing; and to print your finished product. Many graphics programs also provide collections of predrawn pictures, known as **clipart** that you can use as is or incorporate in other drawings. Aldus Corporation's Aldus FreeHand, Corel Systems CorelDRAW, and Adobe Illustrator are three

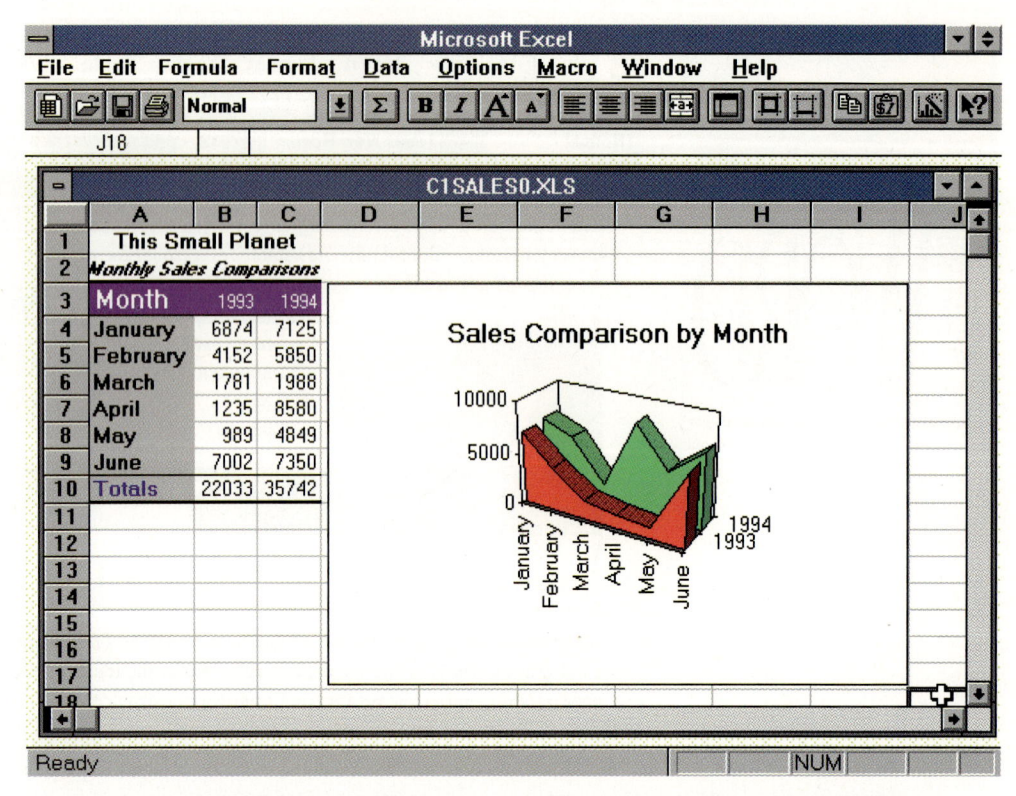

Figure 36:
A Microsoft Excel for Windows screen

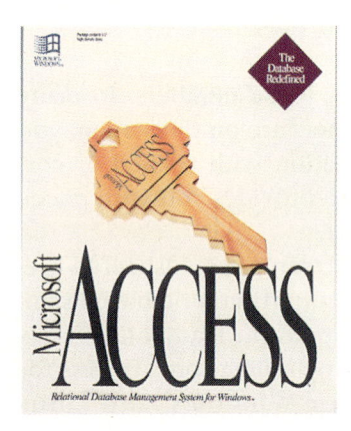

Figure 37:
A Microsoft Access for Windows screen

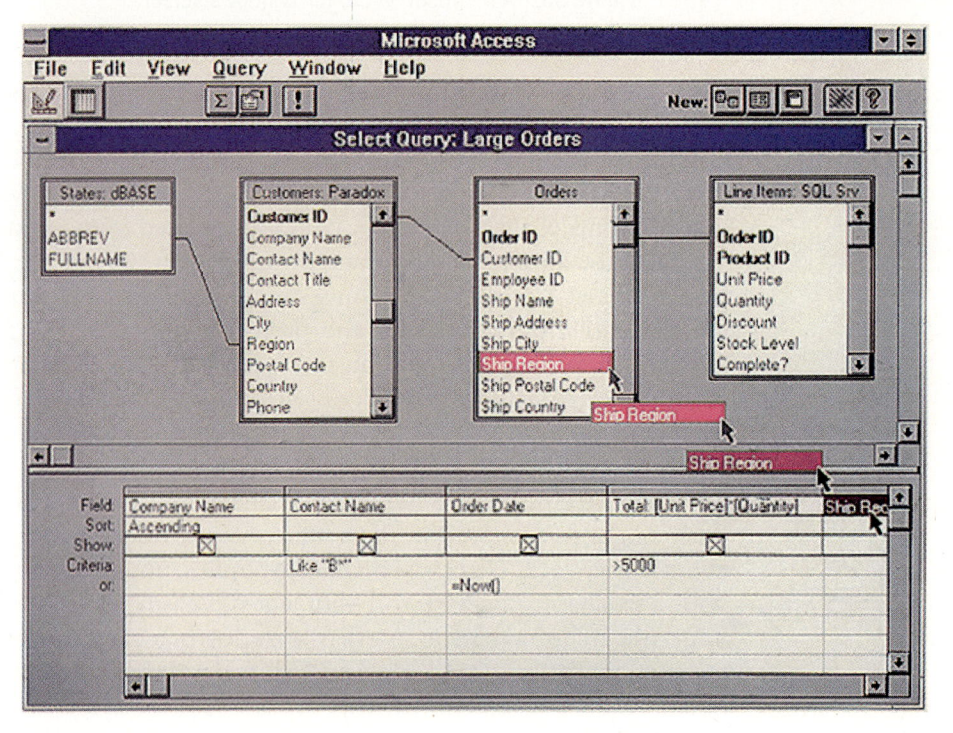

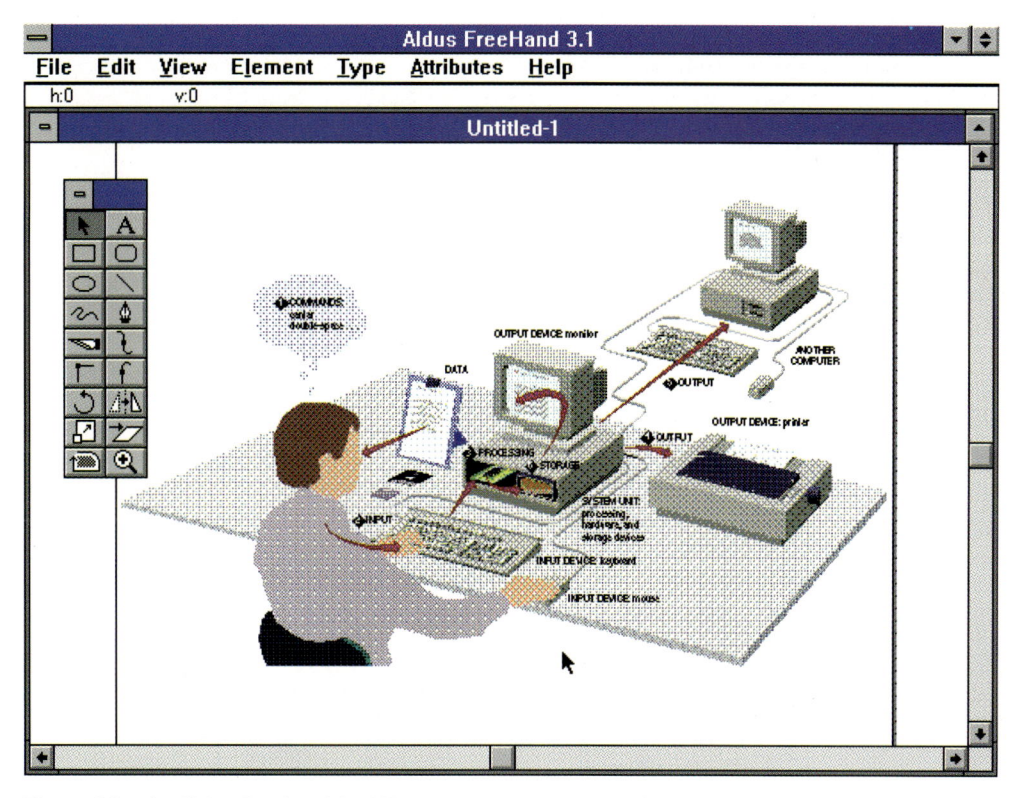

Figure 38: An Aldus Freehand for Windows screen

popular Windows graphics programs. A screen from a popular graphics program is shown in Figure 38.

What types of software are included with the computer described in the ad that accompanied PR #516859? What operating system is provided? Is there an operating environment? Is there any applications software? You are correct if you said that the only software included with the system is the DOS 6.2 operating system. No operating environment or applications software is included.

Now that you have completed this chapter on essential computer concepts, you should have a basic understanding of the hardware and software components of a computer system. You should also be able to understand the terminology in a computer ad, such as the one at the beginning of the chapter. You have seen that the ad attached to PR #516859 includes all the components necessary for a basic computer system, though network hardware and software are not included. Would this be a good system for Tenzing to purchase for International ComAir? To answer that question, you must become familiar with current microcomputer pricing. You will have an opportunity to do some comparison shopping as you work through the questions at the end of this chapter.

Questions

1. What is the key to the computer's versatility?
   a. software
   b. hardware
   c. price
   d. super VGA
2. Keyboards, screens, hard disk drives, printers, and main circuit boards are all examples of which of the following?
   a. input devices
   b. output devices
   c. peripherals
   d. hardware
3. Moving text, sorting lists, and performing calculations are examples of which of the following?
   a. input
   b. output
   c. processing
   d. storage
4. What telecommunications hardware is needed to convert digital signals to analog signals?
   a. mouse
   b. device driver
   c. modem
   d. slot
5. What is a collection of data stored on a disk under a name that you assign called?
   a. a file
   b. the operating system
   c. a protocol
   d. a pixel
6. Which one of the following would not be considered a microcomputer?
   a. desktop
   b. notebook
   c. PC
   d. mainframe
7. The selection of components that make up a particular computer system is referred to as
   a. the configuration
   b. the specification
   c. the protocol
   d. the device driver
8. Which of the following maintains data only on a temporary basis?
   a. ROM
   b. a disk
   c. RAM
   d. a hard disk

9. Which one of the following microprocessors is fastest?
   a. 4.77-MHz 8088
   b. 12-MHz 80286
   c. 33-MHz 80386
   d. 50-MHz 80486
10. What is each 1 or 0 used in the representation of data called?
    a. a bit
    b. a byte
    c. an ASCII
    d. a pixel
11. What usually represents one character of data?
    a. a bit
    b. a byte
    c. an integer
    d. a pixel
12. What is a kilobyte?
    a. 100 megabytes
    b. 1,024 bytes
    c. one-half a gigabyte
    d. one million bits
13. Which one of the following would you not expect to find in RAM while the computer is on?
    a. operating system instructions
    b. data the user has entered
    c. application program instructions
    d. write-protect window
14. What connects a monitor to a computer?
    a. a parallel port
    b. a network card
    c. a graphics adapter
    d. near-letter quality mode
15. Which disk has the highest storage capacity?
    a. 5.25" DS/HD
    b. 5.25" DS/DD
    c. 3.5" DS/HD
    d. 3.5" DS/DD
16. Which one of the following statements best defines a peer-to-peer network?
    a. A central file server acts as a repository for all files and applications programs used on the network.
    b. Your messages travel to a mainframe computer and then are routed to their destinations.
    c. The task of storing data and files is distributed among all the computers that are attached to the network.
    d. The messages travel around a ring until they reach their destination.
17. Which one of the following is systems software?
    a. Lotus 1-2-3
    b. DOS 5.0
    c. WordPerfect for Windows
    d. Corel Draw

18. Which one of the following is an operating environment but not an operating system?
    a. DOS 3.3
    b. Windows 3.1
    c. Windows NT
    d. OS/2
19. Computer memory is measured in _____.
20. Diskette, hard disk, and tape storage capacity is measured in _____.
21. Disk access time is measured in _____.
22. The resolution of computer monitors is measured in _____.
23. The microprocessor clock rate is measured in _____.
24. The transmission of text, numeric, voice, or video data from one computer to another is called _____.
25. Connecting a computer to peripheral devices is called _____.
26. List the four essential components of communication.
27. For each of the following data items, indicate how many bits and how many bytes of storage would be required:

Data Item	Bits	Bytes
North		
Scissors		
CEO		
U.S.A.		
General Ledger		
123 N. Main St.		

28. Read the following requirements for using Microsoft Windows 3.1 (taken from the documentation that accompanies the Microsoft Windows 3.1 program). Then turn back to Figure 1 and determine if the computer specifications listed in the ad are sufficient to run Windows 3.1.
    Windows requires:
    - Microsoft MS-DOS version 3.1 or later.
    - For 386 enhanced mode, a personal computer with an 80386 processor (or higher) and 640 kilobytes (K) of conventional memory plus 1024K of extended memory, 8 megabytes (MB) of free disk space (10.0 is recommended), and at least one floppy disk drive.
    - A display adapter that is supported by Windows.
    - A printer that is supported by Windows, if you want to print with Windows.

- A Hayes, Multi-tech, Trail Blazer, or compatible modem, if you want to use Terminal, the Windows communications Application.
- A mouse that is supported by Windows. Though it is not required, a mouse is highly recommended so that you can take full advantage of the easy-to-use Windows graphical interface.

29. Using the Windows specifications in Question 28, look through a recent computer magazine and find the least expensive computer that will run this operating environment. Make a photocopy of the ad showing the specifications, price, and vendor. Write the name of the magazine and the issue date on the top of the ad.

30. Look through the ads in a computer magazine to find a variety of peripheral devices. Note the type of port to which they connect, then add the devices to the appropriate column of the following chart:

Types of Ports and Their Connecting Devices

Type of Port	Device
Serial Port	
Parallel Port	
MIDI Port	
SCSI Port	

Essential Computer Concepts Index

A

access time EC 21
Adobe Illustrator EC 29
Aldus FreeHand EC 29
American Standard Code for Information Interchange (ASCII) code EC 12
Ami Pro EC 28
analog signals EC 26
applications software EC 28-31
    database EC 29
    electronic spreadsheets EC 28-29
    graphics EC 29, EC 31
    word processing EC 28
Approach EC 29
Arcnet EC 26
ASCII (American Standard Code for Information Interchange) code EC 12

B

baud rate EC 26
binary digit EC 12
bit EC 12
byte(s) EC 12-14
byte values EC 13

C

cables EC 22
cathode ray tube (CRT) EC 15
CD-ROM drives EC 21
    installing EC 24
CDs (compact discs) EC 21
central processing unit (CPU) *See* microprocessors
CGA (color graphics adapter) monitors EC 16
channel EC 22
characters per second (cps) EC 16
chips EC 12
clipart EC 29
clock rate EC 12
color graphics adapter (CGA) monitors EC 16
COM1-COM4 EC 22, EC 26
communications devices EC 7
communications software EC 26
compact discs (CDs) EC 21
computer(s)
    definition of EC 5
    expandability of EC 24
    hardware for. *See* hardware
    software for. *See* software
    types of EC 7-9
computer system EC 5
    components of EC 5
configuration EC 5
controller cards EC 22
Corel DRAW EC 29
cps (characters per second) EC 16
CPU (central processing unit). *See* microprocessors
CRT (cathode ray tube) EC 15

D

data EC 5-6
data communications EC 7, EC 22-27
    network communication EC 25-26
    peripheral interfaces EC 22-24
    telecommunications EC 26-27
data representation EC 12-14
database software EC 29
desktop computers EC 7
device drivers EC 22
digital signals EC 26
disk(s), hard. *See* hard disks
disk drives
    letter designations of EC 21
    speed of EC 21
disk jacket EC 18
disk operating system (DOS) EC 27-28
    versions of EC 27
diskette(s) EC 18
    distinguishing between types of EC 20
    sizes of EC 18, EC 20
    types of EC 18
    write protecting EC 20
diskette drives EC 18, EC 20
display adapter EC 16
display card EC 16
DOS (disk operating system) EC 27-28
    versions of EC 27
dot-matrix printers EC 16
double-sided, double-density (DS/DD) diskettes EC 18
double-sided, high-density (DS/HD) diskettes EC 18
draft mode EC 16
drives EC 18, EC 20
DS/DD (double-sided, double-density) diskettes EC 18
DS/HD (double-sided, high-density) diskettes EC 18

E

electronic spreadsheets EC 28-29
enhanced keyboards EC 10
Ethernet EC 26
Excel EC 29

expansion cards EC 22
expansion slots EC 22, EC 24

F

file EC 7
file server EC 26
fixed disks. *See* hard disks
floppy disks. *See* diskette(s)

G

GEM EC 28
graphics adapter EC 16
graphics software EC 29, EC 31

H

hard copy EC 16
hard disks EC 20-21
    capacity of EC 21
    speed of EC 21
hardware EC 5, EC 10-21
    input devices EC 6,
        EC 10-11, EC 22
    output devices EC 7,
        EC 15-18, EC 22
    processing EC 6, EC 11-15
    storage devices and media
        EC 7, EC 18-21
hierarchical network EC 26

I

ink-jet printers EC 16
input EC 6
input devices EC 6, EC 10-11, EC 22
integrated circuit EC 12
Intel microprocessors EC 12
interface cards EC 22

K

keyboards EC 10
kilobyte EC 14

L

LAN (local-area network) EC 25-26
laser discs EC 21
laser printers EC 17
LCD (liquid crystal display) EC 15
liquid crystal display (LCD) EC 15
local-area network (LAN) EC 25-26
Lotus 1-2-3 for Windows EC 29
LPT1-LPT2 EC 22

M

main board EC 6
main circuit board EC 6
mainframe computers EC 8
megabyte EC 14
megahertz (MHz) EC 12
memory EC 11, EC 14-15
MHz (megahertz) EC 12
microcomputers EC 7-8
    ports EC 22-24
microprocessors EC 11, EC 12
MIDI (musical instrument digital interface) ports EC 23
milliseconds EC 21
mini-tower case EC 7
minicomputers EC 8
modems EC 26
monitors EC 15-16
mother board EC 6
mouse EC 10-11
MS-DOS EC 27
musical instrument digital interface (MIDI) ports EC 23

N

near-letter-quality (NLQ) mode EC 16
NetWare EC 26
network(s) EC 25-26
network cards EC 26
network software EC 26
NLQ (near-letter-quality) mode EC 16
notebook computers EC 7-8

O

operating environments EC 28
operating system EC 14, EC 27-28
optical storage devices EC 21
Oracle Card EC 29
OS/2 EC 28
output EC 7
output devices EC 7, EC 15-18, EC 22

P

pages per minute (ppm) EC 17
parallel ports EC 22
PC-DOS EC 27
PCs (personal computers). *See* microcomputers
peer-to-peer network EC 26
peripheral(s). *See* input devices; output devices
peripheral interfaces EC 22-24
personal computers (PCs). *See* microcomputers
pixels EC 15
pointer EC 10
ports EC 22-24
    adding to computer EC 24
    for modem EC 26
ppm (pages per minute) EC 17
printers EC 16-17
processing EC 6

processing hardware EC 6,
   EC 11-15
      data representation EC 12-14
      memory EC 14-15
      microprocessor EC 11, EC 12
programs. *See* software
protocols EC 22

Q

Quattro Pro for Windows EC 29

R

random-access memory (RAM)
   EC 14-15
read-only memory (ROM) EC 14
receiver EC 22
resolution EC 16
ROM (read-only memory) EC 14

S

SCSI (small computer system
   interface) port EC 22-23
sender EC 22
serial ports EC 22
small computer system
   interface (SCSI) port EC 22-23
software EC 5, EC 27-31
   applications EC 28-31
   communications EC 26
   device drivers EC 22
   network EC 26
   systems EC 27-28
specifications EC 5
speed
   of disk drives EC 21
   of dot matrix printers EC 16
   of ink-jet printers EC 16
   of laser printers EC 17
   of microprocessor EC 12
   of modem EC 26
storage devices EC 7, EC 18-21
storage media EC 7, EC 18-21
super VGA monitors EC 16
supercomputers EC 9
systems software EC 27-28

T

tape drives EC 21
telecommunications EC 26-27
Token-Ring EC 26
toner EC 17

V

VGA (video graphics array)
   monitors EC 16
video controller EC 16
video graphics array (VGA)
   monitors EC 16
Vines EC 26

W

Windows EC 28
Windows NT EC 28
Word for Windows EC 28
word processing software EC 28
WordPerfect for Windows EC 28
write protection EC 20

Photography Credits

Figure	Credit	Page
1	Courtesy of Hewlett-Packard Company	EC 4
	Courtesy of Hewlett-Packard Company	EC 4
2	Courtesy of International Business Machines	EC 5
4	Courtesy of International Business Machines	EC 7
5	Courtesy of International Business Machines	EC 8
6	Courtesy of Toshiba American Information Systems, Inc.	EC 8
7	Courtesy of International Business Machines	EC 8
8	Courtesy of International Business Machines	EC 9
9	Photo by Paul Shambroom, courtesy of Cray Research, Inc.	EC 9
12	Courtesy of Microsoft Corporation	EC11
13	Courtesy of Intel Corporation	EC 12
18	Courtesy of NEC Technologies, Inc.	EC 16
20	Courtesy of Panasonic Communications Systems Company	EC 16
22	Photo Courtesy of Hewlett-Packard Company	EC 17
23	Photo Courtesy of Hewlett-Packard Company	EC 17
26	Richard Morgenstein	EC 19
27	Richard Morgenstein	EC 20
28	Photo courtesy of Seagate Technology, Inc.	EC 20
32	Toshiba's XM-3301 Series CD-ROM disc drive	EC 24
35	Courtesy of Microsoft Corporation	EC 29
36	Courtesy of Microsoft Corporation	EC 30
37	Courtesy of Microsoft Corporation	EC 30

Introduction to DOS

Introduction to DOS

Using the DOS Operating System and Essential DOS Commands

OBJECTIVES

In this tutorial you will:
- Start your computer
- Work from the DOS prompt
- Enter DOS commands
- Get Help from DOS
- View your disk using the DIR command
- Create a file using the EDIT utility
- Use file-related commands
- Create and use subdirectories
- Format and use floppy disks

Getting Started with DOS

DOS is a comprehensive control program, or **operating system**, that manages the resources of your personal computer and helps you run useful **application programs**, such as a word processor or a spreadsheet. DOS is active whenever your computer is running and allows you to accomplish useful work on your computer. You communicate with DOS by issuing special **DOS commands** typed from the keyboard, such as VER, DIR, and FORMAT. DOS communicates with you by displaying information on the screen and prompting you for additional information. In this tutorial, you will learn how DOS manages the different parts of your computer system, and you'll use the primary DOS commands. Familiarity with DOS will be useful to you later as you work with application programs and as you learn Microsoft Windows, a popular graphical operating environment based on DOS.

Starting Your Computer

DOS comes pre-installed on most personal computers and runs automatically when you turn on, or **boot**, your computer. Every computer system is different, so ask your instructor or technical support person for the location of any components or switches you can't find.

To start your computer and run DOS:

❶ Make sure the disk drives are empty.

❷ Locate and turn on the monitor power switch.

❸ Locate and turn on the computer power switch. Your computer will display some technical information as it starts up and tests its circuitry. DOS loads automatically and displays the **DOS prompt** when it is ready to accept your commands. See Figure 1-1.

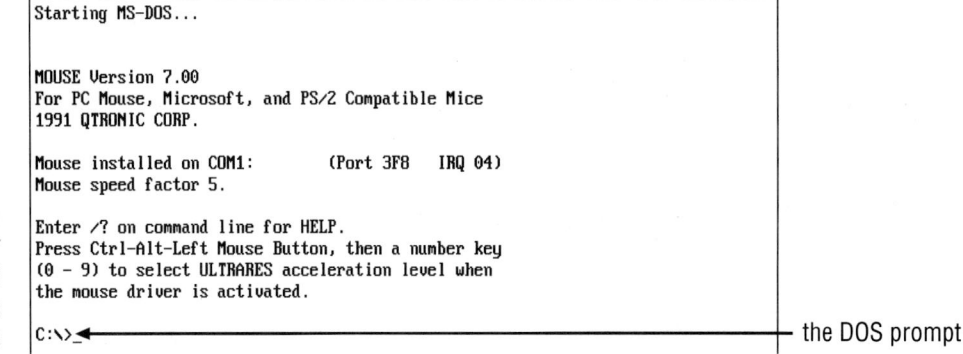

```
Starting MS-DOS...

MOUSE Version 7.00
For PC Mouse, Microsoft, and PS/2 Compatible Mice
1991 QTRONIC CORP.

Mouse installed on COM1:      (Port 3F8   IRQ 04)
Mouse speed factor 5.

Enter /? on command line for HELP.
Press Ctrl-Alt-Left Mouse Button, then a number key
(0 - 9) to select ULTRARES acceleration level when
the mouse driver is activated.

C:\>_                                                  ← the DOS prompt
```

Figure 1-1
Your computer displays the DOS prompt when it is ready for commands

The DOS Prompt

The DOS prompt is your gateway to the functionality of the DOS operating system. At the DOS prompt, you type in instructions known as **DOS commands**, which tell DOS the tasks you want to accomplish. When you type a command and press the Enter key, DOS carries out, or **executes**, the command you requested. When the execution of that command is complete, DOS displays the DOS prompt again and waits for your next command. You can take as long as you like to enter DOS commands—there is no time limit.

In Figure 1-2 on the following page, the DOS prompt is represented by the four characters **C:\>**. The characters that make up the DOS prompt give you information about the disk and directory you are using, and it will change when you use a different disk or directory. The **C:** indicates that the primary hard disk in your system is the **current**, or active, disk. The backslash character (\) indicates that the **root**, or primary, directory is the current directory on the current disk. We'll talk more about these useful characters later in the tutorial. The > character separates the DOS prompt from the characters you type in DOS commands. The **blinking cursor** to the right of the DOS prompt is your current working position on the screen, the place you type in DOS commands. DOS commands can be typed in either uppercase or lowercase. If you make a typing mistake, press the Backspace key to erase any incorrect letters, and try again.

Figure 1-2
Anatomy of the DOS prompt

- a separator symbol
- indicates drive C is the primary drive
- you type at the blinking cursor
- indicates the root directory

```
C:\>_
```

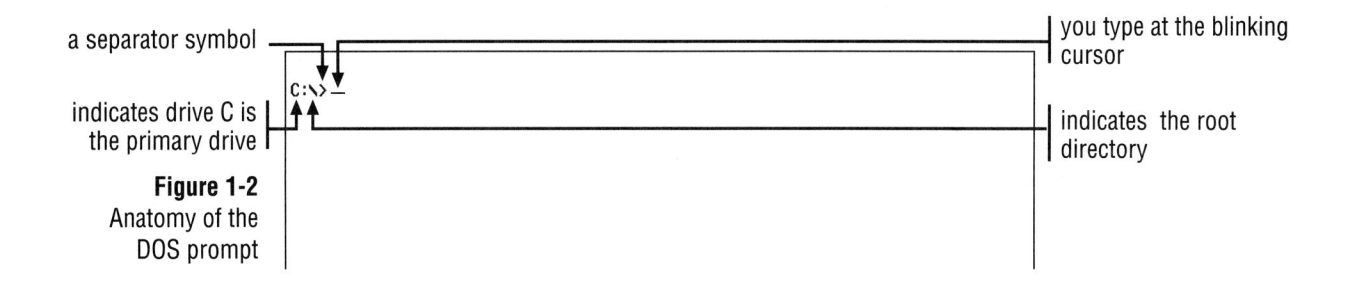

Checking the DOS Version

Now let's try entering the VER command. VER displays the version of DOS that is installed on your computer. This book was written with MS-DOS version 6.0, the most popular version of DOS. Because DOS has been released in several versions by dozens of manufacturers, the versions and the manufacturer of the versions of DOS that you are using may be different. However, most of the essential DOS commands that you will be using in this tutorial will be the same, because they have changed very little since DOS was first released in 1981. So that you can follow the examples in this tutorial exactly, we recommend you use DOS version 5.0 or later.

To check your version of DOS:

❶ Type **VER** and press **[Enter]**. DOS displays the version of DOS on your computer, then redisplays the DOS prompt. See Figure 1-3.

TROUBLE? If you make a typing mistake, you can stop and use the Backspace key to correct the error before you press the Enter key. If DOS displays the message "Bad command or file name," then you mistyped the command.

Figure 1-3
The VER command identifies your version of DOS

```
C:\>VER

MS-DOS Version 6.00

C:\>
```

Setting the Time and Date

Some DOS commands ask you to supply more information while the command is working. Common examples are the TIME and DATE commands, which allow you to display and modify the time and date maintained internally by your computer. In the early years of personal computing, the time and date had to be entered every time a computer was turned on because there was no way to permanently store these settings. But in recent years the technology has been developed to store the time, date, and other important information permanently in the computer memory using special long-life batteries.

The TIME and DATE commands let you view the current time and date stored in your computer and change them if needed. Although the date shouldn't need updating very often, you may need to change the time twice a year for daylight savings time or whenever you move the computer out of your current time zone.

To check and change the current time:

❶ Type **TIME** and press **[Enter]**. DOS displays the current time stored in memory, accurate to $1/100$ of a second, and prompts you to enter a new time in the specified format. See Figure 1-4.

Figure 1-4
The TIME command prompts for a new time

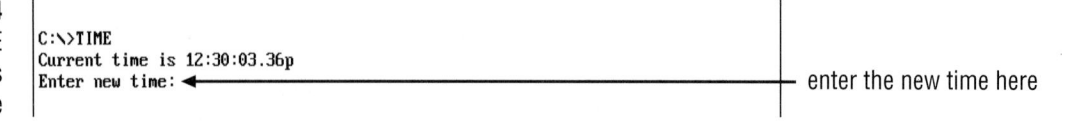

```
C:\>TIME
Current time is 12:30:03.36p
Enter new time: ◄
```
— enter the new time here

❷ Type **1:30pm** and press **[Enter]**. DOS changes the time to 1:30 pm and returns you to the DOS prompt. Time can be entered in military format, which is based on the 24-hour clock, or with trailing AM or PM designations. Specifying seconds or hundredths of a second is optional.

❸ Type **TIME** and press **[Enter]** again to display the time you just entered in memory. If you were to press [Enter] now, without typing in a new time, the time displayed on the screen would be retained in memory. (Do this when you only want to check the time.)

❹ Ask your instructor or technical support person for the current local time, then type it in at the TIME prompt and press **[Enter]** to change the time back to the correct time. DOS updates the clock and returns you to the DOS prompt.

The DATE command works like the TIME command. It displays the current date, then prompts you for a new one in the two-digit format *mm-dd-yy* (month, date, year). If the date displayed by DOS is correct and you don't want to change it, press [Enter] to retain it in memory.

Getting Help from DOS

The secret to using DOS is learning the essential DOS commands and understanding how they work. But if you ever forget a detail, don't worry; help is just a command away. All of the DOS commands are documented in a complete on-line reference accessed through the HELP command. To use HELP to get specific information on a DOS command, type HELP, followed by a space and the name of the command you want help with, then press [Enter]. To get a general list of all DOS commands, type HELP and press [Enter]. Note that the HELP command is available only in DOS versions 5.0 and later, and that the format of the information displayed by HELP is slightly different between DOS versions 5.0 and 6.0.

To use HELP to get documentation for the DATE command:

❶ Type **HELP DATE** and press **[Enter]**. DOS displays documentation for the DATE command. With DOS versions 6.0 and later, a navigation window appears, complete with a title bar, menu bar, scroll bar, cursor, and navigation instructions. See Figure 1-5 on the following page.

Figure 1-5
The contents of the HELP command navigation window

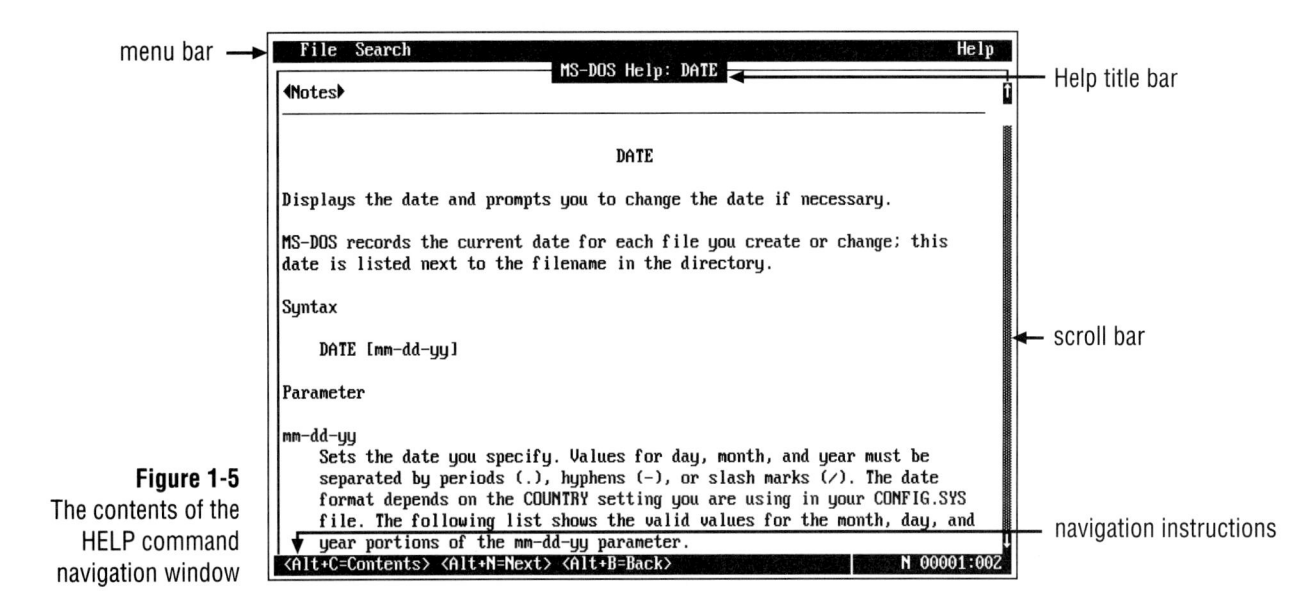

```
menu bar →  File  Search                                    Help
                         MS-DOS Help: DATE                       ← Help title bar
            ◄Notes►
            
                              DATE
            
            Displays the date and prompts you to change the date if necessary.
            
            MS-DOS records the current date for each file you create or change; this
            date is listed next to the filename in the directory.
            
            Syntax
                                                                  ← scroll bar
                DATE [mm-dd-yy]
            
            Parameter
            
            mm-dd-yy
                Sets the date you specify. Values for day, month, and year must be
                separated by periods (.), hyphens (-), or slash marks (/). The date
                format depends on the COUNTRY setting you are using in your CONFIG.SYS
                file. The following list shows the valid values for the month, day, and
            ▼ year portions of the mm-dd-yy parameter.                ← navigation instructions
            <Alt+C=Contents> <Alt+N=Next> <Alt+B=Back>      N 00001:002
```

❷ Press [↓] (Down Arrow key) to move the cursor down the screen. When the cursor reaches the bottom edge of the screen, the HELP window scrolls vertically until more documentation for the DATE command comes into view. Press [↓] (Down Arrow key) to scroll the HELP window to view the remainder of the DATE documentation.

❸ Now press [↑] (Up Arrow key) to move the cursor back to the top of the screen until the cursor is on the word <**Notes**> and press [**Enter**]. The HELP command displays additional information of interest about the DATE command. Use [↑] and [↓] to view the notes on the DATE command, and when you have finished, place the cursor on the word <**Syntax**> and press [**Enter**] to return to the initial HELP screen.

❹ Now exit the Help command by choosing the Exit command from the File menu. Press [**Alt**] to activate the menu bar; then select **F** to drop down the File menu, and **X** to choose the Exit command. The HELP command closes and the DOS prompt appears.

To access a general list of all DOS commands, type HELP and press [Enter] without specifying a command name. As a result, HELP displays a general list of DOS commands. If you're using DOS 6.0 or later you can access detailed information for each command in the list by placing the cursor on the command you're interested in and pressing [Enter]. A navigation window then displays that command, as shown in Figure 1-6 on the following page. To exit the Help command, press [Alt] to activate the menu bar; then select F to drop down the File menu, and X to choose the Exit command.

Viewing Your Disk Using the DIR Command

Information is stored permanently in your computer on a record-like collection of platters known as a **hard disk**. Hard disks come in different sizes and are usually prepared for use by the manufacturer of your computer. Part of this preparation process includes installing the operating system software, such as DOS, on the hard disk. Useful application software, such as a word processor or a spreadsheet, can be installed on the computer later with smaller, portable disks known as **floppy disks**. (Floppy disks will be discussed in detail later in this tutorial.)

All computer programs and data, whether operating system software, application software, or data documents, are stored on disks in electronic containers called **files**. Each file has a unique name and location on the disk. Groups of similar files can be organized in a directory or a subdirectory. Because files are central to personal computing, there are many important DOS commands that pertain to them. One such command—the DIR command—lets you examine the organization of your files and directories on disk.

To use the DIR command to examine the files on your hard disk:

❶ Type **DIR** and press **[Enter]**. DOS displays a directory listing of your files. See Figure 1-6. The directory listing provides a wealth of information about the files stored on your computer, as described below. Because each computer contains a different collection of files, the contents of your directory listing will be slightly different from the one shown in Figure 1-6, but the general structure will be the same.

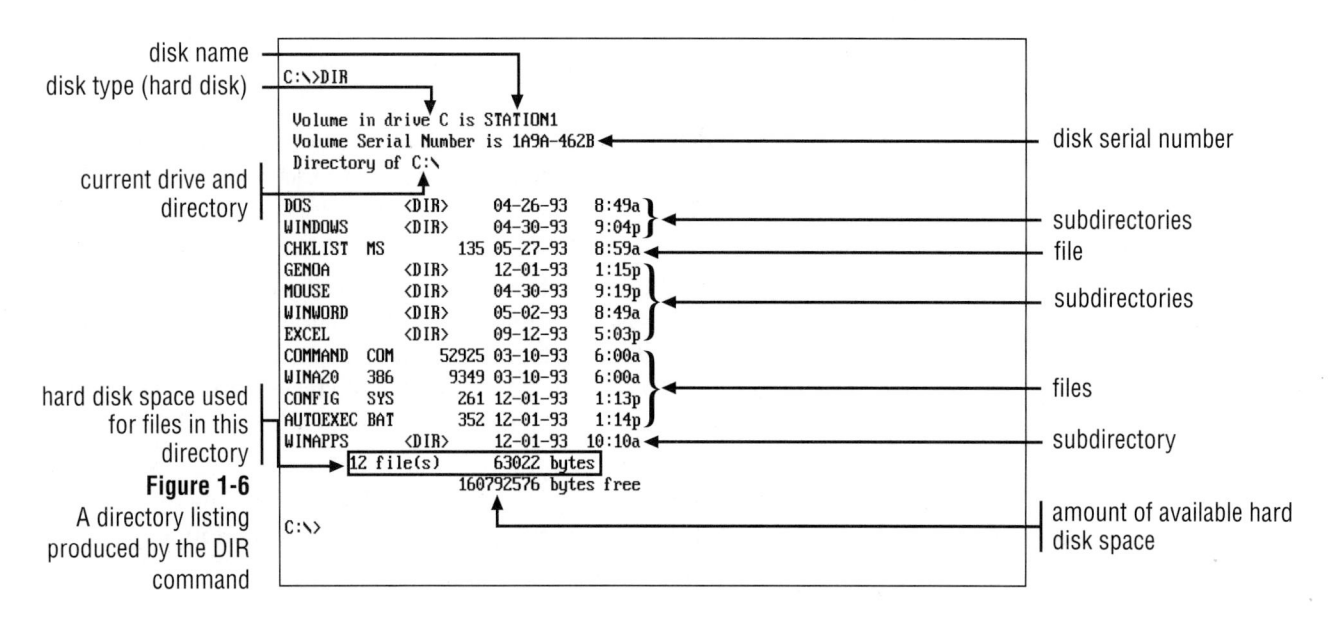

```
C:\>DIR

 Volume in drive C is STATION1
 Volume Serial Number is 1A9A-462B
 Directory of C:\

DOS          <DIR>     04-26-93   8:49a
WINDOWS      <DIR>     04-30-93   9:04p
CHKLIST  MS            135 05-27-93   8:59a
GENOA        <DIR>     12-01-93   1:15p
MOUSE        <DIR>     04-30-93   9:19p
WINWORD      <DIR>     05-02-93   8:49a
EXCEL        <DIR>     09-12-93   5:03p
COMMAND  COM      52925 03-10-93   6:00a
WINA20   386       9349 03-10-93   6:00a
CONFIG   SYS        261 12-01-93   1:13p
AUTOEXEC BAT        352 12-01-93   1:14p
WINAPPS      <DIR>     12-01-93  10:10a
       12 file(s)       63022 bytes
                    160792576 bytes free

C:\>
```

- disk name
- disk type (hard disk)
- current drive and directory
- hard disk space used for files in this directory
- **Figure 1-6** A directory listing produced by the DIR command
- disk serial number
- subdirectories
- file
- subdirectories
- files
- subdirectory
- amount of available hard disk space

At the top of the directory listing is the name and type of disk being examined. **Drive C** indicates you are looking at the primary volume, or **hard disk**, of the computer. In Figure 1-7 on the following page, the hard disk is named STATION1. The name of your hard disk will be different, and it has been chosen by your instructor or technical support person because it easily and logically identifies the contents of the disk. Following the name of the hard disk is the **serial number** used to identify the hard disk. This is assigned when the disk is prepared for use in a process called **formatting**.

The part of the hard disk you are currently looking at is known as the primary or **root directory**, identified by the backward slash character (\) that follows the disk label (C:), as shown on line three. The root directory is the master directory of a disk and provides a look at the overall structure of a disk. The contents of the root directory are listed in the following lines of the directory listing. The directory list is made up both of individual files located in the root directory and the names of other directories, known as **subdirectories**, on the hard disk. A well-organized hard disk will contain dozens of subdirectories, each containing files with a similar function or purpose.

The root directory is listed as the "current directory." The **current directory** is the directory in which the user is working. The root directory happens to be the current directory in this illustration because you haven't yet created any other directories or subdirectories. But, the current directory can be changed to any other directory or subdirectory on the hard disk if the need arises. (You will work with changing directories later in the tutorial.)

DIR displays four important pieces of information about files in the current directory. In the first and second columns of the directory listing DIR displays the **base name** and **extension** of the file. These names identify the contents of the file and the type of the file, respectively, and are used together to spell out a file's name in applications and DOS commands. The directory listing also lists the size of the file in **bytes**, which are the binary equivalents of alphabetic characters and is the form in which all information is stored in the computer. Listed next are the date and time at which the contents of the file were last changed.

The directory also lists information about subdirectories. Subdirectories are identified by the characters <DIR>. These are also listed with their date and time of creation.

The last two lines of a directory listing indicate the total number of files in the directory and the number of bytes used by DOS to store these files. Finally, the directory lists the number of bytes on the disk that are free to store additional information. The amount of space left on this hard disk, as shown in Figure 1-7 on the following page, is 160,792,576 bytes, or approximately 160 **megabytes** of space. Should the amount of free space drop below 10 megabytes or so, you'll need to take action to free up disk space, either by running a compression program such as DOS DoubleSpace, deleting unneeded files, or buying a larger hard disk. (See the section of this tutorial called "Floppy disk capacities" for more information on bytes and disk capacity.)

Creating a File Using the EDIT Utility

Now, you can create a text file with the DOS EDIT utility. EDIT is a simple word processor that lets you create and edit simple documents, including memos, notes, and DOS system files. EDIT does not support text formatting commands (such as bold or italic) or sophisticated word processing commands, but it does provide an effective way to quickly create and modify simple files. Follow these steps to create a text file using EDIT that you will use throughout the rest of this tutorial.

To create a text file with EDIT:

❶ Type **EDIT** and press **[Enter]**. The screen clears, and the EDIT text editor appears. See Figure 1-7 on the following page.

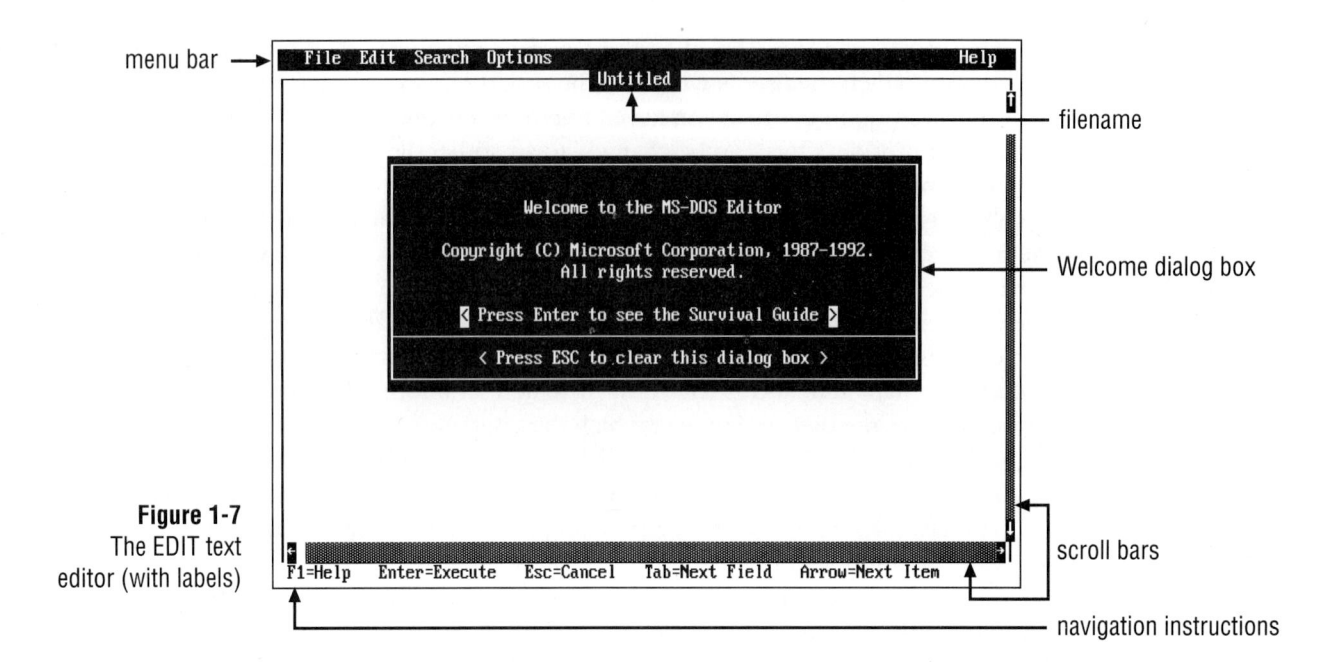

DOS 10 Introduction to DOS

Figure 1-7
The EDIT text editor (with labels)

menu bar → [File Edit Search Options ... Help / Untitled]
filename
Welcome dialog box — Welcome to the MS-DOS Editor / Copyright (C) Microsoft Corporation, 1987-1992. All rights reserved. / ◄ Press Enter to see the Survival Guide ► / < Press ESC to clear this dialog box >
scroll bars
navigation instructions — F1=Help Enter=Execute Esc=Cancel Tab=Next Field Arrow=Next Item

❷ In the center of the screen, you'll see a rectangular window, known as a dialog box, containing the message "Welcome to the MS-DOS Editor." Press **[Esc]** to remove this dialog box from the screen so you can start working with EDIT. (You might want to review the on-line EDIT Survival Guide mentioned in the dialog box if you'd like additional help with EDIT.)

❸ The EDIT screen contains a blinking cursor in the upper-left corner. This is where you'll begin typing text. Along the top of the screen is the menu bar, which contains all the commands available in the EDIT text editor. Directly below the menu bar is the name of the file you're editing, which is listed as *Untitled* in Figure 1-8.

❹ Type the following text in the EDIT text editor, pressing **[Enter]** after each line. If you make a mistake, use the Right Arrow or Left Arrow keys to move the cursor directly after the word you misspelled, then erase it using the Backspace key and begin retyping.

The Inferno, by Dante Alighieri
(Press [Enter])
Midway through our life's journey, I went astray
from the straight road and woke to find myself
alone in a dark wood.

Your screen should look like Figure 1-8.

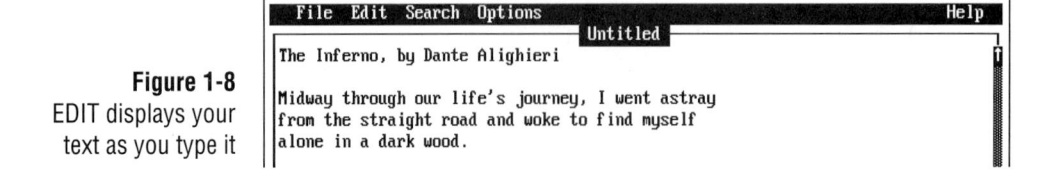

Figure 1-8
EDIT displays your text as you type it

[File Edit Search Options ... Help / Untitled / The Inferno, by Dante Alighieri / Midway through our life's journey, I went astray / from the straight road and woke to find myself / alone in a dark wood.]

Saving a File in EDIT

You'll use the lines you just entered to create a text file called INFERNO.TXT on the hard disk. Of course, EDIT can accommodate much longer text files. In large files, as the lines of text fill the screen, EDIT scrolls through the document, making room on the bottom of the screen for more lines and removing lines from view at the top. To see the lines that have scrolled by, use [↑] (Up Arrow key) and [↓] (Down Arrow key).

To save a file with EDIT, you can use the **Save As** command located on the File menu in the menu bar. When you save a file using EDIT, you create a permanent file on disk that you can use later. This file is visible to the DIR command and other DOS commands that work specifically with files (as will be discussed later in this tutorial). The name for your file should be something related to the content that you can easily remember later and that adheres to DOS naming conventions. A valid filename contains a base name of no more than eight characters, followed by a period and an extension no more than three characters long, as shown in Figure 1-9. Filenames can include letters, numbers, and any one of the following symbols:

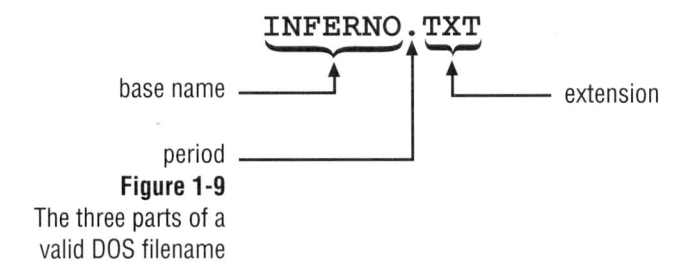

( ) { } _ - & ^ % $ # @ ! `

INFERNO.TXT

base name ⎯⎯⎯⎯⎯⎯⎯⎯⎯↑　　↑⎯⎯⎯⎯⎯ extension
　　　　　　　　　　　　　　period

Figure 1-9
The three parts of a valid DOS filename

To save a text file using the EDIT utility:

❶ Press **[Alt]** to activate the menu bar. This action tells EDIT you want to select a command from one of the menus on the menu bar. In response, EDIT highlights the first letter of each menu name on the menu bar and the entire File menu name.

❷ Press **F** to choose the File menu. EDIT pulls down the File menu, displaying its commands. See Figure 1-10. Note that a unique letter in each command is highlighted. This is the letter, or **hot key**, you type to choose that command. (You can also use the mouse to click on menus and commands if you have one attached to your system.) Feel free to experiment with commands such as print and save.

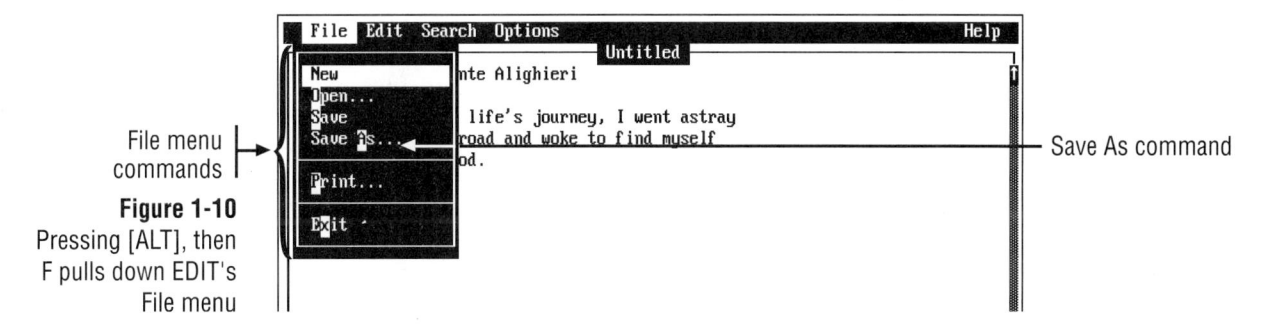

File menu commands

Figure 1-10
Pressing [ALT], then F pulls down EDIT's File menu

File menu showing: New, Open..., Save, Save As..., Print..., Exit — Save As command

❸ Press **A** to choose the Save As command. When the Save As command is initiated, a dialog box is displayed with a prompt asking you for the name of your new text file. See Figure 1-11 on the following page.

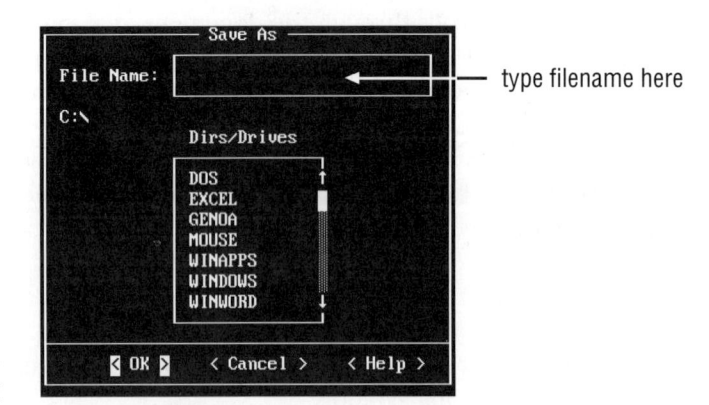

Figure 1-11
The Save As dialog box

❹ Type **INFERNO.TXT** and press **[Enter]** to save your text file to disk under the name INFERNO.TXT. After the text file is saved to disk, the Save As dialog box disappears, and the name INFERNO.TXT appears in the filename box at the top of the screen.

Now you can close the EDIT text editor and return to DOS:

❺ Press **[Alt]** to activate the menu bar. EDIT highlights the first letter of each menu name.

❻ Press **F** to choose the File menu. EDIT pulls down the File menu and displays its commands.

❼ Press **X** to choose the Exit command. The Exit command is executed and EDIT closes.

Note: Be sure to save your file with the name INFERNO.TXT before you exit EDIT. EDIT will prompt you to save the file you've created before you quit. (If you don't save your file before you exit, your work will be lost.) We'll be using the INFERNO.TXT file in the exercises remaining in this tutorial.

Viewing a File Using the TYPE Command

Now that you've created a sample text file, you'll need to know some of the DOS commands that work specifically with files. The most fundamental of these commands is the TYPE command, which displays the contents of a file on the screen. TYPE can only display a text file, however, so don't try to use it to look at program files, such as COMMAND.COM. (If you try to use it with program files, you'll see gibberish on your screen and hear beeps.) Before you use the TYPE command, it's a good idea to use the DIR command to ensure that the file you want to view is actually on the disk you are using. Let's start by verifying that the INFERNO.TXT file is in the current directory.

To verify that INFERNO.TXT is in the current directory:

❶ Type **DIR INFERNO.TXT** and press **[Enter]**. A directory listing for the INFERNO.TXT text file is displayed. See Figure 1-12 on the followng page. A few details of this directory listing, such as the exact size of the file and the time and date you created INFERNO.TXT, will be slightly different from the listing shown in Figure 1-12 on the following page. If the directory listing doesn't include INFERNO.TXT, however, ask your instructor or technical support person for help. You will need access to this file in order to complete the remaining exercises in this tutorial.

Figure 1-12
A directory listing for the INFERNO.TXT text file

```
C:\>DIR INFERNO.TXT

 Volume in drive C is STATION1
 Volume Serial Number is 1A9A-462B
 Directory of C:\

INFERNO  TXT         156 12-01-93   3:14p
        1 file(s)           156 bytes
                       157827072 bytes free

C:\>
```

To view the contents of a file with the TYPE command, simply type the command, leave a space, and type the name of the file you want to look at.

To view INFERNO.TXT using the TYPE command:

❶ Type **TYPE INFERNO.TXT** and press **[Enter]**. The contents of the INFERNO.TXT text file are displayed on the screen. See Figure 1-13. The contents of your file should match the file exactly as you last saw it in EDIT.

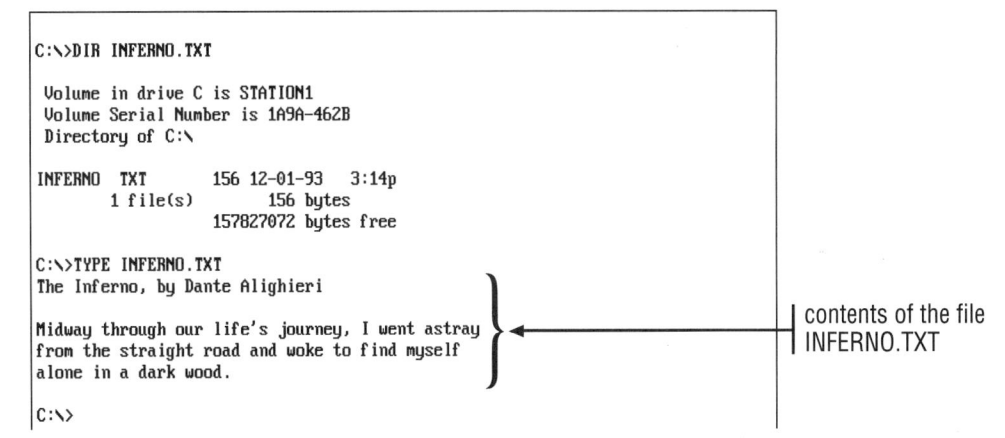

Figure 1-13
Viewing a file with the TYPE command

```
C:\>DIR INFERNO.TXT

 Volume in drive C is STATION1
 Volume Serial Number is 1A9A-462B
 Directory of C:\

INFERNO  TXT         156 12-01-93   3:14p
        1 file(s)           156 bytes
                       157827072 bytes free

C:\>TYPE INFERNO.TXT
The Inferno, by Dante Alighieri

Midway through our life's journey, I went astray
from the straight road and woke to find myself
alone in a dark wood.

C:\>
```

contents of the file INFERNO.TXT

Renaming a File Using the RENAME Command

The RENAME command lets you change the name of a file on disk. This is useful when a file's contents have changed or the original name is no longer appropriate. To use the RENAME command, type the command, followed by a space, the name of the file you want to change, another space, and the new filename. DOS assumes the file is in the current directory, and you can verify this first by using the DIR command. The RENAME command may be abbreviated to REN.

To use RENAME to change INFERNO.TXT to DANTE.TXT:

❶ Type **RENAME INFERNO.TXT DANTE.TXT** and press **[Enter]**. DOS changes the name of the file to DANTE.TXT. See Figure 1-14 on the following page. Notice that when the DOS prompt reappears, the line after it is blank. You will only see a message here if there was a problem renaming the file.

Figure 1-14
Using the RENAME command to rename a file

```
C:\>RENAME INFERNO.TXT DANTE.TXT
C:\>
```

Duplicating a File Using the COPY Command

The DOS COPY command is used to create a copy of a file on disk. The copied file is identical to the original file in all ways but one: it has a different name. COPY is useful when you want to use a document (such as an invoice) as a template for other files, or when you want to move a file from one location to another (moving a file will be discussed in more detail later in this tutorial).

To use COPY to duplicate the file DANTE.TXT:

❶ Type **COPY DANTE.TXT CANTO.TXT** and press [Enter]. A duplicate of the file DANTE.TXT is created on disk under the name CANTO.TXT.

❷ Type **DIR** and press [Enter] to display all files in the current directory. The directory listing contains the files DANTE.TXT and CANTO.TXT. See Figure 1-15. Note that both files are the same size—156 bytes—and that they were both created on the same date. The duplicate file is identical to the original file, except for its name.

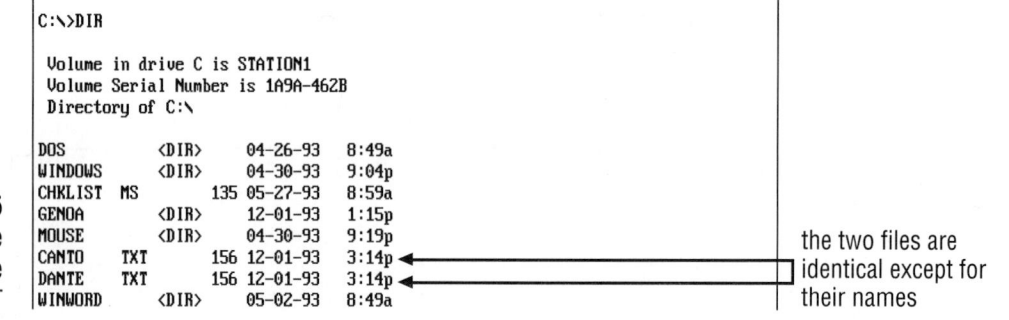

Figure 1-15
COPY creates the duplicate file CANTO.TXT

```
C:\>DIR

 Volume in drive C is STATION1
 Volume Serial Number is 1A9A-462B
 Directory of C:\

DOS          <DIR>     04-26-93   8:49a
WINDOWS      <DIR>     04-30-93   9:04p
CHKLIST  MS        135 05-27-93   8:59a
GENOA        <DIR>     12-01-93   1:15p
MOUSE        <DIR>     04-30-93   9:19p
CANTO    TXT      156 12-01-93   3:14p   ◄─────
DANTE    TXT      156 12-01-93   3:14p   ◄─────
WINWORD      <DIR>     05-02-93   8:49a
```

the two files are identical except for their names

Deleting a File Using the DEL Command

When you no longer need a file, you can remove it from your hard disk by using the DEL command. This command is both simple and permanent, so be absolutely sure you want to remove a file before you use it. Never delete a file unless you know exactly what it contains or what function it performs. A typical application program contains hundreds of files, each important to the program's operation, so an ill-advised deletion could cause major problems. Also, before you delete any files on your computer (other than the one named in the following exercise), first check with your instructor or technical support person. Now, delete the duplicate file (CANTO.TXT) that you created in the last exercise.

To delete the CANTO.TXT file:

❶ Type **DEL CANTO.TXT** and press **[Enter]**. The CANTO.TXT file is removed from the hard disk, and the DOS prompt reappears.

❷ Type **DIR** and press **[Enter]**. A directory listing for the root directory appears. Note that the file CANTO.TXT has been deleted.

Creating Subdirectories

Because a single application can contain several hundred support files, DOS provides an intuitive mechanism for storing files on disk in an organized way: the subdirectory. A **subdirectory** can be compared to the drawers in a filing cabinet, because each subdirectory has a name and has room inside for files and additional subdirectories. A well-organized hard disk will contain dozens of subdirectories, each containing files grouped by function or purpose. Some subdirectories, such as those containing files for DOS and Windows, are created automatically by software during its installation. Others are created deliberately by computer users as they organize data files related to ongoing projects. Subdirectories are created with the MD command and accessed with the CD command, as we'll see in the following exercises.

To create a subdirectory on your hard disk:

❶ Type **DIR** and press **[Enter]**. DOS displays a directory listing for the current directory. Remember, this directory is identified by the backslash character (\) and is also called the root directory.

❷ Type **MD ITALIANS** and press **[Enter]**. A subdirectory named ITALIANS in the root directory of drive C. See Figure 1-16.

Figure 1-16
The contents of a root directory (label root slash)

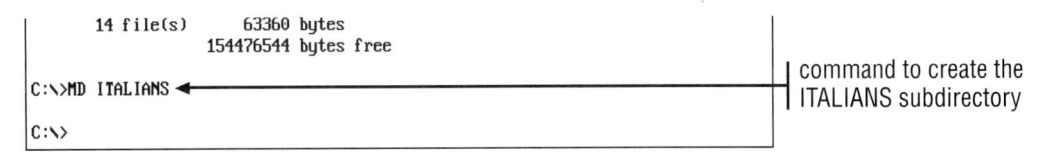

```
         14 file(s)       63360 bytes
                     154476544 bytes free
C:\>MD ITALIANS  ◄────────────────────────── command to create the
                                             ITALIANS subdirectory
C:\>
```

❸ Type **DIR** and press **[Enter]**. DOS displays a directory listing for the current directory, including a listing for our new subdirectory. The subdirectory has been given the same time and date as its point of creation and is identified as a subdirectory with the characters <DIR>.

Copying Files to a Subdirectory

To demonstrate how a subdirectory can be used to store files, let's copy the DANTE.TXT sample file to the ITALIANS subdirectory. We'll do this with the COPY command, which, as you may remember, can be used not only to duplicate files in the current directory, but also to copy files to subdirectories. To use the COPY command in this way, type COPY, a space, the name of the file you want to copy, another space, and the destination subdirectory's name. DOS will copy the file to the subdirectory and give the duplicate file the same name as the original file.

To copy DANTE.TXT to the ITALIANS subdirectory:

❶ Type **COPY DANTE.TXT ITALIANS** and press **[Enter]**. DOS copies DANTE.TXT to the ITALIANS subdirectory.

❷ Type **DIR ITALIANS** and press **[Enter]** to verify the file was copied to the ITALIANS subdirectory. DOS displays a directory listing of the ITALIANS subdirectory, including a listing for the file DANTE.TXT. See Figure 1-17. As you can see, in addition to displaying the contents of the current directory, the DIR command also can be used to display the contents of a subdirectory.

```
C:\>COPY DANTE.TXT ITALIANS                    ← COPY command moves
        1 file(s) copied                          DANTE.TXT to the ITALIANS
                                                  subdirectory
C:\>DIR ITALIANS                               ← DIR command displays
                                                  contents of ITALIANS
 Volume in drive C is STATION1
 Volume Serial Number is 1A9A-462B
 Directory of C:\ITALIANS

 .            <DIR>        12-01-93   4:50p
 ..           <DIR>        12-01-93   4:50p
 DANTE    TXT       156    12-01-93   3:14p
         3 file(s)         156 bytes
                    154443776 bytes free

C:\>
```

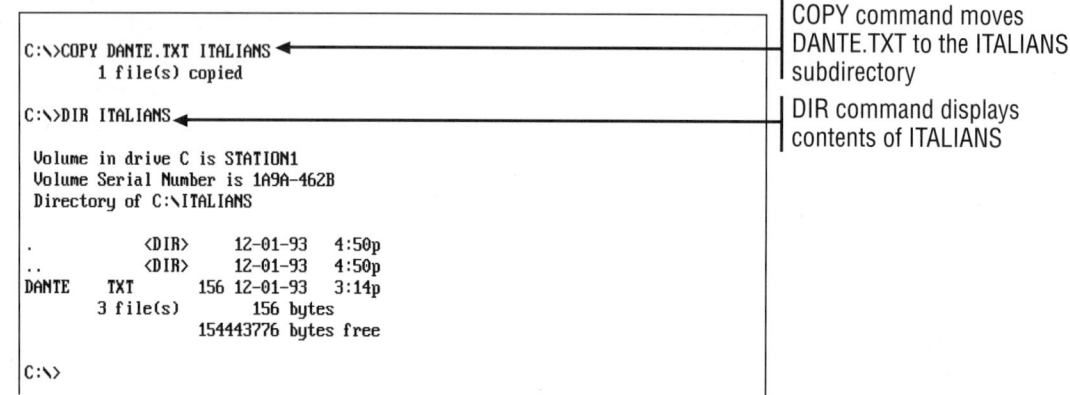

Figure 1-17
The contents of the ITALIANS subdirectory

The file DANTE.TXT has successfully been copied from one directory to another. Now let's delete the original DANTE.TXT file in the root directory, to avoid the unneeded duplication of this file on the hard disk.

❸ Type **DEL DANTE.TXT** and press **[Enter]**. DOS deletes the DANTE.TXT file from the root directory.

Note: Although you examined the ITALIANS subdirectory with the DIR command in Step 2 above, the current directory is still the root directory where you have been working throughout this tutorial. The current directory is the place where DEL and other commands take effect, unless a different subdirectory is *specifically* chosen, as it was in Step 2 above (you specifically chose the ITALIANS subdirectory in the DIR command).

Now let's look at the command used to change the current directory on the hard disk.

Changing Directories

To change to a different directory, use the CD (Change Directory) command. CD changes the current directory so you can work on files stored in a different place on your hard disk. To use the CD command, type CD followed by a space and the name of the subdirectory you want to change to. If you don't know the name of the subdirectory you're looking for, use the DIR command first. If you don't know where you are in the directory structure, you can type the CD command without specifying a subdirectory name, and DOS will display the name of the current directory.

To use the CD command to change to the ITALIANS subdirectory:

❶ Type **CD ITALIANS** and press **[Enter]**. DOS sets the current directory to the ITALIANS subdirectory.

❷ Type **DIR** and press **[Enter]**. DOS displays the new current directory. See Figure 1-18. Notice that both the DOS prompt and the third line of the directory listing confirm you are currently in the C:\ITALIANS subdirectory. The phrase—C:\ITALIANS—is spoken as "the Italians subdirectory on drive C" and is known as the subdirectory's **pathname**.

```
C:\>CD ITALIANS

C:\ITALIANS>DIR

 Volume in drive C is STATION1
 Volume Serial Number is 1A9A-462B
 Directory of C:\ITALIANS

.            <DIR>        12-01-93   4:50p
..           <DIR>        12-01-93   4:50p
DANTE    TXT         156  12-01-93   3:14p
        3 file(s)          156 bytes
                   154443776 bytes free

C:\ITALIANS>
```

— Change Directory command

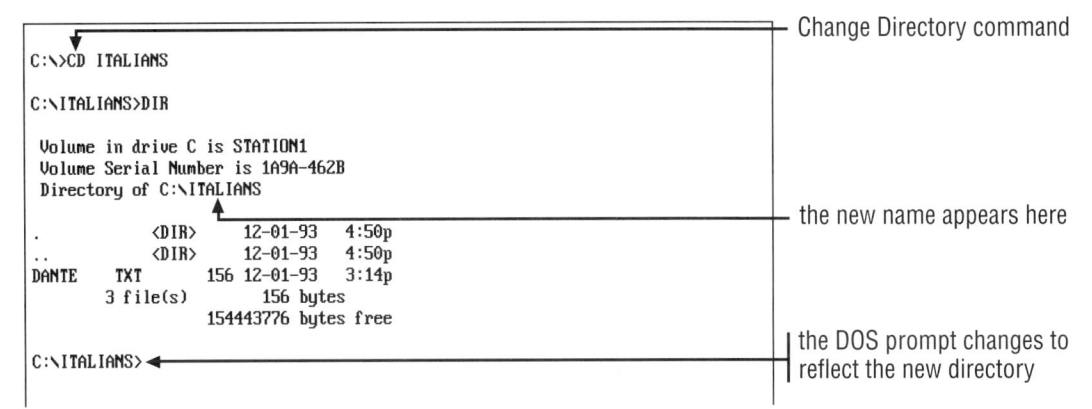

— the new name appears here

— the DOS prompt changes to reflect the new directory

Figure 1-18
Using the CD command to change the current directory

❸ Type **CD** and press **[Enter]**. DOS displays the current directory again. See Figure 1-19. Since this command produces the same pathname information already displayed by the DOS prompt, this command is redundant.

```
C:\>CD ITALIANS

C:\ITALIANS>DIR

 Volume in drive C is STATION1
 Volume Serial Number is 1A9A-462B
 Directory of C:\ITALIANS

.            <DIR>        12-01-93   4:50p
..           <DIR>        12-01-93   4:50p
DANTE    TXT         156  12-01-93   3:14p
        3 file(s)          156 bytes
                   154443776 bytes free

C:\ITALIANS>CD
C:\ITALIANS
C:\ITALIANS>
```

— output of the CD command with parameters

Figure 1-19
CD used to display the current directory

❹ Type **CD** and press **[Enter]**. This command returns you to the root (\) directory, the directory you started in. You can also return to the root (\) directory by typing CD .. and pressing [Enter]. DOS uses the two dots (..) as shorthand for "the directory above the current one." (You may have noticed these dots in the output of previous directory listings.) You may find times when typing the two dots is quicker than spelling out the directory name to which you want to go.

Understanding Floppy Disks

Most of the application and data files you use on your computer will be stored on your hard disk, but from time to time you'll want to use portable **floppy disks** to transfer files from one computer to another or to install new software. You'll also want to use floppy disks to make backup copies of your work. If your hard disk ever fails, having duplicate copies of your important documents on floppy disks will save you time and money.

Before you can use floppy disks, they must be prepared for storage, or formatted, by DOS. **Formatting** is initiated by the FORMAT command and involves the organization of your disk into allocation units known as sectors, tracks, and clusters, as shown in Figure 1-20. The more clusters on a disk, the more storage space on the disk. Information is stored (written) and retrieved (read) from the disk by a mechanical arm controlled by the circuitry in the **hard disk controller**.

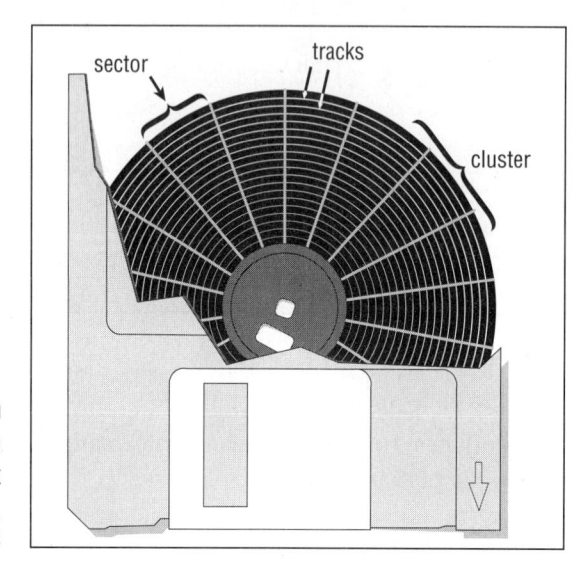

Figure 1-20
Formatting organizes a disk into sectors, tracks, and clusters

Floppy Disk Capacities

Modern floppy disks come in two physical sizes, 3.5" and 5.25", and can be either **high** or **low density** (a high-density disk can hold more data). The four resulting disk types are listed in Table 1-1, with their storage capacities expressed in **kilobytes** (thousands of bytes) or **megabytes** (millions of bytes). You'll generally want to use the disk with the most capacity, but you also have to use a disk that fits in your floppy disk drive. All personal computers have at least one floppy disk drive, and this is designated by DOS as **drive A**. If you have a second floppy drive, it will be designated and referenced as **drive B**. Most modern floppy drives work equally well with high- and low-density disks, although some older drives were designed for only one density and should be used only for the disks for which they were designed. When a floppy disk drive formats a floppy disk, by default it formats the disk at the highest capacity it can.

Table 1-1
Floppy disk types and capacities

Physical size	Density	Capacity
3.5"	low-density	720KB
3.5"	high-density	1.44MB
5.25"	low-density	360KB
5.25"	high-density	1.2MB

Take a minute now to determine what type of floppy disk drive(s) you have in your computer and what type of floppy disk you'll be using in the following exercise. It will be either a 3.5" or 5.25" disk, whichever fits in drive A, your primary floppy disk drive. If possible you should select a high-density disk. If you have any questions, ask your instructor or technical support person for help.

Formatting Floppy Disks

To format a high-density floppy disk:

❶ Put a blank, unformatted high-density floppy disk in drive A and close the **drive latch** (if there is one). The disk should fit snugly inside the disk drive.

❷ Type **FORMAT A:** and press **[Enter]**. FORMAT will prompt you to put a disk in drive A and press [Enter] to continue.

❸ Press **[Enter]** to format the disk. FORMAT checks the disk in drive A and begins the format process. See Figure 1-21. The formatting will take a few minutes. When the process is complete, FORMAT asks you to name the disk. You may use up to 11 letters or numbers in the name.

Figure 1-21
FORMAT checks the disk and starts formatting

```
C:\>FORMAT A:
Insert new diskette for drive A:
and press ENTER when ready...

Checking existing disk format.
Formatting 1.44M
 38 percent completed.
```

❹ Type **POETS** and press **[Enter]**. DOS records the label POETS on the disk and displays some information about the new disk's storage capacity. You will notice that the disk formatted in this example is a 3.5" high-density disk, so the number of bytes available for storage is 1,457,664 (approximately 1.44 megabytes). Each disk has some space set aside for **bad sectors**, or imperfections. From time to time you may see a few less bytes available for storage after formatting a disk because the DOS file system carefully tracks any bad sectors and avoids storing data in them. In addition to the number of bytes free, FORMAT also displays the unique serial number for the disk. You can use this number later, if necessary, to identify the disk. Finally, FORMAT asks you if you'd like to format another disk.

❺ Press **N** to indicate no. The FORMAT command ends and the DOS prompt appears. Now you're ready to work with the floppy disk.

Working with Floppy Disks

Earlier in this tutorial, when you learned how to work with directories, you were introduced to the concept of the current directory. DOS uses a similar concept to identify the drive you are actively working on, which is called the **current drive**. The current drive is the drive currently affected by the commands you are typing. For the majority of this tutorial, drive C—your hard disk—has been the current drive. Now, however, you are going to work with the floppy disk, which is in drive A. To do that you need to make drive A the current drive. Doing this is easy—you just type in the letter associated with the drive you want to change to (A) and a colon.

To change the current drive to drive A:

❶ Type **A:** and press **[Enter]**. DOS checks for a disk in drive A (you might see the drive light flicker) and changes the current drive to drive A. As a result, the drive letter in the DOS prompt changes. See Figure 1-22 on the following page.

Figure 1-22
Changing drives

```
C:\>A:
A:\>
```

❷ Type **DIR** and press **[Enter]** to view the contents of the disk in drive A. DOS displays a directory listing for the root (\) directory of the floppy disk. See Figure 1-23. The directory listing indicates there are no files on the new disk. Notice the disk label is POETS, the name you entered while formatting the disk.

Figure 1-23
A directory listing for the disk in drive A

```
C:\>A:

A:\>DIR

Volume in drive A is POETS
Volume Serial Number is 0C2B-18DF
Directory of A:\

File not found

A:\>
```

❸ Type **C:** and press **[Enter]**. DOS changes the current drive back to drive C (the hard disk). The DOS prompt changes to reflect the new current drive.

Copying Files to a Floppy Disk

Files can be copied from a hard drive to a floppy disk by using the COPY command. To copy files to a floppy disk, type COPY, a space, the name of the file you want to copy, another space, and the letter associated with the drive that contains the floppy disk. Copying files from a hard drive to a floppy disk is a good way to keep them safe. If the hard disk ever fails mechanically, or if you should accidentally delete files from it, your work will not be lost because you will have backup copies on floppy disk.

To copy DANTE.TXT from the hard drive to the floppy disk in drive A:

❶ Type **CD ITALIANS** and press **[Enter]** to change the current directory to the ITALIANS subdirectory on drive C. The DOS prompt changes to C:\ITALIANS, indicating the current directory is now ITALIANS on the hard disk.

❷ Type **DIR** and press **[Enter]**. DOS displays the contents of the ITALIANS subdirectory, including DANTE.TXT. See Figure 1-24. It's always a good idea to verify a file's location before you use the COPY command.

Figure 1-24
DIR verifies DANTE.TXT is in the ITALIANS subdirectory

```
C:\>CD ITALIANS

C:\ITALIANS>DIR

Volume in drive C is STATION1
Volume Serial Number is 1A9A-462B
Directory of C:\ITALIANS

.            <DIR>     12-01-93   4:50p
..           <DIR>     12-01-93   4:50p
DANTE    TXT      156  12-01-93   3:14p
        3 file(s)         156 bytes
                    154337280 bytes free

C:\ITALIANS>
```

❸ Type **COPY DANTE.TXT A:** and press **[Enter]**. DOS copies the file DANTE.TXT to the floppy disk in drive A. During the copy operation, both disk drives (drive C and drive A) will be active. When the copy process is complete, the DOS prompt appears.

❹ Type **A:** and press **[Enter]** to change the current drive to drive A. The DOS prompt changes to reflect the new current drive.

❺ Type **DIR** and press **[Enter]**. DOS displays the contents of the root directory of drive A. See Figure 1-25. The presence of DANTE.TXT in the directory listing verifies that you've successfully copied a file from the hard disk to the floppy disk.

```
C:\ITALIANS>COPY DANTE.TXT A:
        1 file(s) copied

C:\ITALIANS>A:

A:\>DIR

 Volume in drive A is POETS
 Volume Serial Number is 0C2B-18DF
 Directory of A:\

DANTE    TXT         156 12-01-93   3:14p
        1 file(s)          156 bytes
                       1457152 bytes free

A:\>
```

Figure 1-25
A directory listing of the POETS floppy disk

❻ Type **C:** and press **[Enter]** to change the current drive to drive C. The DOS prompt changes to reflect the new current drive.

❼ Remove the floppy disk from drive A (press the button or unhook the latch) and put the disk in a safe place.

Note: Always store your floppy disks, especially the 5.25" disks, which are less sturdy than the 3.5" disks, in a safe place when you're finished using them. Take care to label them properly and keep them away from magnetic fields, excessive temperatures, and locations that could crimp or damage them. With proper care, floppy disks can last for many years.

Questions

1. Identify two important types of operations performed by operating system software.
2. What are the two common storage capacities for double-density and high-density diskettes?
3. What is a filename and why is it important?
4. What information does the DOS prompt provide?
5. Name one reason for identifying the version of DOS that you use on your computer system. How do you find out what the version is?
6. If you make a typing mistake as you enter a DOS command, how can you correct that mistake?

Tutorial Assignments

1. **Issuing DOS Commands:** After you boot your computer system and see the DOS prompt, use DOS commands to answer the following questions. List the full command that you use for each step.
   a. What version of DOS is installed on the computer system?
   b. Are the date and time settings correct? If not, how did you correct them?
   c. What happens when you clear the screen?
   d. What files and directories are located in the root directory of your hard disk?
2. **Setting the Time:** Assume that the time on your computer system is incorrect. Adjust the time in each of the following steps and answer the questions.
   a. Check the current setting for the time. What command did you enter? What time is your computer system using?
   b. If the time is an a.m. time, change it to a p.m. time. If the time is a p.m. time, change it to an a.m. time. What command did you enter? Did DOS change the time? How did you verify it?
   c. Change the time to 7:30 without specifying an a.m. or p.m. time. What command did you enter? Check the time. Is DOS using an a.m. or a p.m. time? What does this feature tell you about DOS?
   d. Assume the time should be 7:30 p.m. What command would you enter to set the time?
   e. Set the time back to the correct time.
3. **Accessing On-Line Help:** From the DOS prompt, obtain help information on the TIME command with the HELP command. As you perform these operations, answer the following questions.
   a. How did you enter the HELP command?
   b. From the type of information that the HELP command displays, you should know whether your computer system uses DOS 5.0 or DOS 6.0. What version does your computer use?
   c. What did you learn about this command from examining the information on the Help screens?

DOS Index

A

application programs, DOS 3
arrow keys, DOS 7

B

backing up, DOS 17
Bad command or file name message, DOS 5
bad sectors, DOS 19
boot, DOS 4

C

C:\, *see* DOS prompt
CD (Change Directory), DOS 15-17
clusters, DOS 18
commands, DOS 3-4
    CD, DOS 15-17
    COPY, DOS 14
    DATE, DOS 5-6
    DEL, DOS 14-15
    DIR, DOS 7-10
    for files, DOS 12-15
    FORMAT, DOS 18-19
    HELP, DOS 6-7
    listing, DOS 6
    MD, DOS 15
    RENAME, DOS 13-14
    TIME, DOS 5-6
    TYPE, DOS 12-13
    VER, DOS 5
computer
    starting, DOS 4
COPY, DOS 14
current directory, DOS 16
current disk, DOS 4
current drive, changing, DOS 19-20
cursor, DOS 4, 6

D

date, setting, DOS 5-6
DEL, DOS 14-15
dialog box, DOS 10
DIR, DOS 7-10
directories, DOS 8
    changing, DOS 16-17
    current, DOS 16
    root, DOS 4
disks. See floppy disks, hard disks.
DOS
    commands, DOS 3-4. *See also* commands.
    definition, DOS 3
    prompt, DOS 4-5
    version, DOS 5
Drive A, DOS 18
Drive B, DOS 18
Drive C, DOS 8
Drive latch, DOS 19

E

EDIT, DOS 10-12
    quitting, DOS 12
    saving files, DOS 10-12
    Survival Guide, DOS 10
erasing characters, DOS 4, DOS 10
execute, DOS 4
Exit command, DOS 7

F

file menu, DOS 7
filenames, DOS 11
files, DOS 8
    commands, DOS 12-15
    copying, DOS 15-16, DOS 20-21
    deleting, DOS 14

duplicating, DOS 14
naming, DOS 11
organization of, DOS 8
renaming, DOS 13-14
saving, DOS 10-12
types of, DOS 12
viewing, DOS 12-13
floppy disks, DOS 7, DOS 17-21
    capacities, DOS 18
    copying to, DOS 20-21
    formatting, DOS 18-19
    naming, DOS 19
    storing, DOS 21
FORMAT, DOS 18-19
formatting, DOS 8, DOS 18-19

H

hard disk, DOS 8-9
    controller, DOS 18
    organization, DOS 8, DOS 15
HELP, DOS 6-7
high-density disk, DOS 18
hot key, DOS 11

L

low-density disk, DOS 18

M

MD, DOS 15
megabytes, DOS 18
menu bar, DOS 6-7
    activating, DOS 7, DOS 11

N

navigation window, DOS 6-7

O

operating system, DOS 3, DOS 7

P

pathname, DOS 17
primary directory. See root directory

R

RENAME, DOS 13-14
root directory, DOS 4, DOS 8
    returning to, DOS 17

S

Save As, DOS 11
scroll bar, DOS 6-7
scrolling, DOS 7
sectors, DOS 18
serial number, disk, DOS 8, DOS 19
subdirectories, DOS 8
    changing, DOS 16-17
    creating, DOS 15-16
Syntax, DOS 7

T

TIME, DOS 5-6
time, setting, DOS 5-6
title bar, DOS 6-7
tracks, DOS 18
TYPE, DOS 12-13

V

VER, DOS 5

W

working position, DOS 4

Microsoft Windows 3.1 Tutorials

1 Essential Windows Skills

2 Effective File Management

Read This Before You Begin

To the Student

To use this book, you must have a Student Disk. Your instructor will either provide you with a Student Disk or ask you to make your own by following the instructions in the section called "Preparing Your Student Disk" in Windows Tutorial 2. See your instructor or lab manager for further information.

Using Your Own Computer If you are going to work through this book using your own computer, you need:

- The Student Disk. **You will not be able to complete the tutorials and exercises in this book using your own computer until you have the Student Disk.** Ask your instructor or lab manager for details on how to get it.
- A computer system running Microsoft Windows 3.1 and DOS.

To the Instructor

Making the Student Disk To complete the tutorials in this book, your students must have a copy of the Student Disk. To relieve you of having to make multiple Student Disks from a single master copy, we provide you with the CTI WinApps Setup Disk, which contains an automatic Student Disk generating program. Once you install the Setup Disk on a network or standalone workstation, students can easily make their own Student Disks by double clicking on the "Make Win 3.1 Student Disk" icon in the CTI WinApps icon group. Double clicking this icon transfers all the data files students will need to complete the tutorials and Tutorial Assignments to a high-density disk in drive A or B. If some of your students will use their own computers to complete the tutorials and exercises in this book, they must first get the Student Disk. The section called "Preparing Your Student Disk" in Windows Tutorial 2 provides complete instructions on how to make the Student Disk.

If you have disk copying resources available, you might choose to use them for making quantities of the Student Disk. The "Make Win 3.1 Student Disk" provides an easy and fast way to make multiple Student Disks.

Installing the CTI WinApps Setup Disk: To install the CTI WinApps icon group from the Setup Disk, follow the instructions either on the disk label or inside the disk envelope that was bundled with your book. By adopting this book, you are granted a license to install this software on any computer or computer network used by you or your students.

Readme File: A Readme.txt file located on the Setup Disk provides additional technical notes, troubleshooting advice, and tips for using the CTI WinApps software in your school's computer lab. You can view the Readme file using any word processor you choose.

System Requirements for installing the CTI WinApps Disk The minimum software and hardware requirements your computer system needs to install the CTI WinApps icon group are as follows:

- Microsoft Windows version 3.1 on a local hard drive or on a network drive
- A 286 (or higher) processor with a minimum of 2 MB RAM (4 MB RAM or more is strongly recommended).
- A mouse supported by Windows
- A printer that is supported by Windows 3.1
- A VGA 640 x 480 16-color display is recommended; an 800 x 600 or 1024 x 768 SVGA, VGA monochrome, or EGA display is also acceptable
- 1.5 MB of free hard disk space
- Student workstations with at least 1 high-density 3.5 inch-disk drive.
- If you wish to install the CTI WinApps Setup Disk on a network drive, your network must support Microsoft Windows.

TUTORIAL 1

Essential Windows Skills

Using the Program Manager, CTI WinApps, and Help

OBJECTIVES

In this tutorial you will:
- Start your computer
- Launch and exit Windows
- Use the mouse and the keyboard
- Identify the components of the Windows desktop
- Launch and exit applications
- Organize your screen-based desktop
- Switch tasks in a multi-tasking environment.
- Use Windows menus
- Explore Windows toolbars

CASE

A New Computer, Anywhere, Inc. You're a busy employee without a minute of spare time. But now, to top it all off, a computer technician appears at your office door, introduces himself as Steve Laslow, and begins unpacking your new computer!

You wonder out loud, "How long is it going to take me to learn this?"

Steve explains that your new computer uses Microsoft Windows 3.1 software and that the **interface**—the way you interact with the computer and give it instructions—is very easy to use. He describes the Windows software as a "gooey," a **graphical user interface (GUI)**, which uses pictures of familiar objects such as file folders and documents to represent a desktop on your screen.

Steve unpacks your new computer and begins to connect the components. He talks as he works, commenting on three things he really likes about Microsoft Windows. First, Windows applications have a standard interface, which means that once you learn how to use one Windows application, you are well on your way to understanding how to use others. Second, Windows lets you use more than one application at a time, a capability called **multitasking**, so you can easily switch between applications such as your word processor and your calendar. Third, Windows lets you do more than one task at a time, such as printing a document while you create a pie chart. All in all, Windows makes your computer an effective and easy-to-use productivity tool.

Using the Windows Tutorials Effectively

This tutorial will help you learn about Windows 3.1. Begin by reading the text that explains the concepts. Then when you come to numbered steps on a colored background, follow those steps as you work at your computer. Read each step carefully and completely *before* you try it.

Don't worry if parts of your screen display are different from the figures in the tutorials. The important parts of the screen display are labeled in each figure. Just be sure these parts are on your screen.

Don't worry about making mistakes—that's part of the learning process. TROUBLE? paragraphs identify common problems and explain how to get back on track. Do the steps in the TROUBLE? paragraph *only* if you are having the problem described.

Starting Your Computer and Launching Windows

The process of starting Windows is sometimes referred to as **launching**. If your computer system requires procedures different from those in the steps below, your instructor or technical support person will provide you with step-by-step instructions for turning on your monitor, starting or resetting your computer, logging into a network if you have one, and launching Windows.

To start your computer and launch Windows:

❶ Make sure your disk drives are empty.

❷ Find the power switch for your monitor and turn it on.

❸ Locate the power switch for your computer and turn it on. After a few seconds you should see C:\> or C> on the screen.

TROUBLE? If your computer displays a "non-system disk" error message, a floppy disk was left in a disk drive at startup. To continue, remove the disk and press [Enter].

❹ Type **win** to launch Windows. See Figure 1-1.

Figure 1-1
Launching Windows
(type win; your screen shows C:\>; C:\>win)

❺ Press the key labeled [Enter]. Soon the Windows 3.1 title screen appears. Next you might notice an hourglass on the screen. This symbol means your computer is busy with a task and you must wait until it has finished.

After a brief wait, the title screen is replaced by one similar to Figure 1-2. Don't worry if your screen is not exactly the same as Figure 1-2. You are ready to continue the Tutorial when you see the Program Manager title at the top of the screen. If you do not see this title, ask your technical support person for assistance.

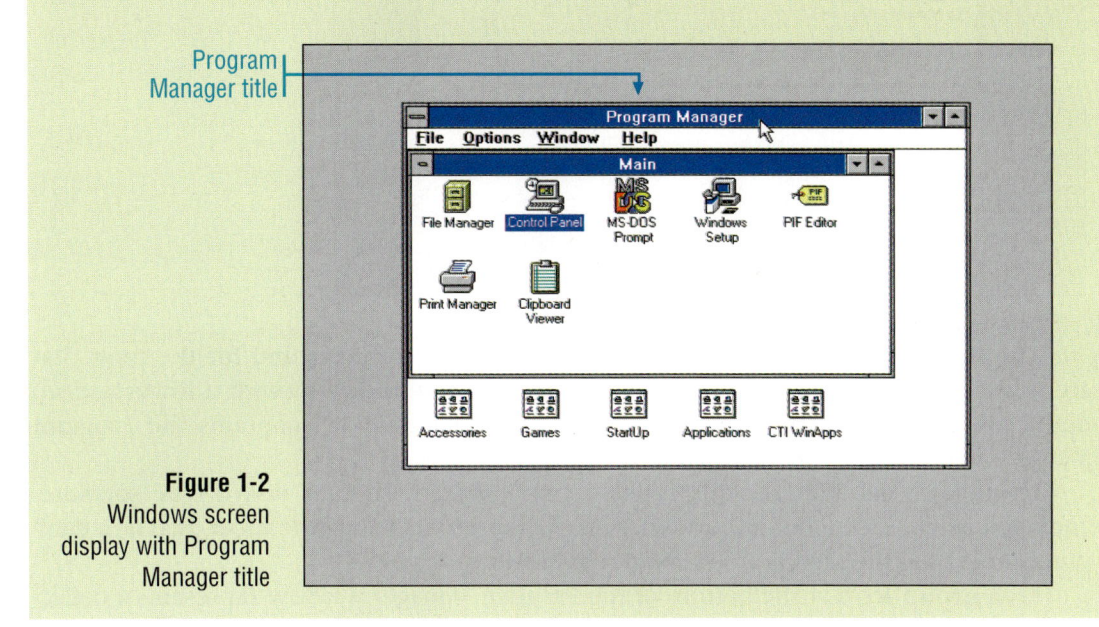

Figure 1-2
Windows screen display with Program Manager title

Basic Windows Controls and Concepts

Windows has a variety of **controls** that enable you to communicate with the computer. In this section you'll learn how to use the basic Windows controls.

The Windows Desktop

Look at your screen display and compare it to Figure 1-3 on the following page. Your screen may not be exactly the same as the illustration. You should, however, be able to locate components on your screen similar to those in Figure 1-3 on the following page.

Figure 1-3
The Windows desktop

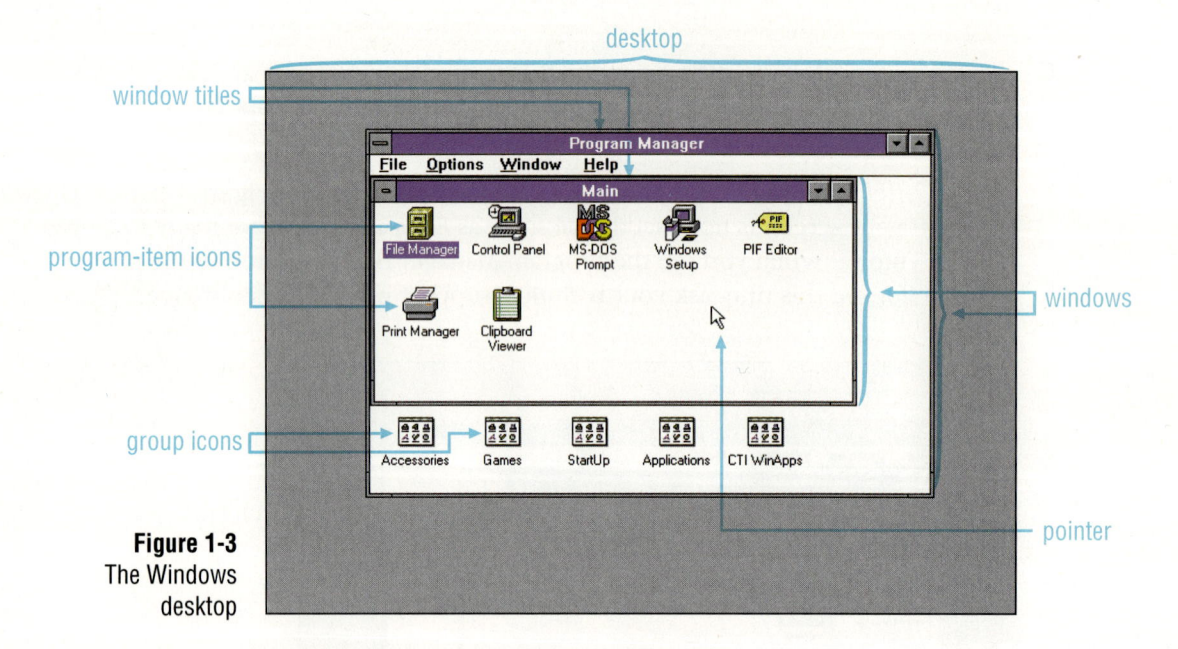

The screen represents a **desktop**, a workspace for projects and for the tools that are needed to manipulate those projects. Rectangular **windows** (with a lowercase *w*) define work areas on the desktop. The desktop in Figure 1-3 contains the Program Manager window and the Main window.

Icons are small pictures that represent real objects, such as disk drives, software, and documents. Each icon in the Main window represents an **application**, that is, a computer program. These icons are called **program-item icons**.

Each **group icon** at the bottom of the Program Manager window represents a collection of applications. For example, the CTI WinApps icon represents a collection of tutorial and practice applications, which you can use to learn more about Windows. A group icon expands into a group window that contains program-item icons.

The **pointer** helps you manipulate objects on the Windows desktop. The pointer can assume different shapes, depending on what is happening on the desktop. In Figure 1-3 the pointer is shaped like an arrow.

The Program Manager

When you launch Windows, the Program Manager application starts automatically and continues to run as long as you are working with Windows. Think of the Program Manager as a launching pad for other applications. The **Program Manager** displays icons for the applications on your system. To launch an application, you would select its icon.

Using the Mouse

The **mouse** is a pointing device that helps you interact with the screen-based objects in the Windows environment. As you move the mouse on a flat surface, the pointer on the screen moves in the direction corresponding to the movement of the mouse. You can also control the Windows environment from the keyboard; however, the mouse is much more efficient for most operations, so the tutorials in this book assume you are using one.

Find the arrow-shaped pointer on your screen. If you do not see the pointer, move your mouse until the pointer comes into view. You will begin most Windows-based operations by **pointing**.

To position the pointer:

❶ Position your right index finger over the left mouse button, as shown in Figure 1-4.

TROUBLE? If you want to use your mouse with your left hand, ask your technical support person to help you. Be sure you find out how to change back to the right-handed mouse setting, so you can reset the mouse each time you are finished in the lab.

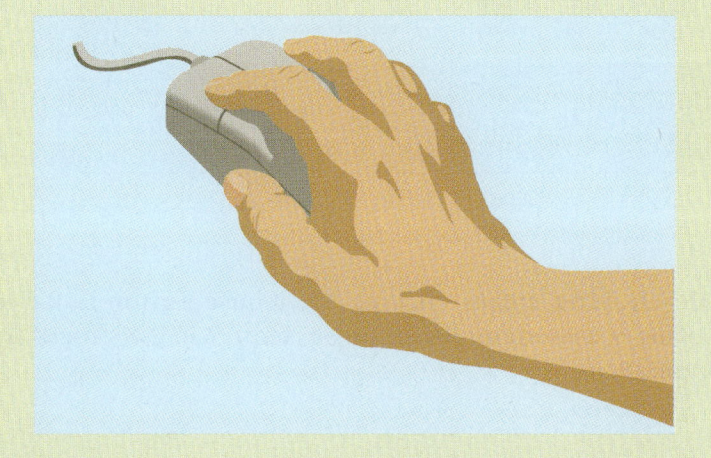

Figure 1-4
How to hold the mouse

❷ Locate the arrow-shaped pointer on the screen.

❸ Move the mouse and watch the movement of the pointer.

❹ Next, move the mouse to each of the four corners of the screen.

TROUBLE? If your mouse runs out of room, lift it, move it into the middle of a clear area on your desk, and then place it back on the table. The pointer does not move when the mouse is not in contact with the tabletop.

❺ Continue experimenting with mouse pointing until you feel comfortable with your "eye-mouse coordination."

Pointing is usually followed by clicking, double-clicking, or dragging. **Clicking** means pressing a mouse button (usually the left button) and then quickly releasing it. Clicking is used to select an object on the desktop. Windows shows you which object is selected by highlighting it.

To click an icon:

❶ Locate the Print Manager icon in the Main window. If you cannot see the Print Manager icon, use any other icon for this activity.

❷ Position the pointer on the icon.

❸ Once the pointer is on the icon, *do not move the mouse*.

❹ Press the left mouse button and then quickly release it. Your icon should have a highlighted title like the one in Figure 1-5 on the following page.

WIN 8   T U T O R I A L   1   Essential Windows Skills

Figure 1-5
Highlighted Print Manager icon

highlighted icon title

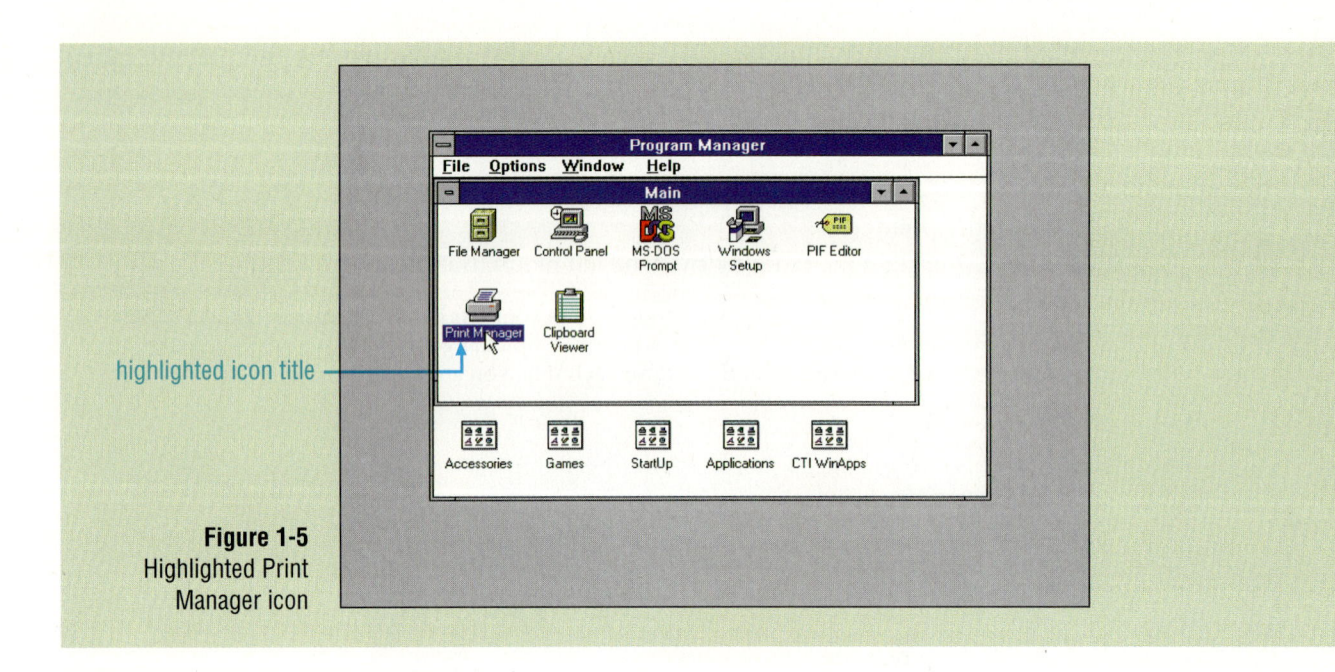

Double-clicking means clicking the mouse button twice in rapid succession. Double-clicking is a shortcut. For example, most Windows users double-click to launch and exit applications.

To double click:

❶ Position the pointer on the Program Manager Control-menu box, as shown in Figure 1-6.

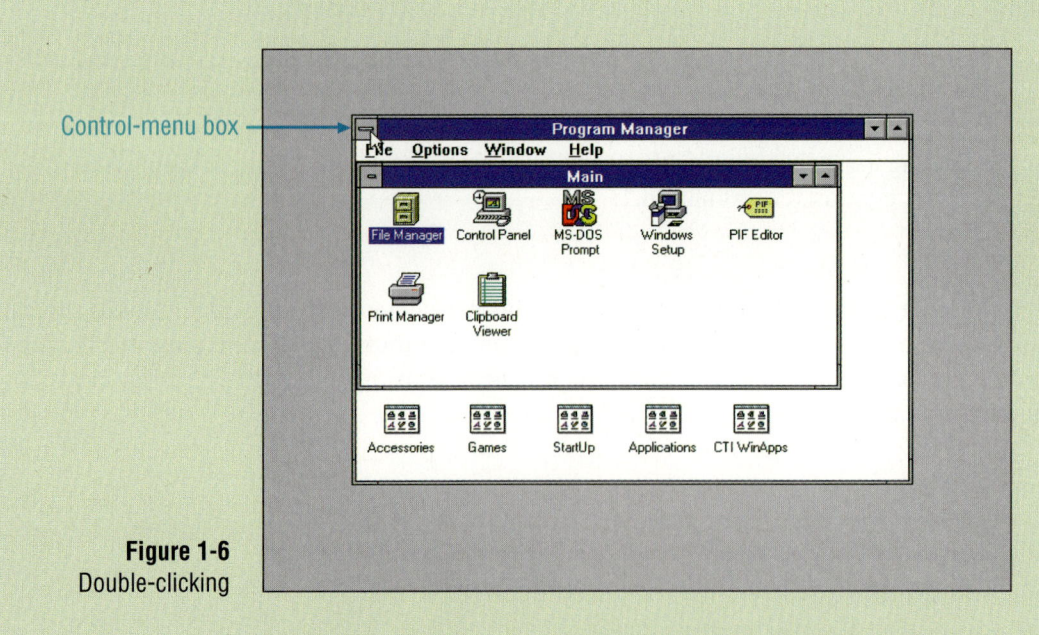

Control-menu box

Figure 1-6
Double-clicking

❷ Click the mouse button twice in rapid succession. If your double-clicking is successful, an Exit Windows box appears on your screen.

❸ Now, single-click the **Cancel button**.

Basic Windows Controls and Concepts **WIN 9**

Dragging means moving an object to a new location on the desktop. To drag an object, you would position the pointer on the object, then hold the left mouse button down while you move the mouse. Let's drag one of the icons to a new location.

To drag an icon:

❶ Position the pointer on any icon on the screen, such as on the Clipboard Viewer icon. Figure 1-7 shows you where to put the pointer and what happens on your screen as you carry out the next step.

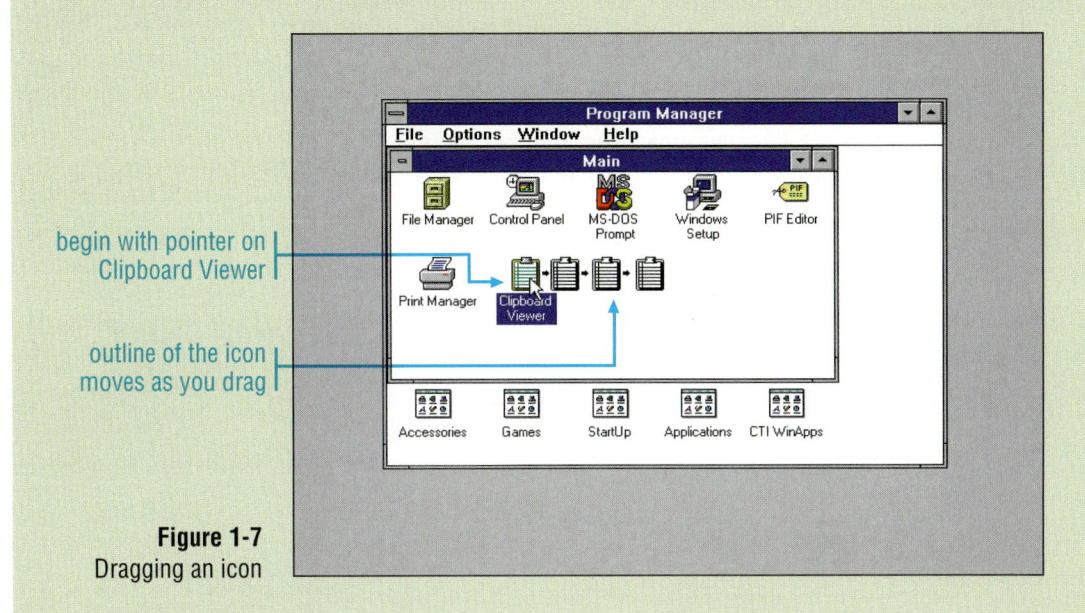

begin with pointer on Clipboard Viewer

outline of the icon moves as you drag

Figure 1-7
Dragging an icon

❷ Hold the left mouse button down while you move the mouse to the right. Notice that an outline of the icon moves as you move the mouse.

❸ Release the mouse button. Now the icon is in a new location.

TROUBLE? If the icon snaps back to its original position, don't worry. Your technical support person probably has instructed Windows to do this. If your icon automatically snapped back to its original position, skip Step 4.

❹ Drag the icon back to its original location.

Using the Keyboard

You use the keyboard to type documents, enter numbers, and activate some commands. You can use the on-screen CTI Keyboard Tutorial to learn the special features of your computer keyboard. To do this, you need to learn how to launch the Keyboard Tutorial and other applications.

Launching Applications

Earlier in this tutorial you launched Windows. Once you have launched Windows, you can launch other Windows applications such as Microsoft Works. When you launch an application, an application window opens. Later, when you have finished using the application, you close the window to exit.

Launching the CTI Keyboard Tutorial

To launch the CTI Keyboard Tutorial, you need to have the CTI WinApps software installed on your computer. If you are working in a computer lab, these applications should already be installed on your computer system. Look on your screen for a group icon or a window labeled "CTI WinApps."

If you don't have anything labeled "CTI WinApps" on your screen's desktop, ask your technical support person for help. If you are using your own computer, you will need to install the CTI WinApps applications yourself. See your technical support person or your instructor for a copy of the Setup Disk and the Installation Instructions that come with it.

To open the CTI Win Apps group window:

❶ Double-click the **CTI WinApps group icon**. Your screen displays a CTI WinApps group window similar to the one in Figure 1-8.

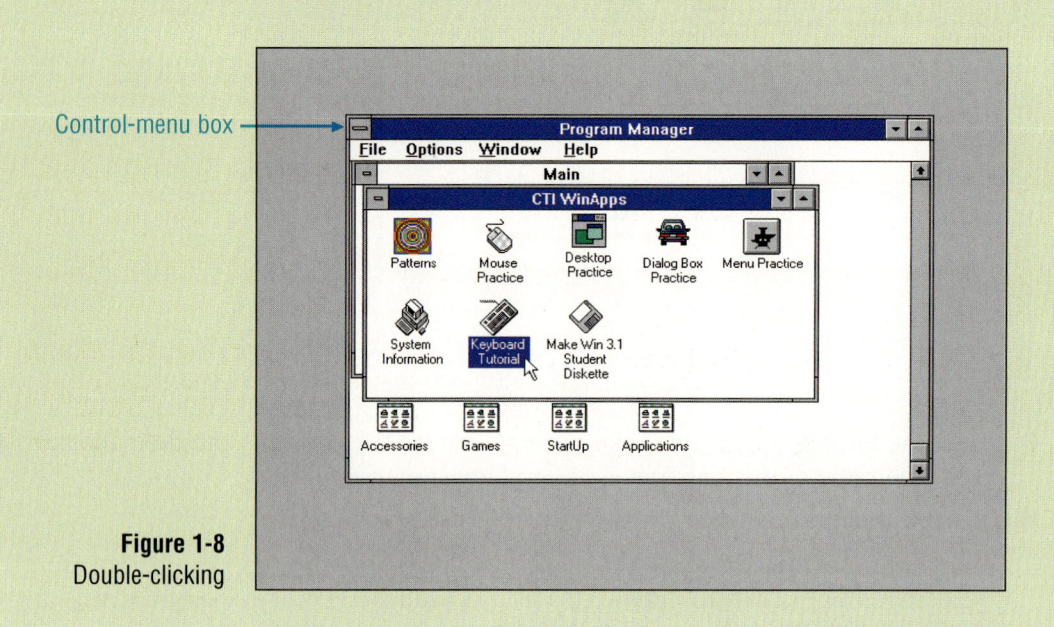

Figure 1-8
Double-clicking

The CTI WinApps group window contains an icon for each application provided with these tutorials. Right now we want to use the Keyboard Tutorial application.

To launch the Keyboard Tutorial:

❶ Double-click the **Keyboard Tutorial icon**. Within a few seconds, the tutorial begins.

❷ Read the opening screen, then click the **Continue button**. The CTI Keyboard Tutorial window appears. Follow the instructions on your screen to complete the tutorial. See Figure 1-9.

Organizing Application Windows on the Desktop   WIN 11

Figure 1-9
Instructions in the CTI Keyboard Tutorial window

Keyboard Tutorial

Your computer keyboard consists of four major parts:
1) The main keyboard
2) The editing keypad
3) The function keys
4) The numeric keypad
Your keyboard may be arranged differently than the keyboard in the diagram.
Try to find the four major parts on your keyboard now.
Click CONTINUE to go to the next screen.

← follow the instructions in this window

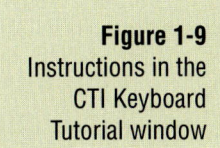

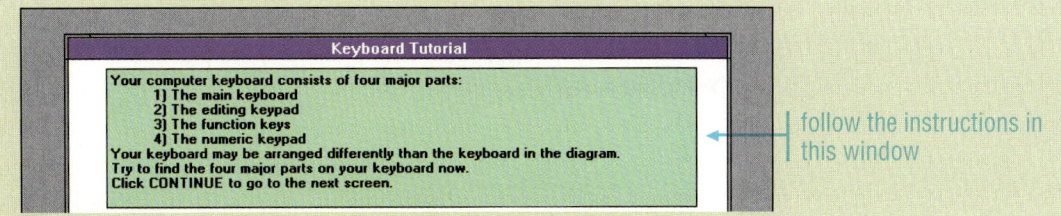

> **TROUBLE?** Click the Quit button at any time if you want to exit the Tutorial.

❸ When you have completed the Keyboard Tutorial, click the **Quit button**. This takes you back to the Program Manager and CTI WinApps group window.

> **TROUBLE?** *If you did not have trouble in Step 3, skip this entire paragraph!* If the Program Manager window is not open, look for its icon at the bottom of your screen. Double-click this icon to open the Program Manager window. To prevent this problem from happening again, click the word Options on the Program Manager menu bar, then click Minimize on Use.

Launching the CTI Mouse Practice

To discover how to use the mouse to manipulate Windows controls, you should launch the Mouse Practice.

To launch the Mouse Practice:

❶ Make sure the Program Manager and the CTI WinApps windows are open. It is not a problem if you have additional windows open.

> **TROUBLE?** If the Program Manager window is not open, look for its icon at the bottom of your screen. Double-click this icon to open the Program Manager window. To prevent this problem from happening again, click the word Options that appears near the top of the Program Manager window, then click Minimize.

❷ Double-click the **Mouse Practice icon**. The Mouse Practice window opens.

> **TROUBLE?** If you don't see the Mouse Practice icon, try clicking the scroll bar arrow button or see your technical support person.

❸ Click, drag, or double-click the objects on the screen to see what happens. Don't hesitate to experiment.

❹ When you have finished using the Mouse Practice, click the **Exit button** to go back to the Program Manager and continue the tutorial steps.

Organizing Application Windows on the Desktop

The Windows desktop provides you with capabilities similar to your desk; it lets you stack many different items on your screen-based desktop and activate the one you want to use.

There is a problem, though. Like your real desk, your screen-based desktop can become cluttered. That's why you need to learn how to organize the applications on your Windows desktop.

Launching the CTI Desktop Practice

The Desktop Practice application will help you learn the controls for organizing your screen-based desktop.

To Launch the Desktop Practice:

❶ Double-click the **Desktop Practice icon** to open the Desktop Practice window, shown in Figure 1-10. Your windows might be a different size or in a slightly different position. Don't worry. What's important is that you see a window with the title "Desktop Practice."

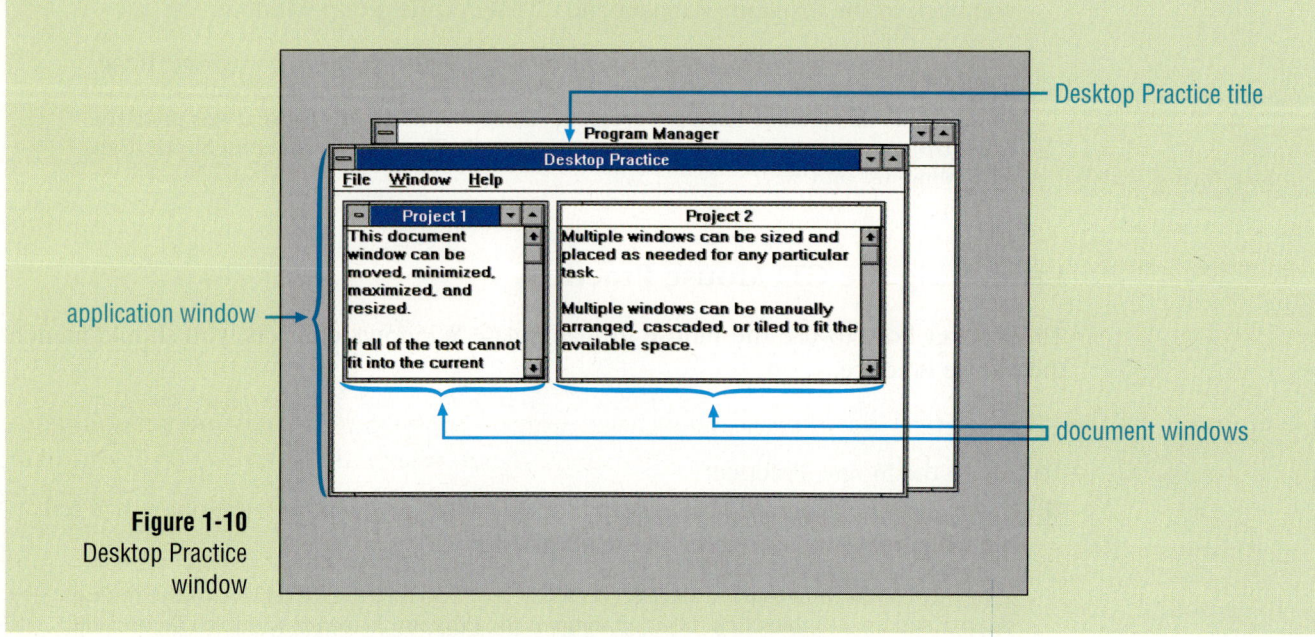

Figure 1-10
Desktop Practice window

Launching the Desktop Practice application opens three new windows on the desktop: Desktop Practice, Project 1, and Project 2. You might be able to see the edges of the Program Manager window "under" the Desktop Practice window. Essentially, you have stacked one project on top of another on your desktop.

The Desktop Practice window is an **application window**, a window that opens when you launch an application. The Project 1 and Project 2 windows are referred to as **document windows**, because they contain the documents, graphs, and lists you create using the application. Document windows are also referred to as **child windows**, because they belong to and are controlled by a "parent" application window.

The ability to have more than one document window open is one of many useful features of the Windows operating environment. Without this capability, you would have to print the documents that aren't being displayed so you could refer to them.

The Anatomy of a Window

Application windows and document windows are similar in many respects. Take a moment to study the Desktop Practice window on your screen and in Figure 1-11 on the following page to familiarize yourself with the terminology. Notice the location of each component but *don't* activate the controls.

Figure 1-11 Anatomy of a window

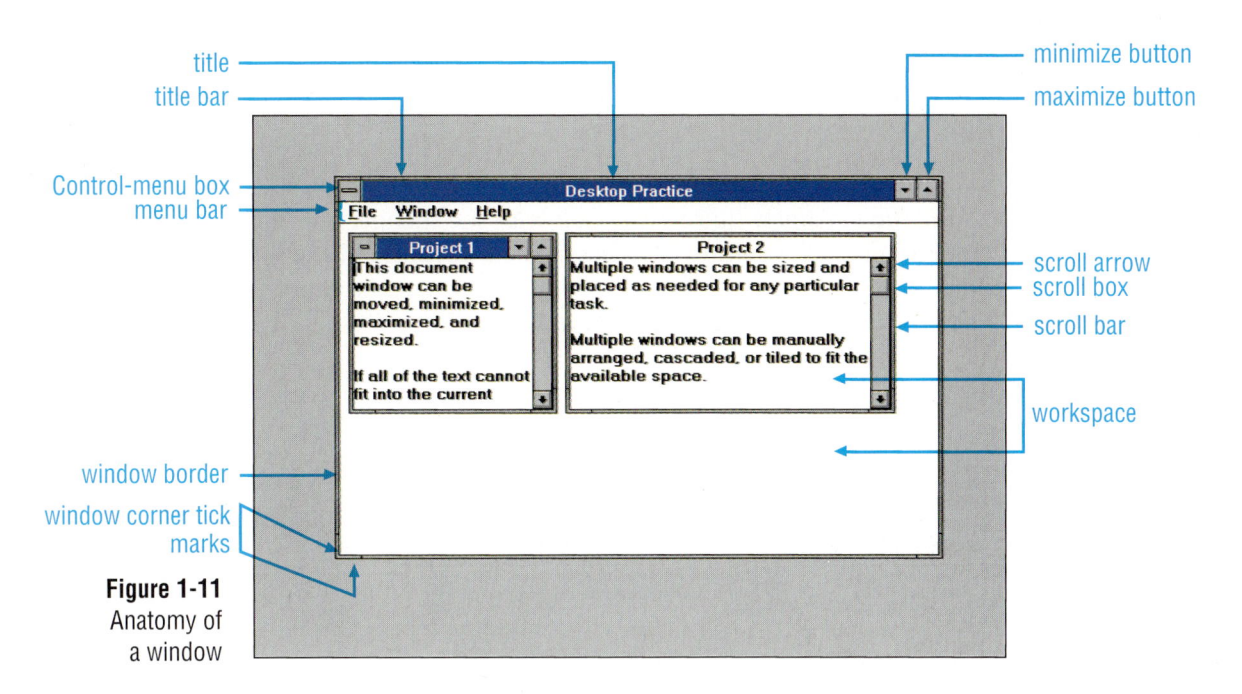

At the top of each window is a **title bar**, which contains the window title. A darkened or highlighted title bar indicates that the application window is active. In Figure 1-11, the Desktop Practice application and the Project 1 document windows are active.

In the upper-right of the application window are two buttons used to change the size of a window. The **minimize button**—a square containing a triangle with the point down—is used to shrink the window. The **maximize button**, with the triangle pointing up, is used to enlarge the window so it fills the screen. When a window is maximized, a **restore button** with two triangles replaces the maximize button. Clicking the restore button reduces a maximized window to its previous size.

The **Control-menu box**, located in the upper-left of the Desktop Practice application window, is used to open the **Control menu**, which allows you to switch between application windows.

The **menu bar** is located just below the title bar on application windows. Notice that child windows do not contain menu bars.

The thin line running around the entire perimeter of the window is called the **window border**. The **window corners** are indicated by tick marks on the border.

The gray bar on the right side of each document window is a **scroll bar**, which you use to view window contents that don't initially fit in the window. Both application windows and document windows can contain scroll bars. Scroll bars can appear on the bottom of a window as well as on the side.

The space inside a window where you type text, design graphics, and so forth is called the **workspace**.

Maximizing and Minimizing Windows

The buttons on the right of the title bar are sometimes referred to as **resizing buttons**. You can use the resizing buttons to **minimize** the window so it shrinks down to an icon, **maximize** the window so it fills the screen, or **restore** the window to its previous size.

Because a minimized program is still running, you have quick access to the materials you're using for the project without taking up space on the desktop. You don't need to launch the program when you want to use it again because it continues to run.

A maximized window is useful when you want to focus your attention on the project in that window without being distracted by other windows and projects.

To maximize, restore, and minimize the Desktop Practice window:

❶ Locate the maximize button (the one with the triangle pointing up) for the Desktop Practice window. You might see a portion of the Program Manager window behind the Desktop Practice window. Be sure you have found the Desktop Practice maximize button. See Figure 1-12.

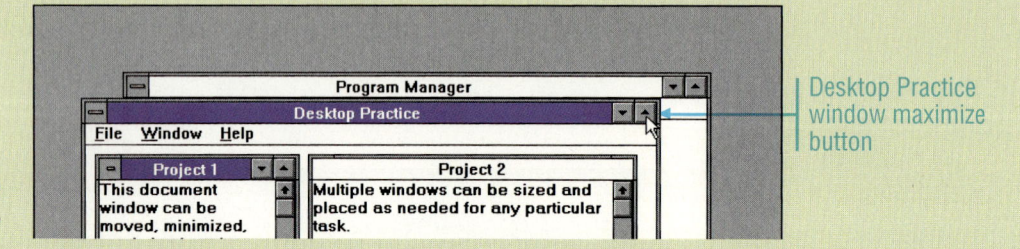

Figure 1-12
Maximizing a window

❷ Click the **maximize button** to expand the window to fill the screen. Notice that in place of the maximize button there is now a restore button that contains double triangles.

❸ Click the **restore button**. The Desktop Practice window returns to its original size.

❹ Next, click the **minimize button** (the one with the triangle pointing down) to shrink the window to an icon.

❺ Locate the minimized Desktop Practice icon at the bottom of your screen. See Figure 1-13.

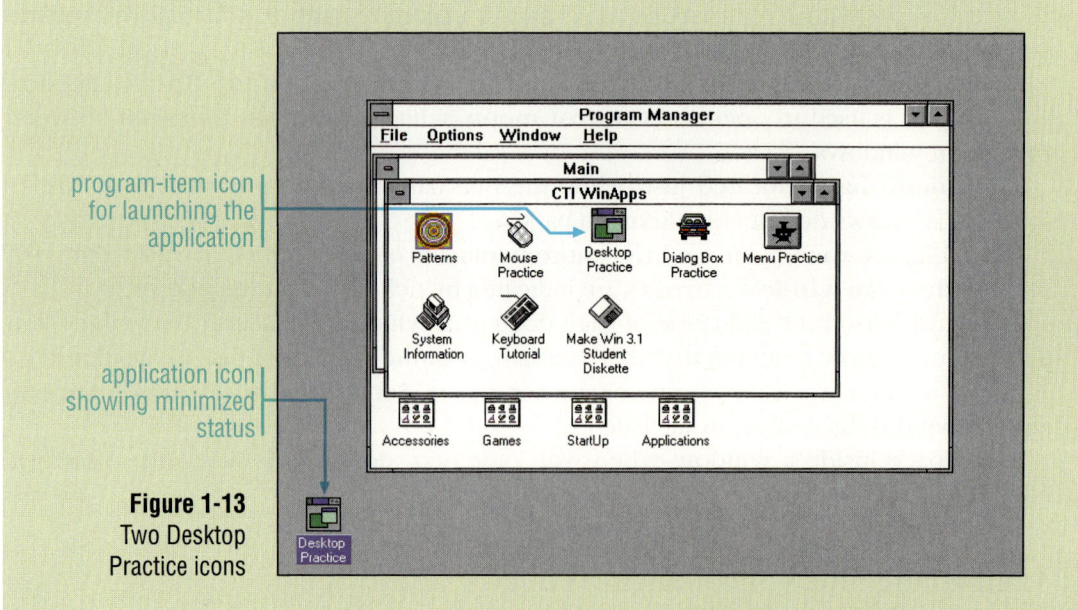

Figure 1-13
Two Desktop Practice icons

TROUBLE? If you cannot locate the Desktop Practice icon at the bottom of your screen, the Program Manager is probably maximized. To remedy this situation, click the restore button on the Program Manager Window.

Organizing Application Windows on the Desktop   WIN 15

When you *close* an application window, you exit the application and it stops running. But when you *minimize* an application, it is still running even though it has been shrunk to an icon. It is important to remember that minimizing a window is not the same as closing it.

The icon for a minimized application is called an **application icon**. As Figure 1-13 illustrates, your screen shows two icons for the Desktop Practice application. The icon at the bottom of your screen is the application icon and represents a program that is currently running even though it is minimized. The other Desktop Practice icon is inside the CTI WinApps window. If you were to double-click this icon, you would launch a second version of the Desktop Practice application. *Don't launch two versions of the same application.* You should restore the Desktop Practice window by double-clicking the minimized icon at the bottom of your screen. Let's do that now.

To restore the Desktop Practice window:
❶ Double-click the minimized **Desktop Practice icon** at the bottom of your screen. The Desktop Practice window opens.

Changing the Dimensions of a Window

Changing the dimensions of a window is useful when you want to arrange more than one project on your desktop. Suppose you want to work with the Desktop Practice application and at the same time view the contents of the Program Manager window. To do this, you will need to change the dimensions of both windows so they don't overlap each other.

To change the dimensions of the Desktop Practice window:
❶ Move the pointer slowly over the top border of the Desktop Practice window until the pointer changes shape to a double-ended arrow. See Figure 1-14.

Figure 1-14
Preparing to change the window dimensions

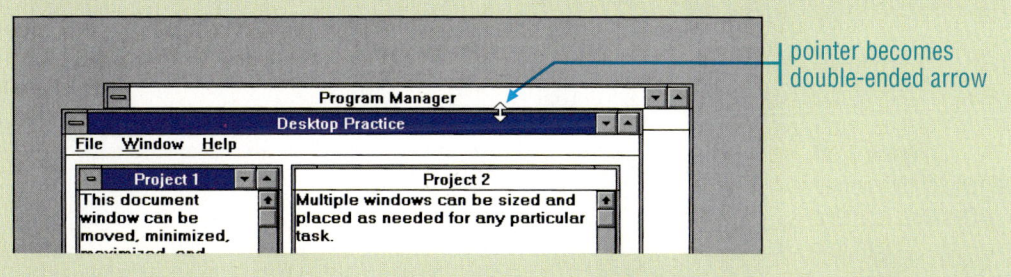

pointer becomes double-ended arrow

❷ Press the left mouse button and hold it down while you drag the border to the top of the screen. Notice how an outline of the border follows your mouse movement.
❸ Release the mouse button. As a result the window adjusts to the new border.
❹ Drag the left border of the Desktop Practice window to the left edge of the screen.
❺ Move the pointer slowly over the lower-right corner of the Desktop Practice window until the pointer changes shape to a double-ended diagonal arrow. Figure 1-15 on the following page shows you how to do this step and the next one.

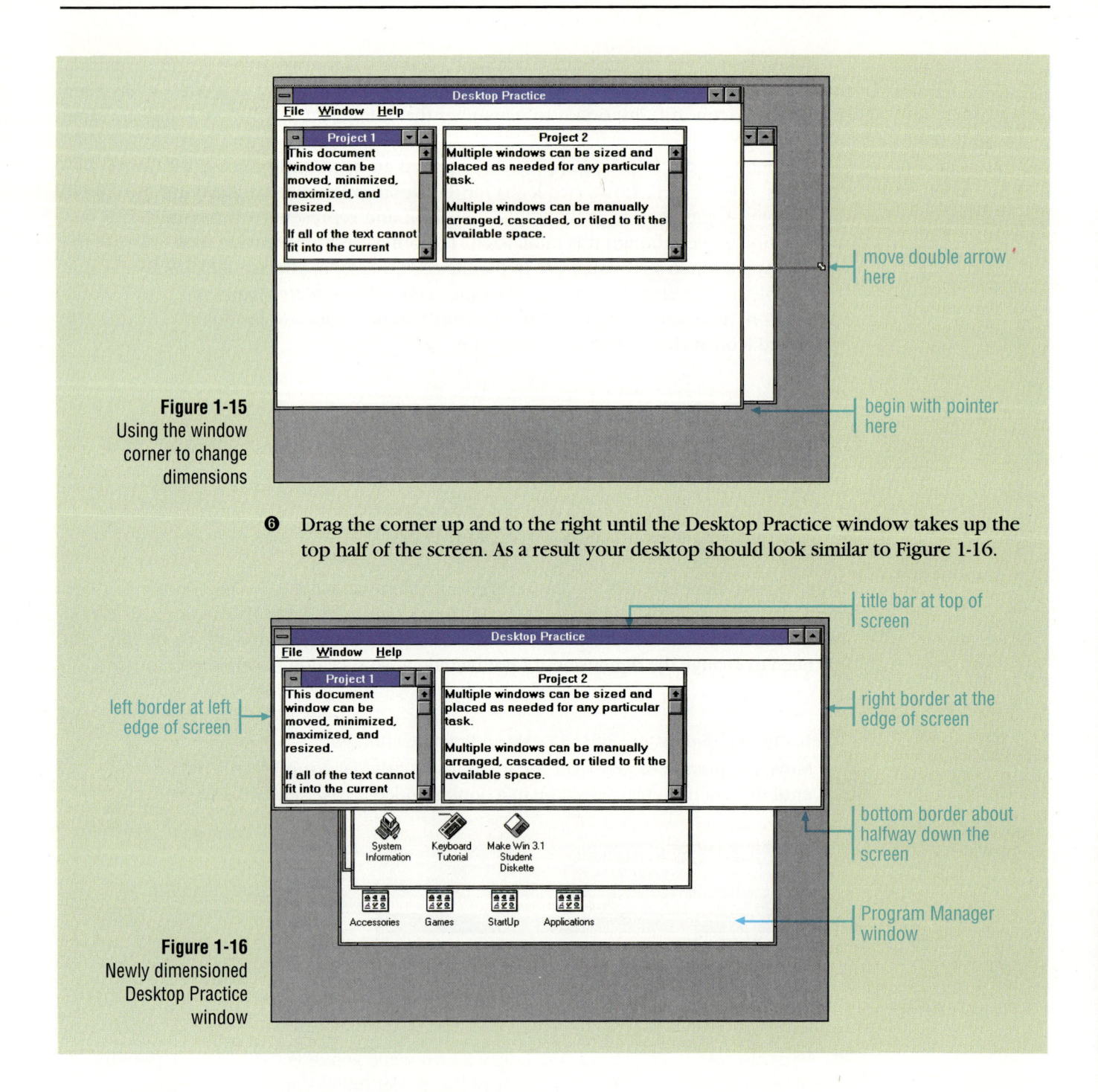

Figure 1-15
Using the window corner to change dimensions

6. Drag the corner up and to the right until the Desktop Practice window takes up the top half of the screen. As a result your desktop should look similar to Figure 1-16.

Figure 1-16
Newly dimensioned Desktop Practice window

Switching Applications

In the preceding steps you arranged the application windows so they were both visible at the same time. A different approach to organizing windows is to maximize the windows and then switch between them using the **Task List**, which contains a list of all open applications.

Let's maximize the Desktop Practice window. Then, using the Task List, let's switch to the Program Manager window, which will be hidden behind it.

Organizing Application Windows on the Desktop **WIN 17**

To maximize the Desktop Practice window and then switch to the Program Manager:

❶ Click the **maximize button** on the Desktop Practice title bar. As a result the maximized Desktop Practice window hides the Program Manager window.

❷ Click the **Control-menu box** on the left side of the Desktop Practice title bar. Figure 1-17 shows you the location of the Control-menu box and also the Control menu, which appears after you click.

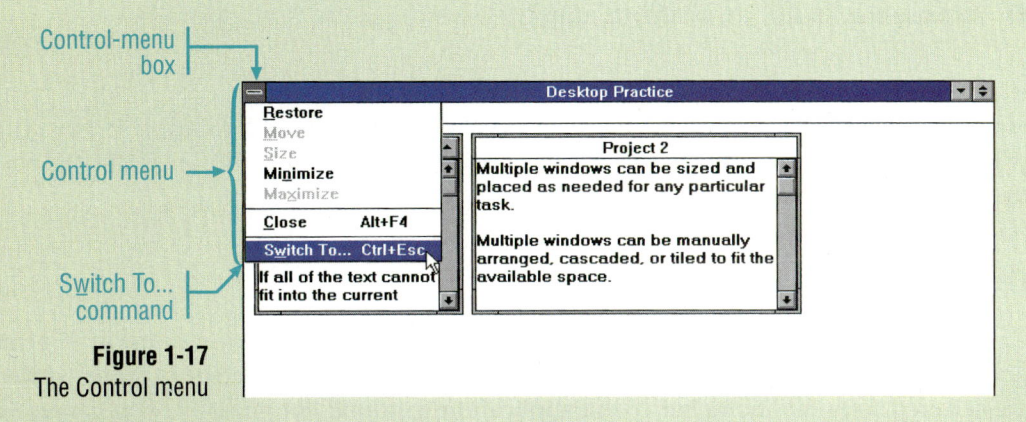

Figure 1-17
The Control menu

❸ Click **Switch To...** The Task List box appears, as shown in Figure 1-18.

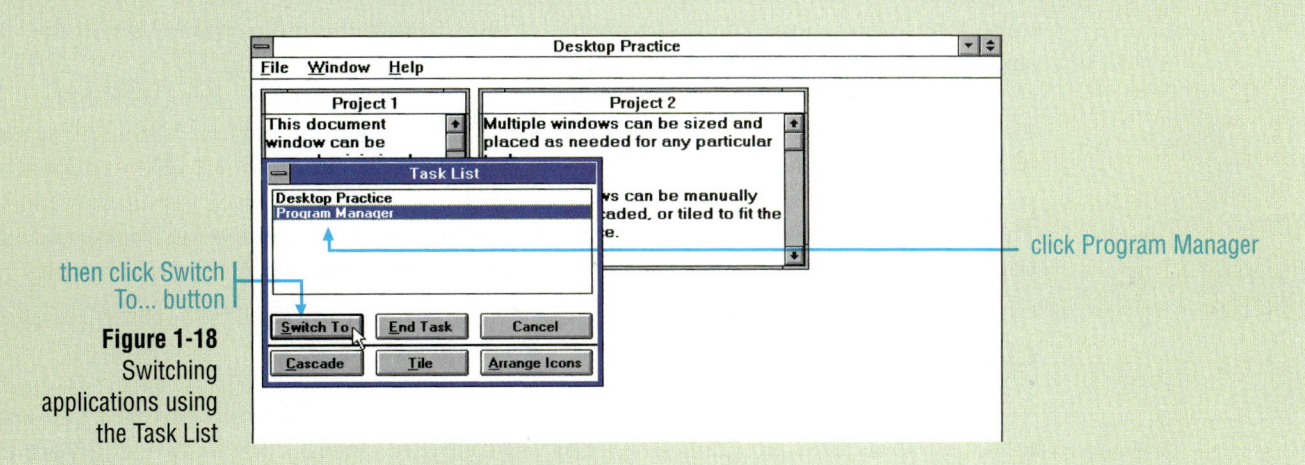

Figure 1-18
Switching applications using the Task List

❹ Click the **Program Manager option** from the list, then click the **Switch To button** to select the Program Manager. As a result the Program Manager reappears on the bottom half of your screen.

❺ If it is not already maximized, click the **maximize button** on the Program Manager window so both applications (Program Manager and Desktop Practice) are maximized.

The Program Manager window is active and "on top" of the Desktop Practice window. To view the Desktop Practice window, you will need to switch application windows again. You could switch tasks using the mouse, as we did in the last set of steps, or you can use the keyboard to quickly cycle through the tasks and activate the one you want. Let's use the keyboard method for switching windows this time, instead of using the Task List.

To switch to the Desktop Practice window using the keyboard:

❶ Hold down **[Alt]** and continue holding it down while you press **[Tab]**. Don't release the Alt key yet! On the screen you should see a small rectangle that says "Desktop Practice."

TROUBLE? Don't worry if you accidentally let go of the Alt key too soon. Try again. Press [Alt][Tab] until the "Desktop Practice" rectangle reappears.

❷ Release the Alt key. Now the maximized Desktop Practice window is open.

When a window is maximized, it is easy to forget what's behind it. If you forget what's on the desktop, call up the Task List using the Control menu or use [Alt][Tab] to cycle through the tasks.

Organizing Document Windows

Think of document windows as subwindows within an application window. Because document windows do not have menu bars, the commands relating to these windows are selected from the menu bar of the application window. For example, you can use the Tile command in the Window menu to arrange windows so they are as large as possible without any overlap. The advantage of tiled windows is that one window won't cover up important information. The disadvantage of tiling is that the more windows you tile, the smaller each tile becomes and the more scrolling you will have to do.

You can use the Cascade command in the Window menu to arrange windows so they are all a standard size, they overlap each other, and all title bars are visible. Cascaded windows are often larger than tiled windows and at least one corner is always accessible so you can activate the window. Try experimenting with tiled and cascading windows. The desktop organizational skills you will learn will help you arrange the applications on your desktop so you can work effectively in the Windows multi-tasking environment.

Closing a Window

You close a window when you have finished working with a document or when you want to exit an application program. The steps you follow to close a document window are the same as those to close an application window. Let's close the Desktop Practice window.

To close the Desktop Practice application window:

❶ Click the **Control-menu box** on the Desktop Practice window.

❷ Click **Close** as shown in Figure 1-19 on the following page. The Desktop Practice window closes and you see the Program Manager window on the desktop.

Using Windows to Specify Tasks **WIN 19**

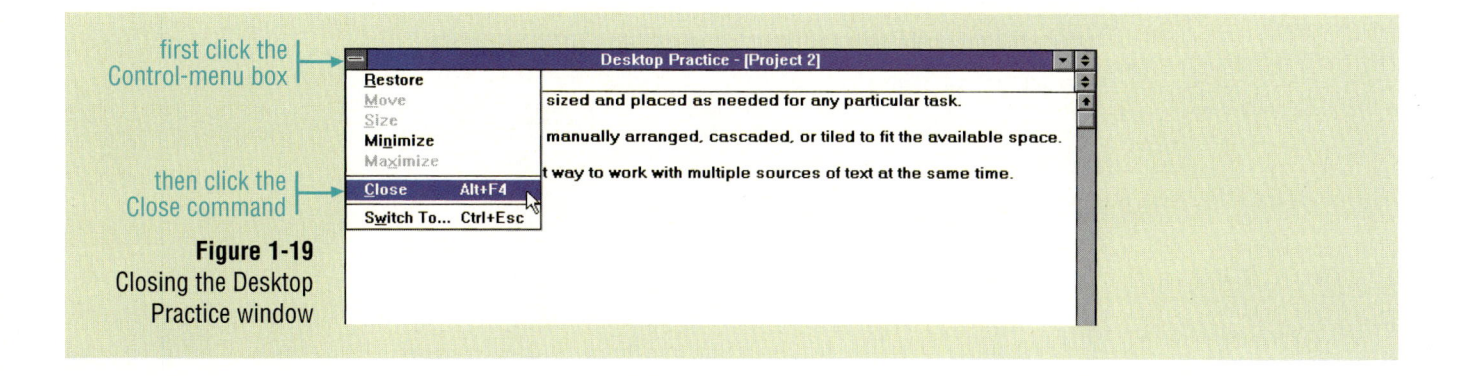

Figure 1-19
Closing the Desktop Practice window

- first click the Control-menu box
- then click the Close command

Using Windows to Specify Tasks

In Windows, you issue instructions called **commands** to tell the computer what you want it to do. Windows applications provide you with lists of commands called **menus**. Many applications also have a ribbon of icons called a **toolbar**, which provides you with command shortcuts. Let's launch the Menu Practice application to find out how menus and toolbars work.

To launch the Menu Practice application:

❶ If the CTI WinApps window is not open, double-click its group icon at the bottom of the Program Manager window.

❷ Double-click the **Menu Practice** icon to open the Menu Practice window. See Figure 1-20.

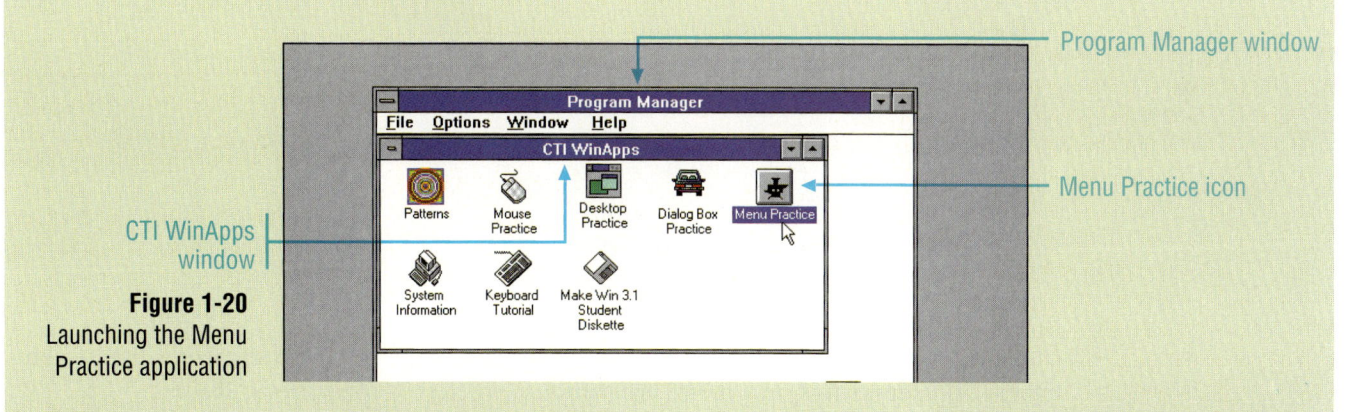

Figure 1-20
Launching the Menu Practice application

- Program Manager window
- Menu Practice icon
- CTI WinApps window

❸ Click the **maximize button** (the one with the triangle point up) for the Menu Practice window. The maximized Menu Practice window is shown in Figure 1-21 on the following page.

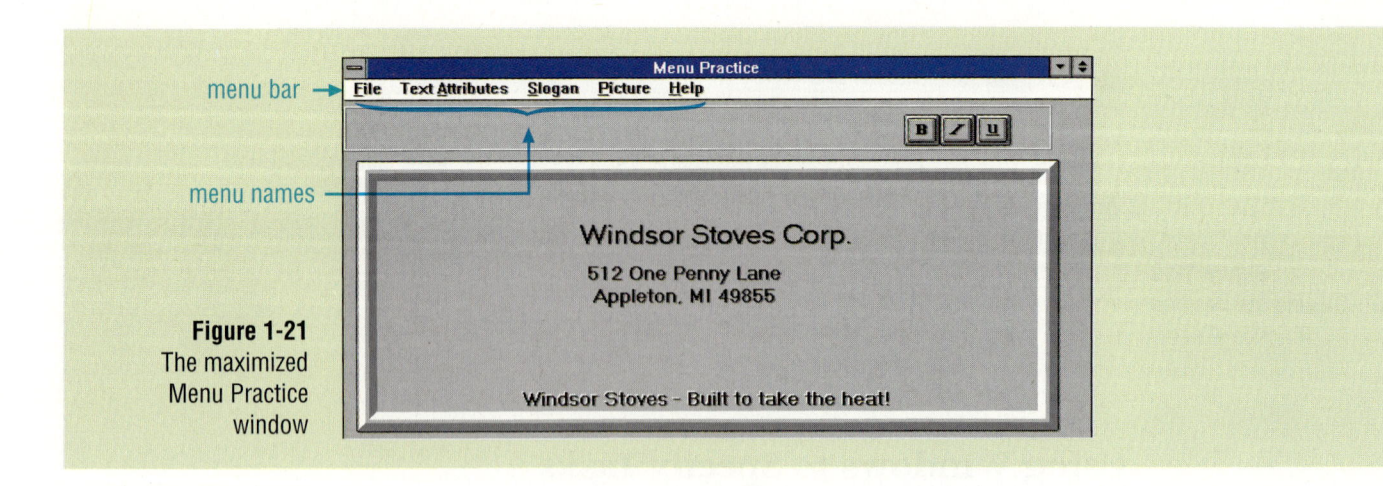

Figure 1-21
The maximized Menu Practice window

Opening and Closing Menus

Application windows, but not document windows, have menu bars such as the one shown in Figure 1-21. The menu bar contains menu names such as File, Text Attributes, Slogan, Picture, and Help. Let's practice opening and closing menus.

To open a menu:
❶ Click **File**. Figure 1-22 shows you where to click and the menu that appears.

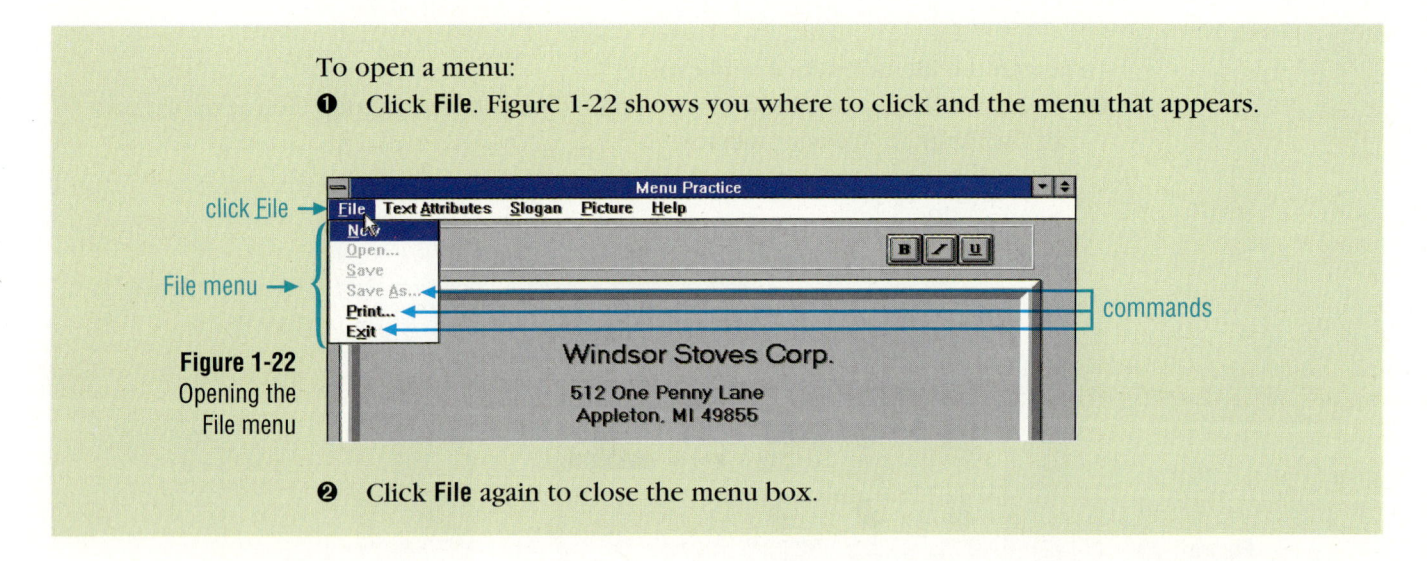

Figure 1-22
Opening the File menu

❷ Click **File** again to close the menu box.

When you click a menu name, the full menu drops down to display a list of commands. The commands on a menu are sometimes referred to as **menu items**.

Menu Conventions

The commands displayed on the Windows menus often include one or more **menu conventions**, such as check marks, ellipses, shortcut keys, and underlined letters. These menu conventions provide you with additional information about each menu command.

A check mark in front of a menu command indicates that the command is in effect. Clicking a checked command will remove the check mark and deactivate the command. For example, the Windsor Stoves logo currently has no graphic because the Show Picture command is not active. Let's add a picture to the logo by activating the Show Picture command.

Using Windows to Specify Tasks   WIN 21

To add or remove a check mark from the Show Picture command:

❶ Click **Picture**. Notice that no check mark appears next to the Show Picture command.

❷ Click **Show Picture**. The Picture menu closes, and a picture of a stove appears.

❸ Click **Picture** to open the Picture menu again. Notice that a check mark appears next to the Show Picture command because you activated this command in Step 2.

❹ Click **Show Picture**. This time clicking Show Picture removes the check mark and removes the picture.

Another menu convention is the use of gray, rather than black, type for commands. Commands displayed in gray type are sometimes referred to as **grayed-out commands**. Gray type indicates that a command is not currently available. The command might become available later, when it can be applied to the task. For example, a command that positions a picture on the right or left side of the logo would not apply to a logo without a picture. Therefore, the command for positioning the picture would be grayed out until a picture was included with the logo. Let's explore how this works.

To explore grayed-out commands:

❶ Click **Picture**. Figure 1-23 shows the Picture menu with two grayed-out choices.

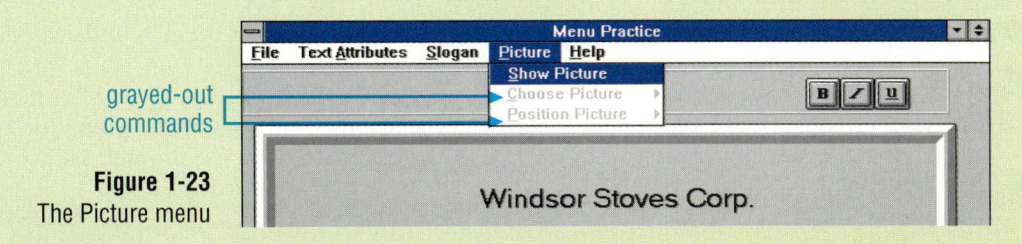

Figure 1-23
The Picture menu

❷ Click the grayed-out command **Position Picture**. Although the highlight moves to this command, nothing else happens because the command is not currently available. You cannot position the picture until a picture is displayed.

❸ Now click **Show Picture**. The Picture menu closes, and a picture is added to the logo.

❹ Click **Picture**. Now that you have opened the Picture menu again, notice that the Choose Picture and Position Picture commands are no longer grayed out.

A **submenu** provides an additional set of command choices. On your screen the Choose Picture and Position Picture commands each have triangles next to them. A triangle is a menu convention that indicates a menu has a submenu. Let's use the submenu of the Position Picture command to move the stove picture to the right of the company name.

To use the position Picture submenu:

❶ Click **Position Picture**. A submenu appears with options for left or right. In Figure 1-24 on the following page, the picture is to the left of the company name.

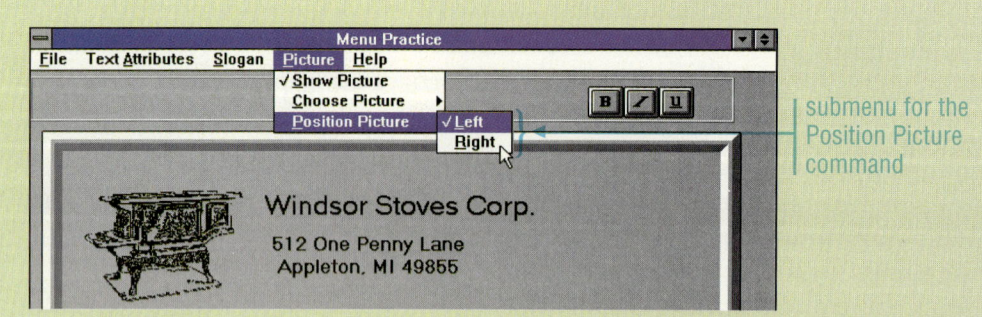

Figure 1-24
Viewing a submenu

submenu for the Position Picture command

❷ Click **Right**. Selecting this submenu command moves the picture to the right of the company name.

Some menu conventions allow you to use the menus without a mouse. It is useful to know how to use these conventions because, even if you have a mouse, in some situations it might be faster to use the keyboard.

One keyboard-related menu convention is the underlined letter in each menu name. If you wanted to open a menu using the keyboard, you would hold down the Alt key and then press the underlined letter. Let's open the Text Attributes menu using the keyboard.

To open the Text Attributes menu this way:
❶ Look at the menu name for the Text Attributes menu. Notice that the A is underlined.
❷ Press **[Alt][A]**. The Text Attributes menu opens.

TROUBLE? Remember from the Keyboard Tutorial that the [Alt][A] notation means to hold down the Alt key and press A. Don't type the brackets and don't use the Shift key to capitalize the A.

You can also use the keyboard to highlight and activate commands. On your screen the Bold command is highlighted. You use the arrow keys on the keyboard to move the highlight. You activate highlighted commands by pressing [Enter]. Let's use the keyboard to activate the Underline command.

To choose the Underline command using the keyboard:
❶ Press **[↓]** two times to highlight the Underline command.
❷ Press **[Enter]** to activate the highlighted command and underline the company name. Now look at the **B**, *I*, and <u>U</u> buttons near the upper-right corner of the screen. The U button has been "pressed" or activated. This button is another control for underlining. You'll find out how to use these buttons later.

Previously you used the Alt key in combination with the underlined letter in the menu title to open a menu. You might have noticed that each menu command also has an underlined letter. Once a menu is open, you can activate a command by pressing the underlined letter—there is no need to press the Alt key.

Using Windows to Specify Tasks **WIN 23**

To activate the Italic command using the underlined letter:

❶ Press **[Alt][A]**. This key combination opens the Text Attributes menu. Next, notice which letter is underlined in the Italic command.

❷ Press **[I]** to activate the Italic command. Now the company name is italicized as well as underlined.

Look at the menu in Figure 1-25. Notice the Ctrl+B to the right of the Bold command. This is the key combination, often called a **shortcut key**, that can be used to activate the Bold command even if the menu is not open. The Windows Ctrl+B notation means the same thing as [Ctrl][B] in these tutorials: hold down the Control key and, while holding it down, press the letter B. When you use shortcut keys, don't type the + sign and don't use the Shift key to capitalize. Let's use a shortcut key to boldface the company name.

Figure 1-25
The Text Attributes menu

shortcut key

To Boldface the company name using a shortcut key:

❶ Press **[Ctrl][B]** and watch the company name appear in boldface type.

The **ellipsis (...)** menu convention means that when you select a command with three dots next to it, a dialog box will appear. A **dialog box** requests additional details about how you want the command carried out. We'll use the dialog box for the Choose Slogan command to change the company slogan.

To use the Choose Slogan dialog box:

❶ Click **Slogan**. Notice that the Choose Slogan command is followed by an ellipsis.

❷ Click **Choose Slogan...** and study the dialog box that appears. See Figure 1-26. Notice that this dialog box contains four sets of controls: the "Use Slogan" text box, the "Slogan in Bold Letters" check box, the "Slogan 3-D Effects" control buttons, and the OK and Cancel buttons. The "Use Slogan" text box displays the current slogan.

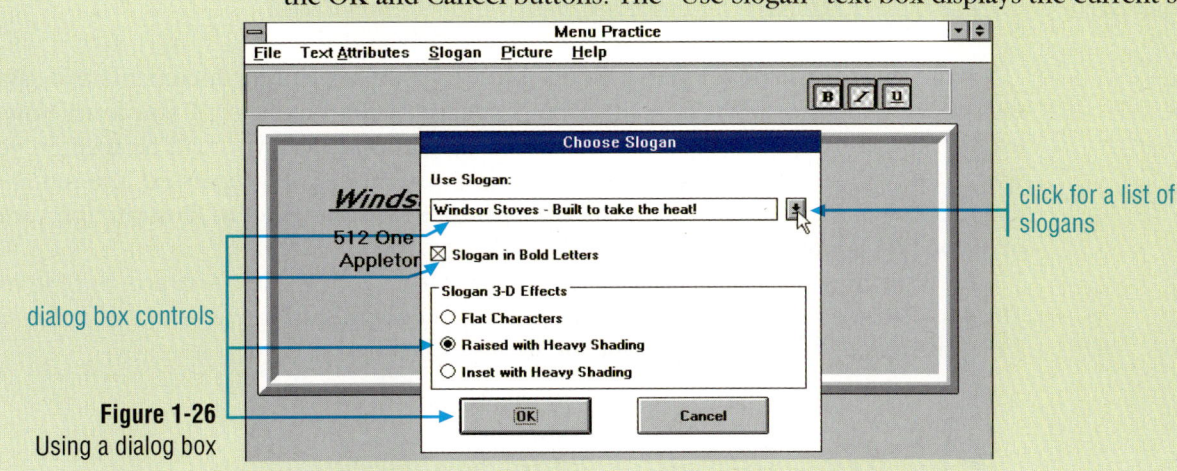

click for a list of slogans

dialog box controls

Figure 1-26
Using a dialog box

WIN 24   TUTORIAL 1   Essential Windows Skills

> ❸ Click the **down arrow button** on the right of the slogan box to display a list of alternative slogans.
>
> ❹ Click the slogan **Windsor Stoves - Built to last for generations!**
>
> ❺ Click the **OK button** and watch the new slogan replace the old.

You have used the Menu Practice application to learn how to use Windows menus, and you have learned the meaning of the Windows menu conventions. Next we'll look at dialog box controls.

Dialog Box Controls

Figure 1-27 shows a dialog box with a number of different controls that could be used to specify the requirements for a rental car. **Command buttons** initiate an immediate action. A **text box** is a space for you to type in a command detail. A **list box** displays a list of choices. A drop-down list box appears initially with only one choice; clicking the list box arrow displays additional choices. **Option buttons**, sometimes called radio buttons, allow you to select one option. **Check boxes** allow you to select one or more options. A **spin bar** changes a numeric setting.

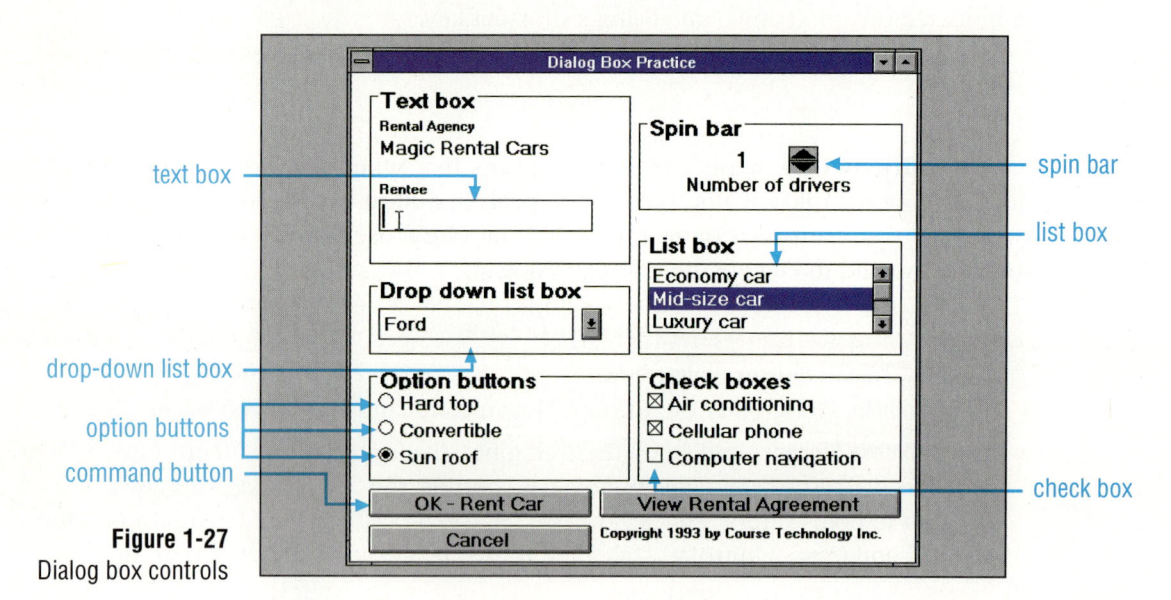

Figure 1-27
Dialog box controls

Windows uses standard dialog boxes for tasks such as printing documents and saving files. Most Windows applications use the standard dialog boxes, so if you learn how to use the Print dialog box for your word processing application, you will be well on your way to knowing how to print in any application. As you may have guessed, the rental car dialog box is not a standard Windows dialog box. It was designed to illustrate the variety of dialog box controls.

Let's see how the dialog box controls work. First, we will use a text box to type text. The Choose Slogan dialog box for the Menu Practice application has a text box that will let us change the slogan on the Windsor Stoves Corp. logo.

Using Windows to Specify Tasks WIN 25

To activate the Use Slogan text box:

① Click **Slogan** to open the Slogan menu.

② Click **Choose Slogan...** and the Choose Slogan dialog box appears.

③ Move the pointer to the text box and notice that it changes to an **I-bar** shape for text entry. See Figure 1-28.

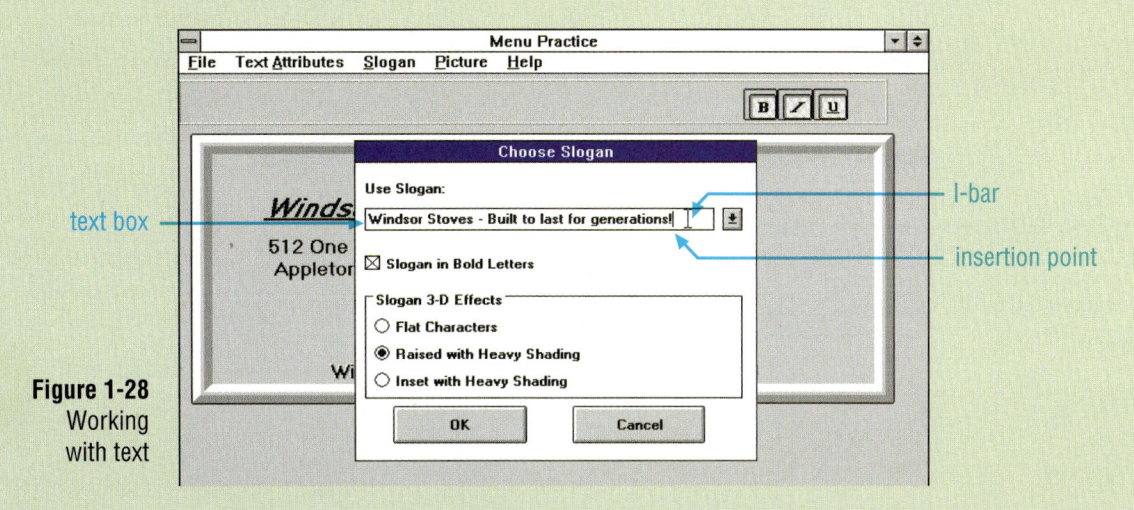

Figure 1-28
Working with text

④ Click the **left mouse button** to activate the text box. A blinking bar called an **Insertion point** indicates that you can type text into the box. Also notice that all the text is highlighted.

⑤ Press **[Del]** to erase the highlighted text of the old slogan.

When you work with a dialog box, be sure to set all the components the way you want them *before* you press the Enter key or click the OK button. Why? Because the Enter key, like the OK button, tells Windows that you are finished with the entire dialog box. Now let's type a new slogan in the text box and change the slogan 3-D effect.

To type a new slogan in a text box:

① Type **Quality is our Trademark!** but don't press [Enter], because while this dialog box is open, you are also going to change the slogan 3-D effect.

TROUBLE? If you make a typing mistake, press [Backspace] to delete the error, then type the correction.

② Look at the Slogan 3-D Effects list. Notice that the current selection is Raised with Heavy Shading.

③ Click **Inset with Heavy Shading**.

④ Click the **OK button** and then verify that the slogan and the 3-D effect have changed.

TROUBLE? If you are working on a monochrome system without the ability to display shade of gray, you may not be able to see the 3-D effect.

Using the Toolbar

A **toolbar** is a collection of icons that provides command shortcuts for mouse users. The icons on the toolbar are sometimes referred to as buttons. Generally the options on the toolbar duplicate menu options, but they are more convenient because they can be activated by a single mouse click. The toolbar for the Menu Practice application shown in Figure 1-29 has three buttons that are shortcuts for the Bold, Italic, and Underline commands. In a previous exercise you underlined, boldfaced, and italicized the company name using the menus. As a result the B, U, and I buttons are activated. Let's see what they look like when we deactivate them.

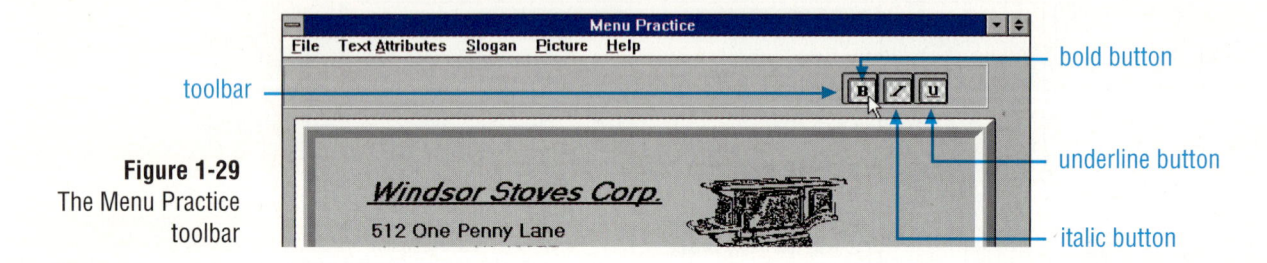

Figure 1-29
The Menu Practice toolbar

To change the type style using the toolbar:
1. Click **B** to remove the boldface.
2. Click **I** to turn off italics.
3. Click **U** to turn off underlining.
4. Click **B** to turn on boldface again.

You might want to spend a few minutes experimenting with the Menu Practice program to find the best logo design for Windsor Stoves Corp. When you are finished, close the Menu Practice window.

To close the Menu Practice window:
1. Click the **Control-menu box**.
2. Click **Close**. The Menu Practice program closes and returns you to Windows Program Manager.

You have now learned about Windows menus, dialog boxes and toolbars. In the next section, you will survey the Paintbrush application, experiment with tools, and access on-line help.

Using Paintbrush to Develop Your Windows Technique

After you have learned the basic Windows controls, you will find that most Windows *applications* contain similar controls. Let's launch the Paintbrush application and discover how to use it.

Using Paintbrush to Develop Your Windows Technique   WIN 27

To launch the Paintbrush application:

❶ Be sure the Program Manager window is open. If it is not open, use the skills you have learned to open it.

❷ You should have an Accessories icon or an Accessories window on the desktop. If you have an Accessories group icon on the desktop, double-click it to open the Accessories group window.

TROUBLE? If you don't see the Accessories icon or window, click the Window menu on the Program Manager menu bar. Look for Accessories in the list. If you find Accessories in this list, click it. If you do not find Accessories, ask your technical support person for help.

❸ Double-click the **Paintbrush icon** to launch the Paintbrush application. Your screen will look similar to the one in Figure 1-30.

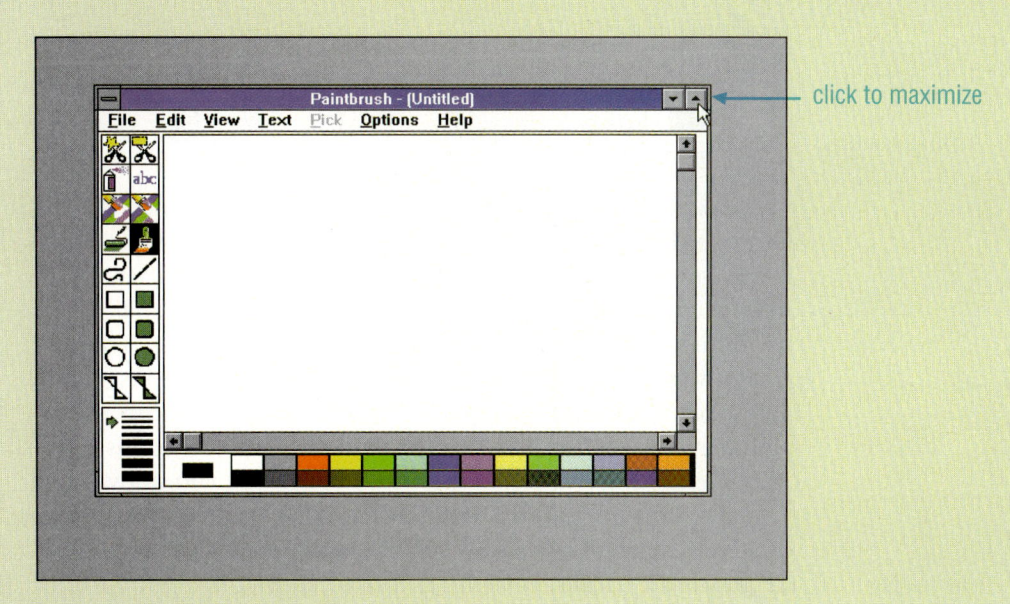

Figure 1-30
The Paintbrush window

click to maximize

❹ Click the Paintbrush window **maximize button** so you will have a large drawing area.

Surveying the Paintbrush Application Window

Whether you are using a reference manual or experimenting on your own, your first step in learning a new application is to survey the window and familiarize yourself with its components.

Look at the Paintbrush window on your screen and make a list of the components you can identify. If you have not encountered a particular component before, try to guess what it might be.

Now refer to Figure 1-31 on the following page, which labels the Paintbrush window components.

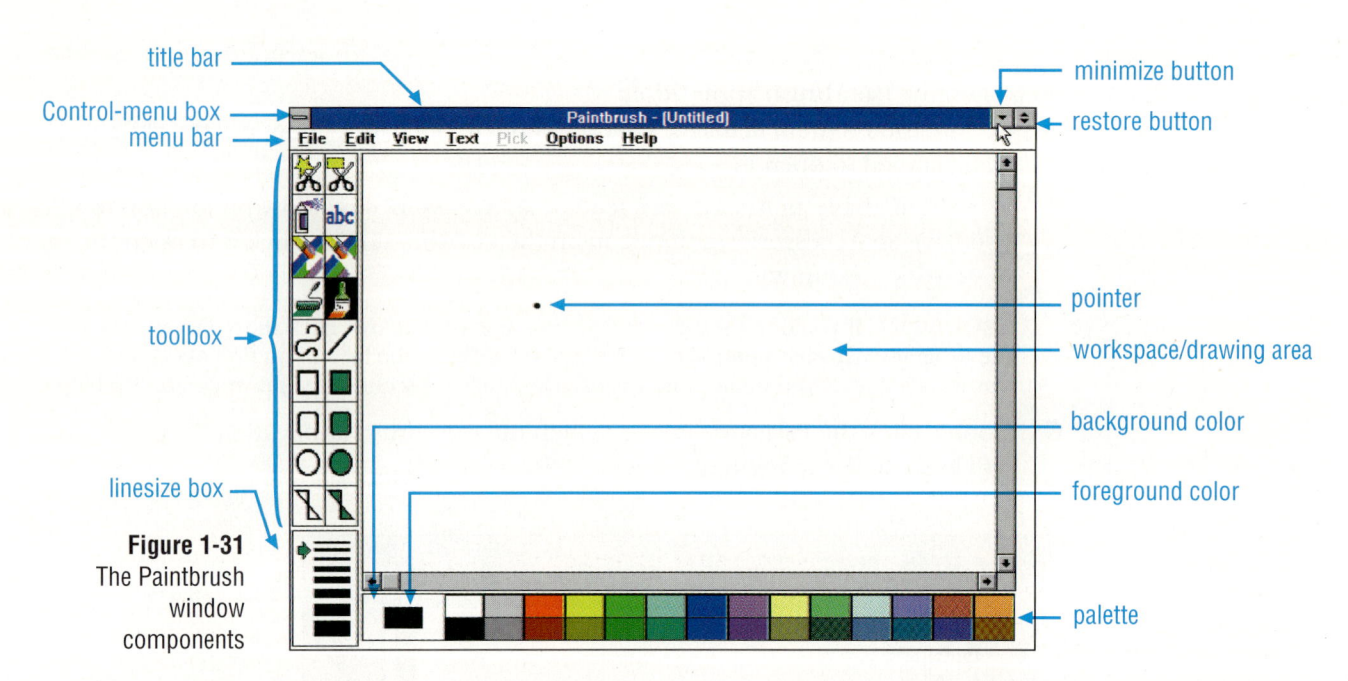

WIN 28   TUTORIAL 1   Essential Windows Skills

Figure 1-31
The Paintbrush window components

Labels: title bar, Control-menu box, menu bar, toolbox, linesize box, minimize button, restore button, pointer, workspace/drawing area, background color, foreground color, palette

The darkened title bar shows that the Paintbrush window is activated. The resizing buttons are in the upper-right corner, as usual. Because there is a restore button and because the window takes up the entire screen, you know that the window is maximized. The Control-menu box is in the upper-left corner, and a menu bar lists seven menus.

On the left side of the window are a variety of icons. This looks similar to the toolbar you used when you created the logo, only it has more icons, which are arranged vertically. The Windows manual refers to this set of icons as the **toolbox**.

Under the toolbox is a box containing lines of various widths. This is the **linesize box**, which you use to select the width of the line you draw.

At the bottom of the screen is a color **palette**, which you use to select the foreground and background colors. The currently selected colors for the foreground and background are indicated in the box to the left of the palette.

The rectangular space in the middle of the window is the drawing area. When the pointer is in the drawing area, it will assume a variety of shapes, depending on the tool you are using.

Experimenting with Tools

The icons on toolbars might be some of the easiest Windows controls, but many people are a little mystified by the symbols used for some of the tools. Look at the icons in the Paintbrush toolbox and try to guess their use.

You can often make good guesses, when you know what the application does. For example, you probably guessed that the brush tool shown in Figure 1-32 is used for drawing a picture. However, you might not be able to guess how the brush and the roller tools differ.

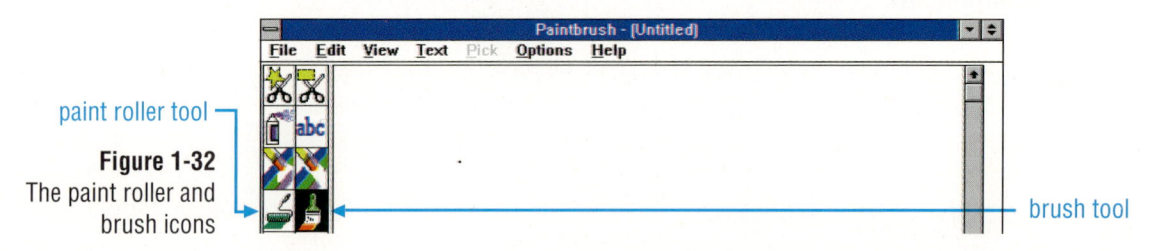

Figure 1-32
The paint roller and brush icons

Labels: paint roller tool, brush tool

If you can make some reasonable guess about how a tool works, it's not a bad idea to try it out. Can you write your name using the paintbrush tool? Let's try it.

To use the brush tool:

❶ Locate and click the **brush tool** in the toolbox. The brush tool becomes highlighted, indicating that it is now the selected tool.

❷ Move the pointer to the drawing area. Notice that it changes to a small dot.

❸ Move the pointer to the place where you want to begin writing your name.

When the left mouse button is down, the brush will paint. When you release the mouse button, you can move the pointer without painting.

❹ Use the mouse to control the brush as you write your name. Don't worry if it looks a little rough. Your "John Hancock" might look like the one in Figure 1-33.

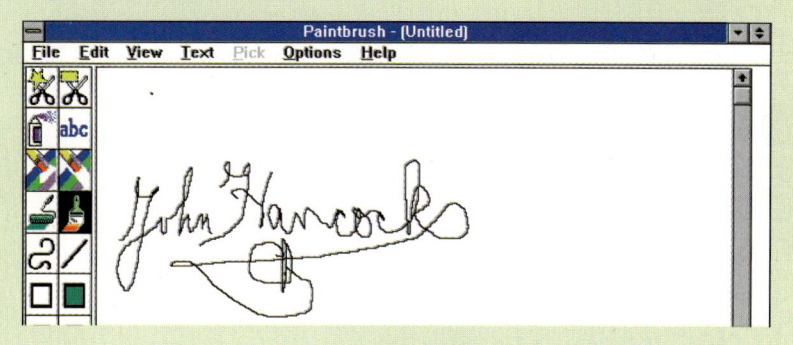

Figure 1-33
Your "John Hancock"

You will recall that we were curious about the difference between the brush and the paint roller. Let's experiment with the paint roller next.

To try the paint roller:

❶ Click the **paint roller** tool.

❷ Position the pointer in the upper-left corner of the drawing area and click. What happened?!

Did you get a strange result? Don't panic. This sort of thing happens when you experiment. Still, we probably should find out a little more about how to control the roller. To do this, we'll use the Paintbrush Help facility.

Using Help

Most Windows applications have an extensive on-line Help facility. A **Help facility** is an electronic reference manual that contains information about an application's menus, tools, and procedures. Some Help facilities also include **tutorials**, which you can use to learn the application.

There are a variety of ways to access Help, so people usually develop their own technique for finding information in it. We'll show you one way that seems to work for many Windows users. Later you can explore on your own and develop your own techniques.

When you use Help, a Help window opens. Usually the Help window overlays your application. If you want to view the problem spot and the Help information at the same time, it is a good idea to organize your desktop so the Help and application windows are side by side.

To access Help and organize the desktop:

❶ Click **Help**. A Help menu lists the Help commands.

❷ Click **Contents** to display a Paintbrush Help window similar to the one in Figure 1-34.

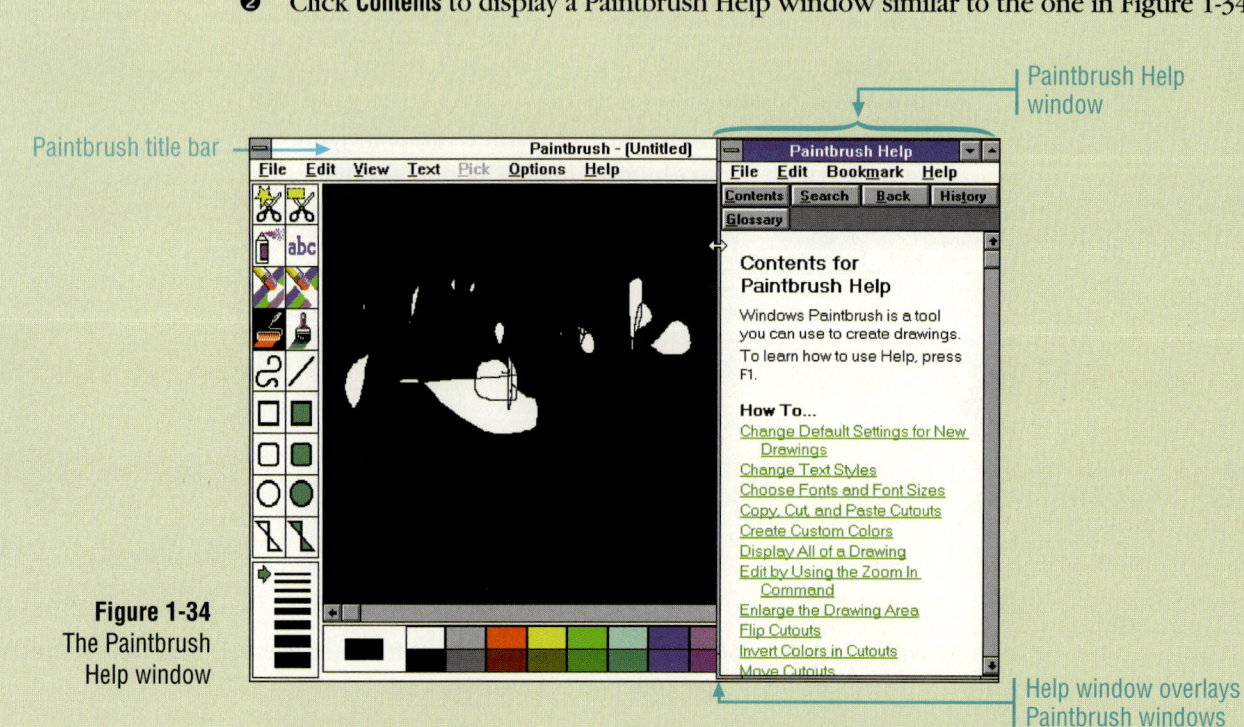

Figure 1-34
The Paintbrush Help window

❸ If the Paintbrush Help window is not the same size and shape as the one in Figure 1-34, drag the corners of the Help window until it looks like the one in the figure.

The Paintbrush application window is partially covered by the Help window. We need to fix that.

❹ Click the **Paintbrush title bar** to activate the Paintbrush window.

❺ Click the **restore button** to display the window borders and corners.

❻ Drag the corners of the Paintbrush application until your screen resembles the one in Figure 1-35 on the following page.

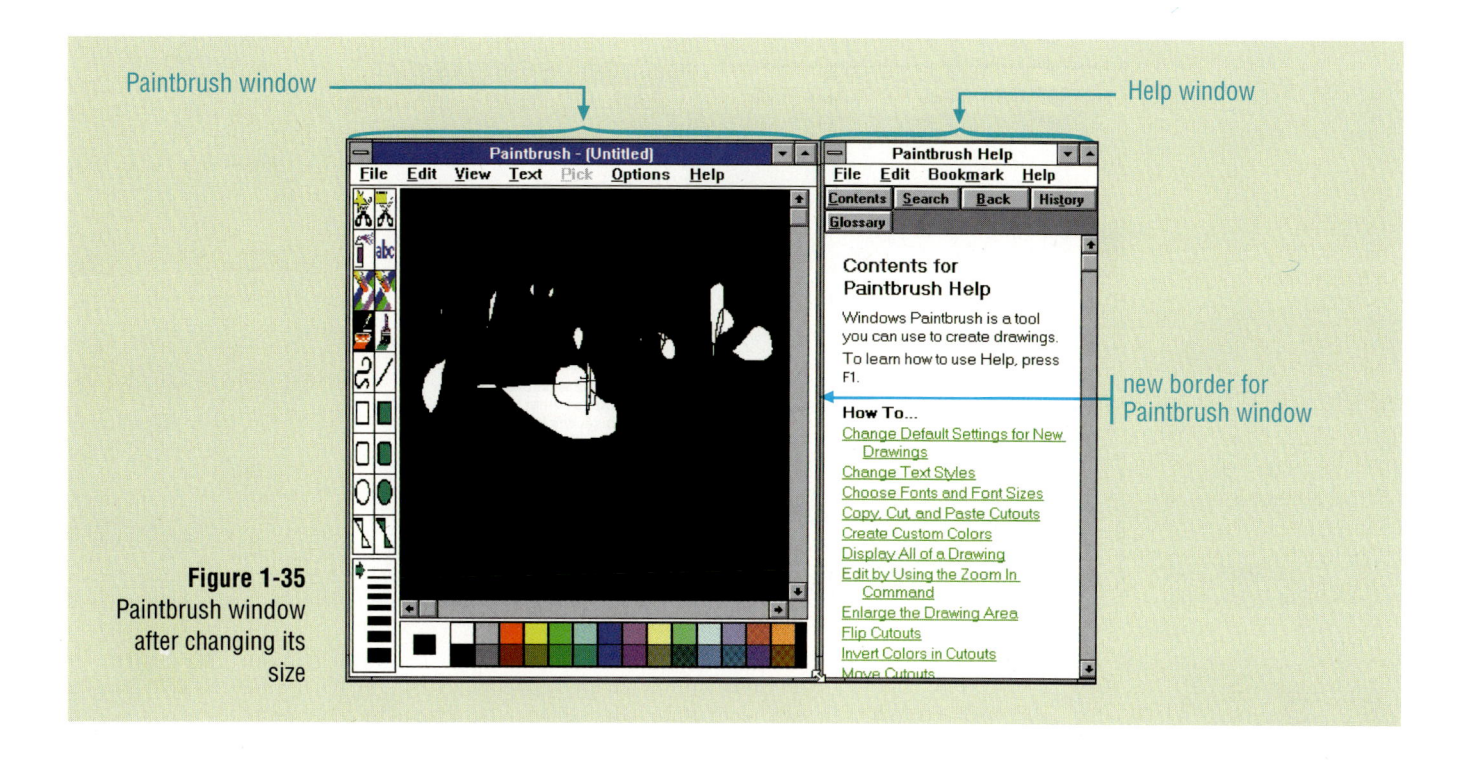

Using Paintbrush to Develop Your Windows Technique   **WIN 31**

Paintbrush window ⎯⎯⎯⎯⎯⎯⎯⎯⎯⎯⎯⎯   Help window

Figure 1-35
Paintbrush window after changing its size

new border for Paintbrush window

Now that the windows are organized, let's find out about the roller tool. The Paintbrush Help window contains a Table of Contents, which is divided into three sections: How To, Tools, and Commands.

The **How To** section is a list of procedures that are explained in the Help facility. Use this section when you want to find out how to do something. The **Tools** section identifies the toolbar icons and explains how to use them. The **Commands** section provides an explanation of the commands that can be accessed from the menu bar.

To find information about the paint roller tool on the Help facility:

❶ Use the scroll box to scroll down the text in the Help window until you see the Tools section heading.

❷ Continue scrolling until the Paint Roller option comes into view.

❸ Position the pointer on the Paint Roller Option. Notice that the pointer changes to a pointing hand, indicating that Paint Roller is a clickable option.

❹ Click the **left mouse button**. The Help window now contains information about the paint roller, as shown in Figure 1-36 on the following page.

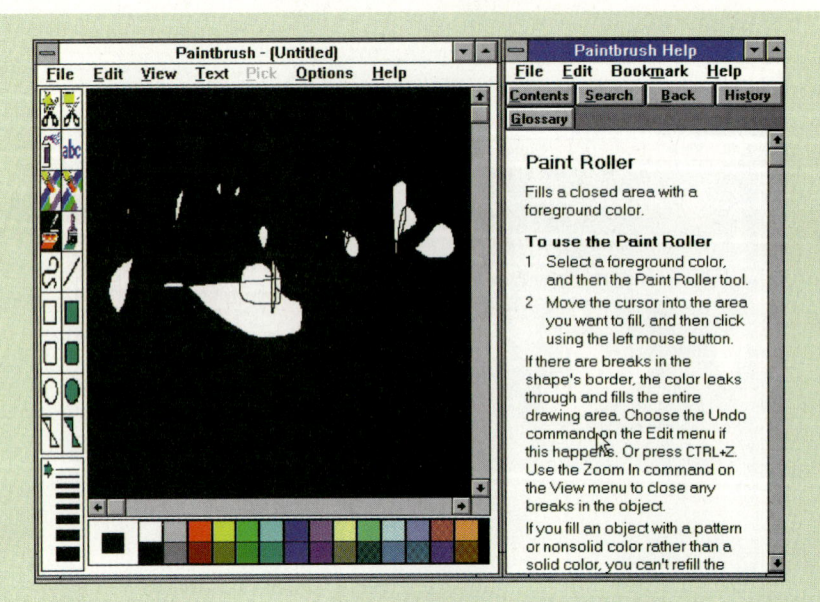

Figure 1-36
Paint Roller Help

❺ Read the information about the Paint Roller, using the scroll bar to view the entire text.

What did you learn about the paint roller? The first item you likely discovered is that the paint roller is used to fill an area. Well, it certainly did that in our experiment. It filled the entire drawing area with the foreground color, black. Next you might have noted that the first step in the procedure for using the paint roller is to select a foreground color. In our experiment, it would have been better if we selected some color other than black for the fill. Let's erase our old experiment so we can try again.

To start a new painting:
❶ Click **File** on the Paintbrush menu bar (not on the Help menu bar) to open the File menu.
❷ Click **New**, because you want to start a new drawing. A dialog box asks, "Do you want to save current changes?"
❸ Click the **No button** to clear the drawing area, because you don't want to save your first experiment.

Now you can paint your name and then use the roller to artistically fill areas. When you have finished experimenting, exit the Paintbrush application.

To exit Paintbrush:
❶ Click the **Control-menu box** and then click **Close**.
❷ In response to the prompt "Do you want to save current changes?" click the **No button**. The Paintbrush window closes, which also automatically closes the Help window.

You've covered a lot of ground. Next, it's time to learn how to exit Windows.

Exiting Windows

You might want to continue directly to the Questions and Tutorial Assignments. If so, stay in Windows until you have completed your work, then follow these instructions for exiting Windows.

To exit Windows:

❶ Click the **Control-menu box** in the upper-left of the Program Manager window.

❷ Click **Close**.

❸ When you see the message "This will end your Windows session," click the **OK button**.

Steve congratulates you on your Windows progress. You have learned the terminology associated with the desktop environment and the names of the controls and how to use them. You have developed an understanding about desktop organization and how to arrange the application and document windows so you will use them most effectively. You have also learned to use menus, dialog boxes, toolbars and Help.

Questions

1. GUI is an acronym for _____.
2. A group window contains which of the following?
    a. application icons
    b. document icons
    c. program-item icons
    d. group icons
3. What is one of the main purposes of the Program Manager?
    a. to organize your diskette
    b. to launch applications
    c. to create documents
    d. to provide the Help facility for applications
4. Which mouse function is used as a shortcut for more lengthy mouse or keyboard procedures?
    a. pointing
    b. clicking
    c. dragging
    d. double-clicking
5. To change the focus to an icon, you _____ it.
    a. close
    b. select
    c. drag
    d. launch

6. What is another name for document windows?
   a. child windows
   b. parent windows
   c. application windows
   d. group windows
7. In Figure 1-37 each window component is numbered. Write the name of the component that corresponds to the number.

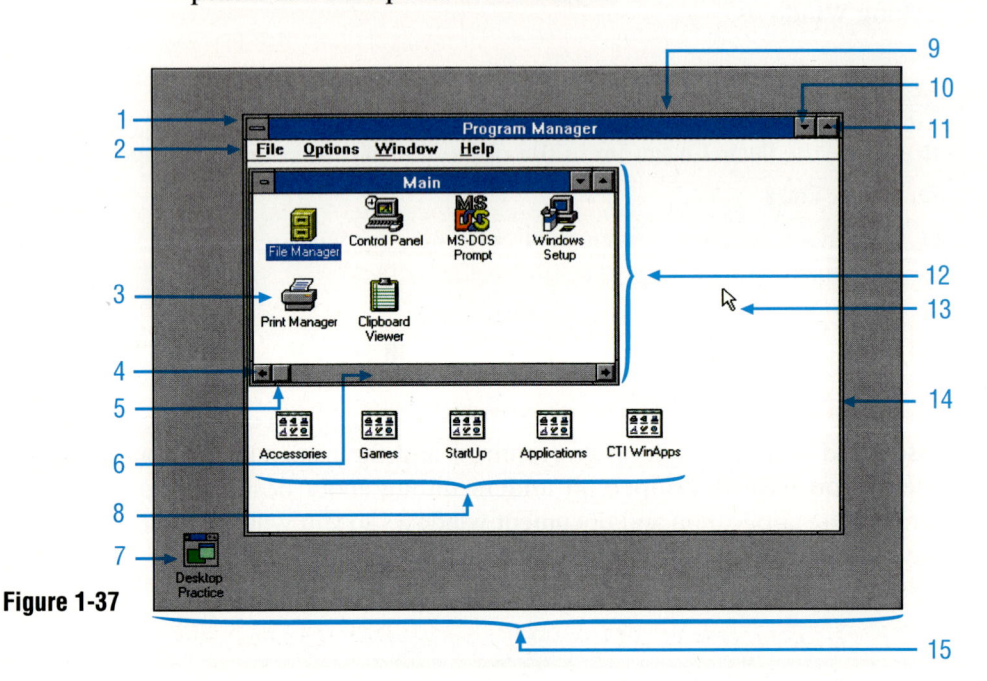

Figure 1-37

8. In Windows terminology you _____ a window when you want to get it out of the way temporarily but leave the application running.
9. You _____ a window when you no longer need to have the application running.
10. The _____ provides you with a way to switch between application windows.
    a. Task List
    b. program-item icon
    c. Window menu
    d. maximize button
11. How would you find out if you had more than one application running on your desktop?
12. _____ refers to the capability of a computer to run more than one application at the same time.
13. Which menu provides the means to switch from one document to another?
    a. the File menu
    b. the Help menu
    c. the Window menu
    d. the Control menu
14. Describe three menu conventions used in Windows menus.
15. The flashing vertical bar that marks the place your typing will appear is _____.
16. If you have access to a Windows reference manual such as the *Microsoft Windows User's Guide*, look for an explanation of the difference between group icons, program-item icons, and application icons. For your instructor's

information, write down the name of the reference, the publisher, and the page(s) on which you found this information. If you were writing a textbook for first-time Windows users, how would you describe the difference between these icons?

E 17. Copy the definition of "metaphor" from any standard dictionary. For your instructor's information, write down the dictionary name, the edition, and the page number. After considering the definition, explain why Windows is said to be a "desktop metaphor."

Tutorial Assignments

If you exited Windows at the end of the tutorial, launch Windows and do Assignments 1 through 15. Write your answers to the questions in Assignments 1, 2, 3, 4, 5, 9, 10, 11, 12, 13, and 15. Also fill out the table in Assignment 7.

1. Close all applications except the Program Manager and shrink all the group windows to icons. What are the names of the group icons on the desktop?
2. Open the Main window. How many program-item icons are in this window?
3. Open the Accessories window. How many program-item icons are in this window?
4. Open, close, and change the dimensions of the windows so your screen looks like Figure 1-38.
   a. How many applications are now on the desktop?
   b. How did you find out how many applications are on the desktop?

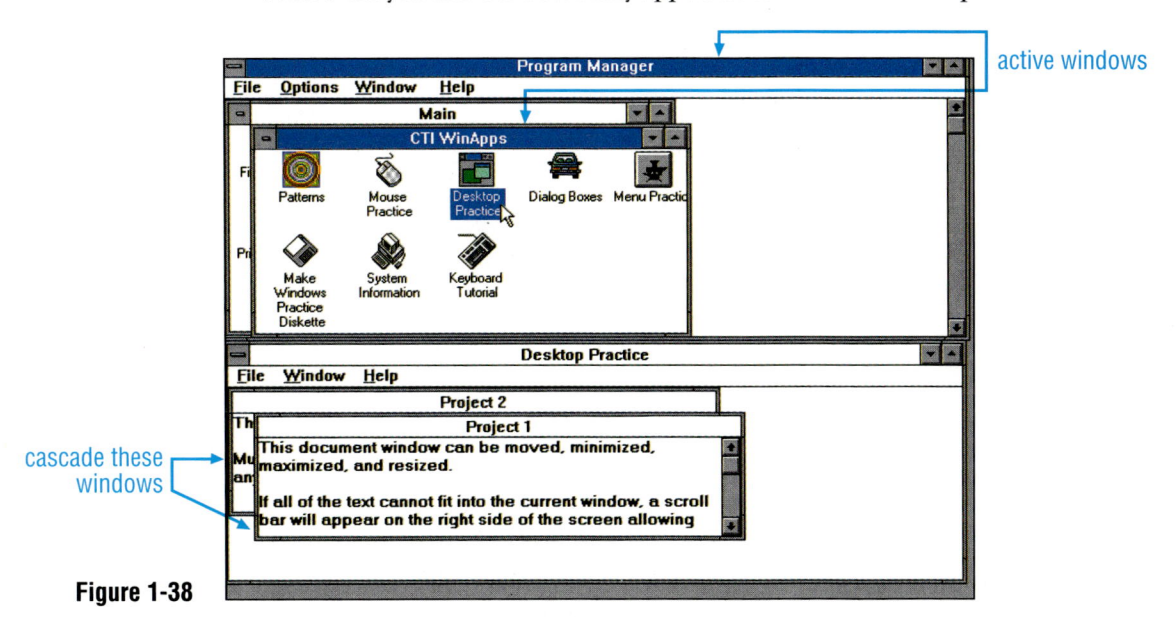

Figure 1-38

5. Open, close, and change the dimensions of the windows so your screen looks like Figure 1-39 on the following page. After you're done, close the Desktop Practice window using the fewest mouse clicks. How did you close the Desktop Practice window?

Open the CTI WinApps window and do Assignments 6 through 8.

WIN 36   TUTORIAL 1   Essential Windows Skills

Figure 1-39

6. Double-click the System Information icon.
7. Using the information displayed on your screen, fill out the following table:

CPU Type:	
Available Memory:	
Number of Diskette Drives:	
Capacity of Drive A:	
Capacity of Drive B:	
Horizontal Video Resolution:	
Vertical Video Resolution:	
Screen Colors or Shades:	
Network Type:	
DOS Version:	
Windows Version:	
Windows Mode:	
Windows Directory:	
Windows Free Resources:	
Available Drive Letters:	
Hard Drive Capacities:	

8. Click the Exit button to return to the Program Manager.

Launch the Mouse Practice application and do Assignments 9 through 14.

9. What happens when you drag the letter to the file cabinet?
10. What happens when you double-click the mouse icon located in the lower-left corner of the desktop?
11. What happens when you click an empty check box? What happens when you click a check box that contains an "X"?
12. Can you select both option buttons at the same time?
13. What happens when you click "Item Fourteen" from the list?
14. Exit the Mouse Practice.

Launch the Desktop Practice and do Assignments 15 through 17.

15. What is the last sentence of the document in the Project 2 window?
16. Close the Desktop Practice window.
17. Exit Windows.

TUTORIAL 2

Effective File Management

Using the File Manager

OBJECTIVES

In this tutorial you will:
- Open and close the File Manager
- Format and make your student disk containing practice files
- Change the current drive
- Identify the components of the File Manager window
- Create directories
- Change the current directory
- Move, rename, delete, and copy files
- Make a disk backup
- Learn how to protect your data from hardware failures

CASE **A Professional Approach to Computing at Narraganset Shipyard** Ruth Sanchez works at the Narraganset Shipyard, a major government defense contractor. On a recent business trip to Washington, DC, Ruth read a magazine article that convinced her she should do a better job of organizing the files on her computer system. The article pointed out that a professional approach to computing includes a plan for maintaining an organized set of disk-based files that can be easily accessed, updated, and secured.

Ruth learns that the Windows File Manager can help to organize her files. Ruth has not used the File Manager very much, so before she begins to make organizational changes to the valuable files on her hard disk, she decides to practice with some sample files on a disk in drive A.

WIN 38   TUTORIAL 2   Effective File Management

In this Tutorial, you will follow the progress of Ruth's File Manager practice and learn how to use Windows to manage effectively the data stored in your computer.

Files and the File Manager

A **file** is a named collection of data organized for a specific purpose and stored on a floppy disk or a hard disk. The typical computer user has hundreds of files.

The Windows File Manager provides some handy tools for organizing files. Ruth's first step is to launch the File Manager. Let's do the same.

To launch the File Manager:

❶ Launch Windows.

❷ Compare your screen to Figure 2-1. Use the skills you learned in Tutorial 1 to organize your desktop so only the Program Manager window and the Main window are open.

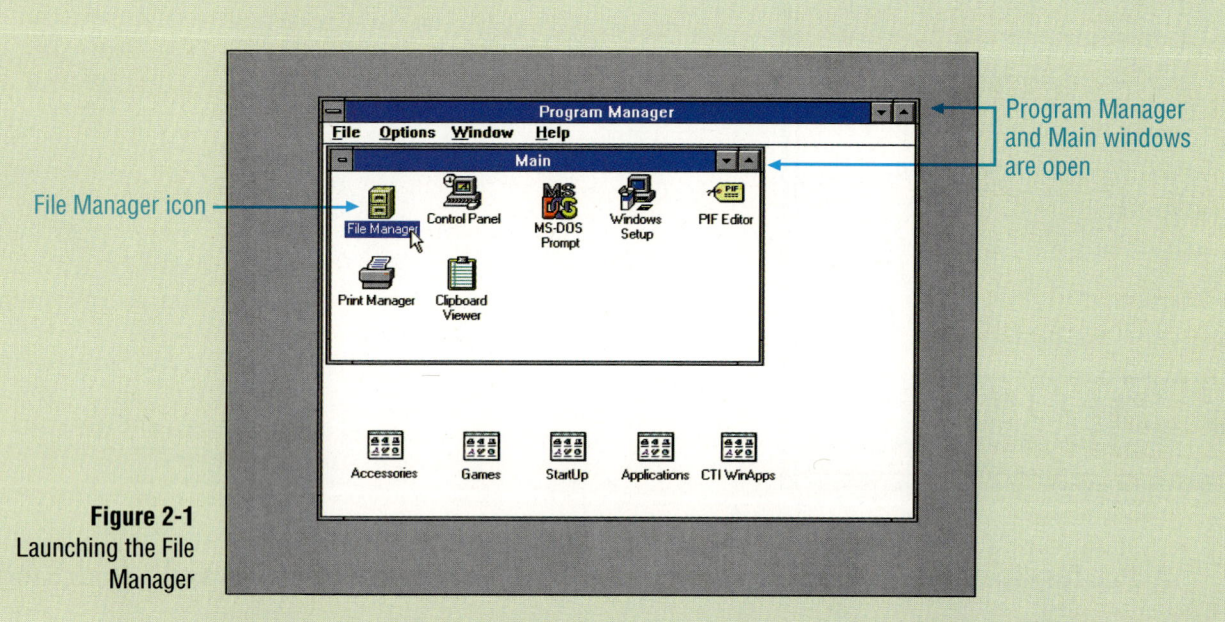

Figure 2-1
Launching the File Manager

❸ Double-click the **File Manager icon** to launch the File Manager program and open the File Manager window.

❹ If the File Manager window is not maximized, click the **maximize button**.

❺ Click **Window**, then click **Tile**. You should now have one child window on the desktop. See Figure 2-2a on the following page. Don't worry if the title of your child window is not the same as the one in the figure.

Files and File Manager **WIN 39**

Figure 2-2a
Desktop with one child window

your child window title might be different

one child window

Figure 2-2b
Desktop with two child windows

double-click to close a child window

child windows

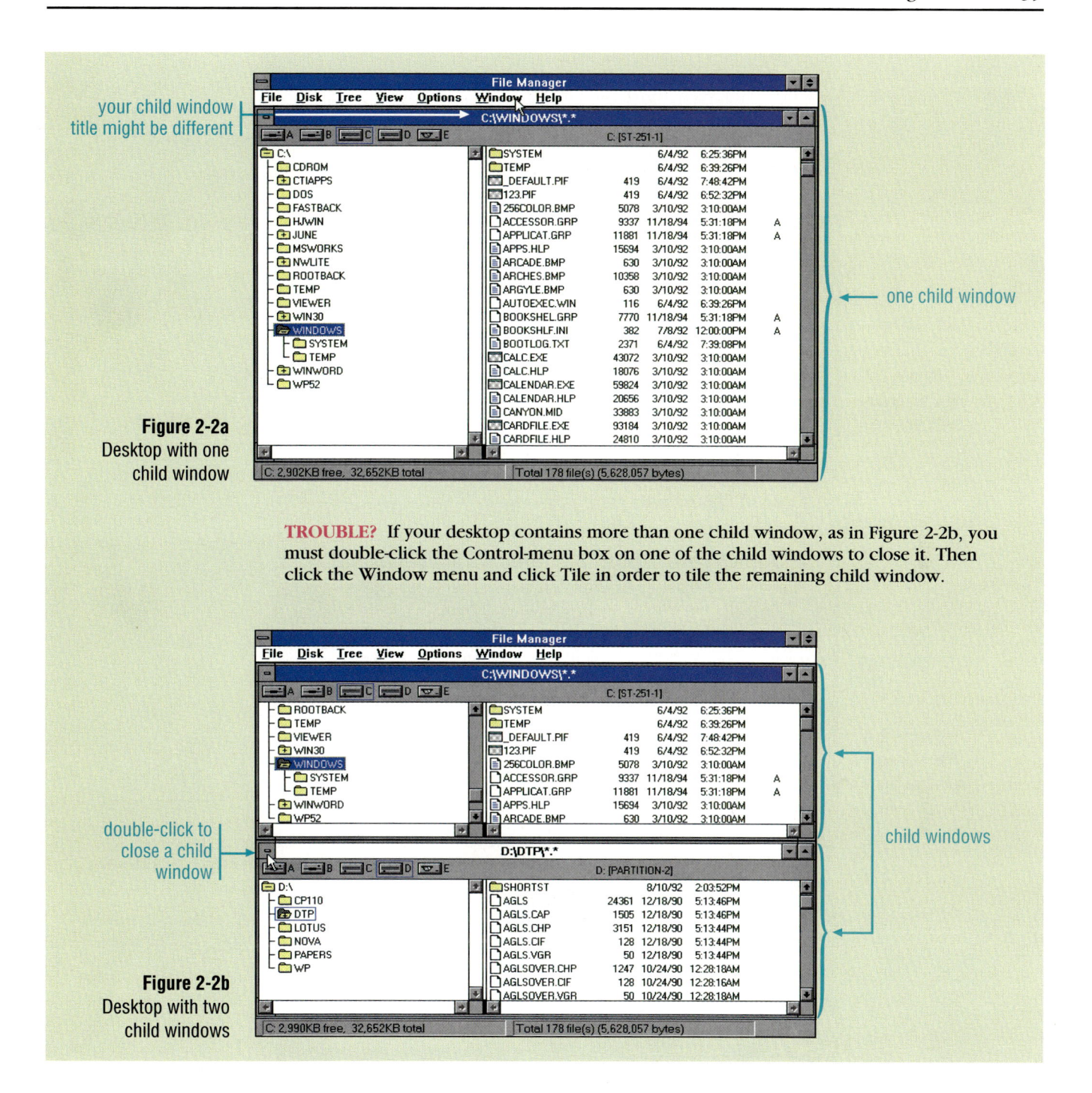

TROUBLE? If your desktop contains more than one child window, as in Figure 2-2b, you must double-click the Control-menu box on one of the child windows to close it. Then click the Window menu and click Tile in order to tile the remaining child window.

Ruth decides to check her File Manager settings, which affect the way information is displayed. By adjusting your File Manager settings to match Ruth's, your computer will display screens and prompts similar to those in the Tutorial. *If you do not finish this tutorial in one session, remember to adjust the settings again when you begin your next session.*

WIN 40   TUTORIAL 2   Effective File Management

To adjust your File Manager settings:

❶ Click **Tree**. Look at the command "Indicate Expandable Branches." See Figure 2-3. If no check mark appears next to this command, position the pointer on the command and click. If you see the check mark, go to Step 2.

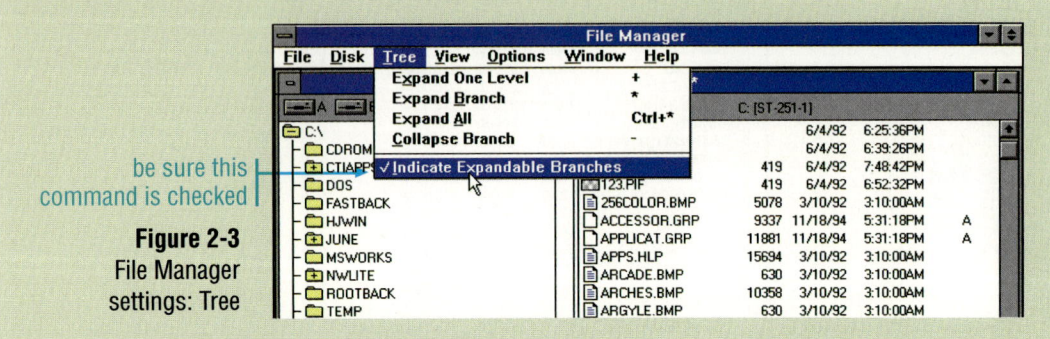

be sure this command is checked

Figure 2-3
File Manager settings: Tree

❷ Click **View**. Make any adjustments necessary so that the settings are the same as those in Figure 2-4.

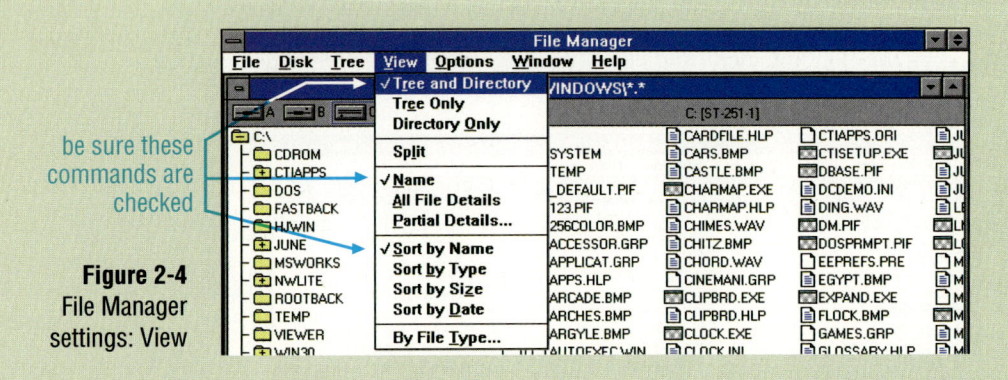

be sure these commands are checked

Figure 2-4
File Manager settings: View

TROUBLE? When you click a command to change the check mark, the menu closes. To change another command in the menu or to confirm your changes, you need to click the View menu again.

❸ Click **Options** and then click **Confirmation...**. Referring to Figure 2-5, make any adjustments necessary so that all the check boxes contain an X, then click the **OK button**.

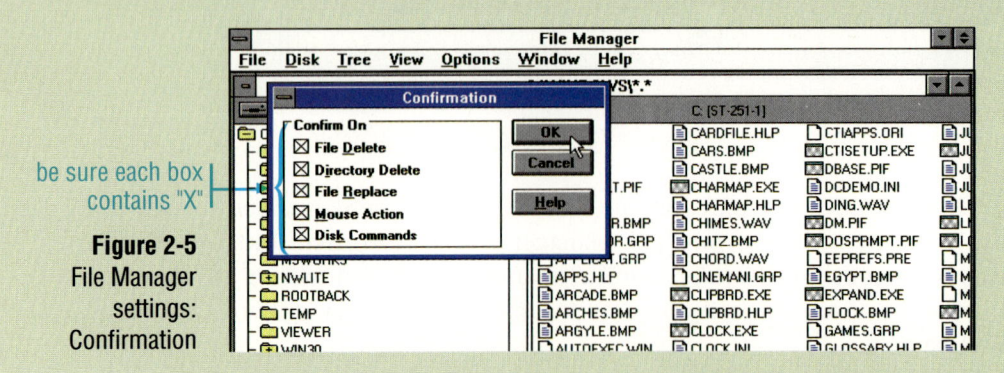

be sure each box contains "X"

Figure 2-5
File Manager settings: Confirmation

❹ Click **Options** again and then click **Font**. Make any adjustments necessary so your font settings match those in Figure 2-6 on the following page. Click the **OK button** whether or not you changed anything in this dialog box.

Formatting a Disk **WIN 41**

Figure 2-6
File Manager settings: Font

- Regular font style
- MS Sans Serif
- size 8
- no "X"

Figure 2-7
File Manager settings: Status Bar

- only Status Bar is checked

❺ Click **Options** again. Make any adjustments necessary so that the settings are the same as those in Figure 2-7. If no adjustments are necessary, click **Options** again to close the menu.

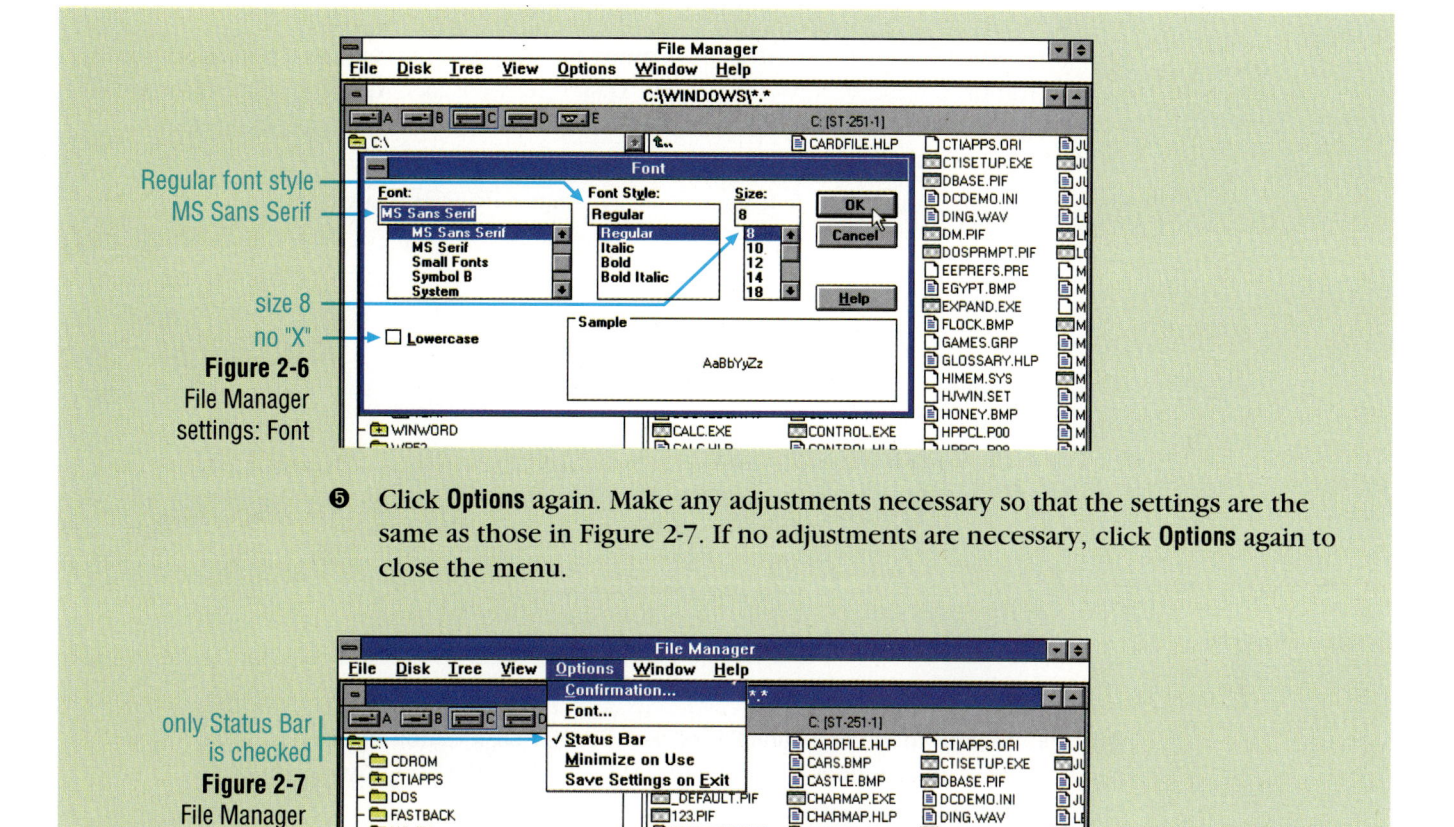

Formatting a Disk

Next, Ruth needs to format the disks she will use for her File Manager practice. Disks must be formatted before they can be used to store data. Formatting arranges the magnetic particles on the disks in preparation for storing data. You need to format a disk when:
- you purchase a new disk
- you want to recycle an old disk that you used on a non-IBM-compatible computer
- you want to erase all the old files from a disk

Pay attention when you are formatting disks. *The formatting process erases all the data on the disk.* If you format a disk that already contains data, you will lose all the data. Fortunately, Windows will not let you format the hard disk or network drives using the Format Disk command.

To complete the steps in this Tutorial you need two disks of the same size and density. You may use blank, unformatted disks or disks that contain data you no longer need. *The following steps assume that you will format the disks in drive A. If you want to use drive B for the formatting process, substitute drive B for drive A* in Steps 3, 4, and 6.

To format the first disk:
❶ Make sure your disk is *not* write-protected. On a 5.25-inch disk the write-protect notch should *not* be covered. On a 3.5-inch disk the hole on the left side of the disk should be *closed*.

WIN 42 TUTORIAL 2 Effective File Management

❷ Write your name, course title, and course meeting time on an adhesive disk label. For the title of the disk, write Student Disk (Source Disk). Apply this label to one of the disks you are going to format. If you are using a 3.5-inch disk, do not stick the label on any of the metal parts.

❸ Put this disk into drive A. If your disk drive has a door or a latch, secure it. See Figure 2-8.

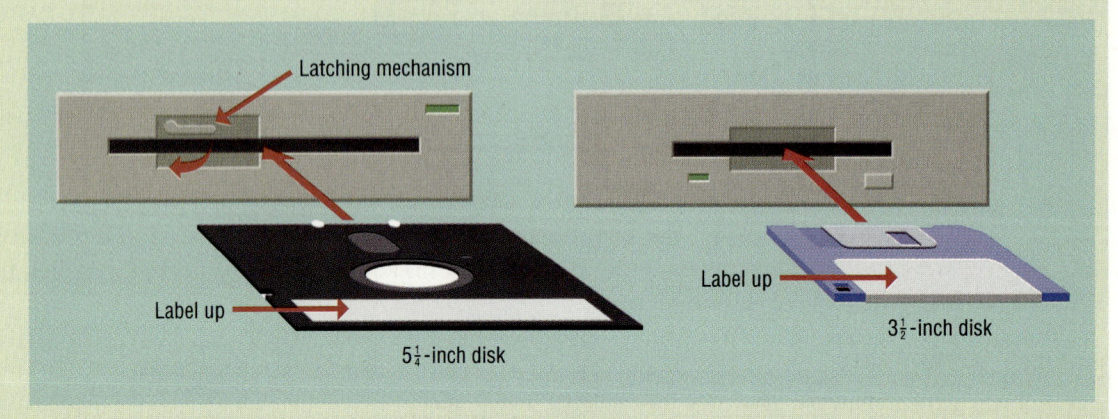

Figure 2-8
Inserting your disk

❹ Click **Disk** and then click **Format Disk....** A Format Disk dialog box appears. See Figure 2-9. If the Disk In box does not indicate Drive A, click the [↓] (down-arrow) button on this box, then click the Drive A option.

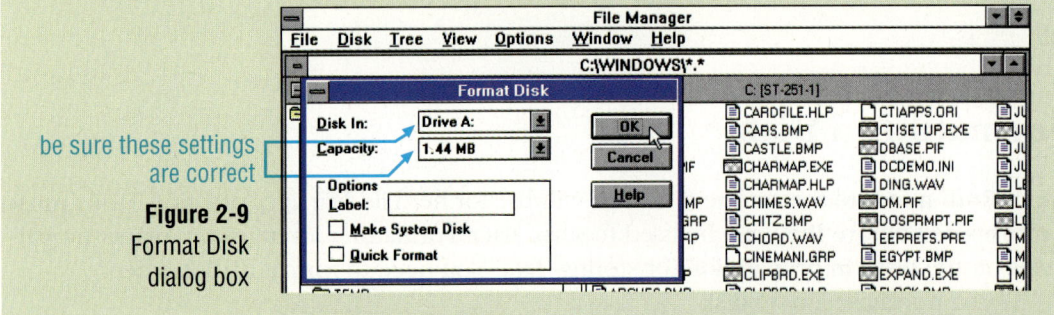

be sure these settings are correct

Figure 2-9
Format Disk dialog box

❺ Look at the number displayed in the Capacity box. If you are formatting a disk that cannot store the displayed amount of data, click the [↓] (down-arrow) button at the right side of the Capacity box and then click the correct capacity from the list of options provided.

TROUBLE? How can you determine the capacity of your disk? The chart in Figure 2-10 (on the next page) will help you. If you still are not sure after looking at the figure, ask your technical support person.

Diskette size	Diskette density	Diskette capacity
5¼-inch	DD	360K
5¼-inch	HD	1.2MB
3½-inch	DD	720K
3½-inch	HD	1.44MB

Figure 2-10
Disk capacities

❻ Click the **OK button**. The Confirm Format Disk dialog box appears with a warning. Read it. Look at the drive that is going to carry out the format operation (drive A). Be sure this is the correct drive. Double-check the disk that's in this drive to be sure it is the one you want to format.

❼ Click the **Yes button**. The Formatting Disk dialog box keeps you updated on the progress of the format.

❽ When the format is complete, the Format Complete dialog box reports the results of the format and asks if you'd like to format another disk. See Figure 2-11.

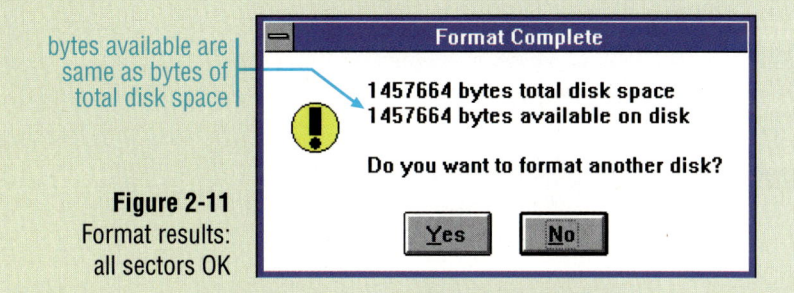

Figure 2-11
Format results: all sectors OK

bytes available are same as bytes of total disk space

Format Complete
1457664 bytes total disk space
1457664 bytes available on disk
Do you want to format another disk?
Yes   No

Let's format your second floppy disk:

❶ Click the **Yes button** after you review the formatting results.

❷ Remove your Student disk from drive A.

❸ Write your name, course title, and course meeting time on the label for the second disk. For the title of this disk write Backup (Destination Disk). Apply this label to your second disk and place this disk in drive A.

❹ Be sure the **Disk In box** is set to drive A and the capacity is set to the capacity of your disk. (Remember to substitute B here if you are formatting your disk in drive B.)

❺ Click the **OK button** to accept the settings. When you see the Confirm Format Disk dialog box, check to be sure you have the correct disk in the correct drive.

❻ Click the **Yes button** to confirm that you want to format the disk. When the format is complete, review the format results.

❼ You do not want to format another disk, so click the **No button** when the computer asks if you wish to format another disk.

❽ *Remove the backup disk from drive A.* You will not need this backup disk until later.

Preparing Your Student Disk

Now that Ruth has formatted her disks, she is going to put some files on one of them to use for her file management exploration. To follow Ruth's progress, you must have copies of her files. A collection of files has been prepared for this purpose. You need to transfer them to one of your formatted disks.

To transfer files to your Student Disk:

❶ Place the disk you labeled Student Disk (Source Disk) in drive A.

The File Manager window is open, but you need to go to the Program Manager window to launch the application that will transfer the files.

❷ Hold down **[Alt]** and continue to press **[Tab]** until Program Manager appears in the box, then release both keys. Program Manager becomes the active window.

❸ If the CTI WinApps window is not open, double-click the **CTI WinApps group icon**. If the CTI WinApps window is open but is not the active window, click it. Your screen should look similar to Figure 2-12.

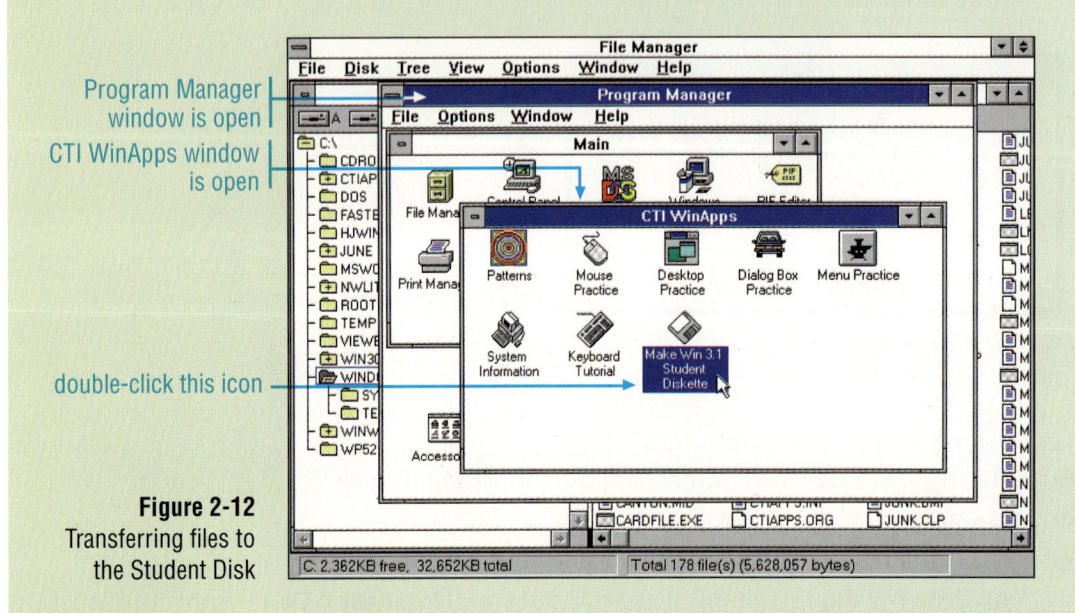

Figure 2-12
Transferring files to the Student Disk

❹ Double-click the **Make Win 3.1 Student Disk icon**. A dialog box appears.

❺ Make sure the drive that is selected in the dialog box corresponds to the drive that contains your disk (drive A or drive B), then click the **OK button**. It will take 30 seconds or so to transfer the files to your disk.

❻ Click the **OK button** when you see the message "24 files copied successfully!"

❼ Double-click on the **CTI WinWorks Apps Control-menu box** to close the window.

Now the data files you need should be on your Student Disk. To continue the Tutorial, you must switch back to the File Manager.

To switch back to the File Manager:

❶ Hold down **[Alt]** and press **[Tab]** until a box with File Manager appears. Then release both keys.

Finding Out What's on Your Disks

Ruth learned from the article that the first step toward effective data management is to find out what's stored on her disks. To see what's on your Student Disk, you will need to be sure your computer is referencing the correct disk drive.

Changing the Current Drive

Each drive on your computer system is represented by a **drive icon** that tells you the drive letter and the drive type. Figure 2-13 shows the drive types represented by these icons.

Figure 2-13
Drive icons

- Floppy Disk
- Hard Disk
- Network Drive
- CD-ROM Drive

Near the top of the File Manager window, a **drive icon ribbon** indicates the drives on your computer system. See Figure 2-14. Your screen may be different because the drive icon ribbon on your screen reflects your particular hardware configuration.

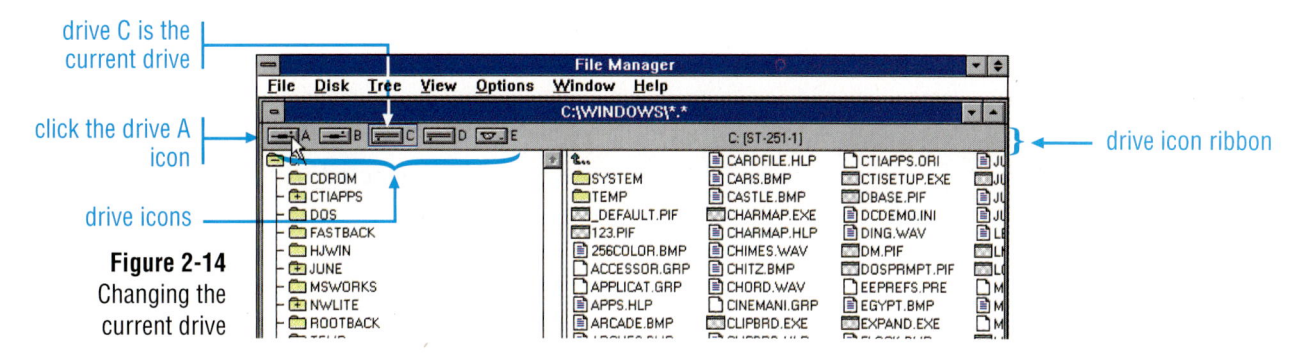

Figure 2-14
Changing the current drive

- drive C is the current drive
- click the drive A icon
- drive icons
- drive icon ribbon

Your computer is connected to a number of storage drives or devices, but it can work with only one drive at a time. This drive is referred to as the **current drive** or **default drive**. You must change the current drive whenever you want to use files or programs that are stored on a different drive. The drive icon for the current drive is outlined with a rectangle. In Figure 2-14, the current drive is C.

To work with Ruth's files, you must be sure that the current drive is the one in which you have your Student Disk. *For this Tutorial we'll assume that your Student Disk is in drive A. If it is in drive B, substitute "drive B" for "drive A" in the rest of the steps for this Tutorial.*

Follow the next set of steps to change the current drive, if your current drive is not the one containing your Student Disk.

To change the current drive to A:
1. Be sure your Student Disk is in drive A.
2. Click the **drive A icon**. Drive A becomes the current drive. See Figure 2-15 on the following page.

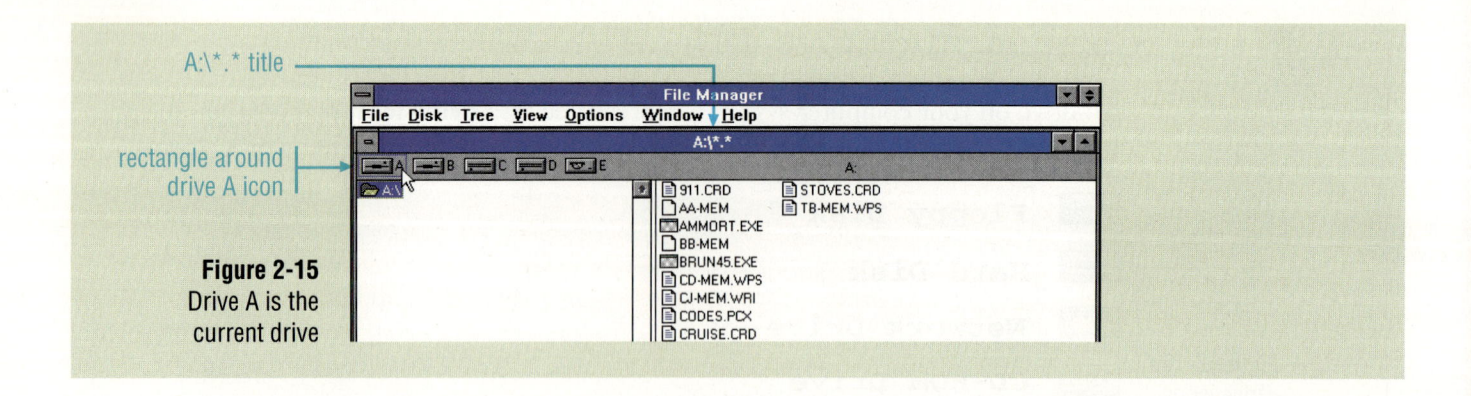

WIN 46   TUTORIAL 2   Effective File Management

Figure 2-15
Drive A is the current drive

After you make drive A the current drive, your screen should look similar to Figure 2-15. Don't worry if everything is not exactly the same as the figure. Just be sure you see the A:*.* window title and that there is a rectangle around the drive A icon (or the drive B icon if drive B contains your floppy disk).

The File Manager Window

The components of the File Manager window are labeled in Figure 2-16. Your screen should contain similar components.

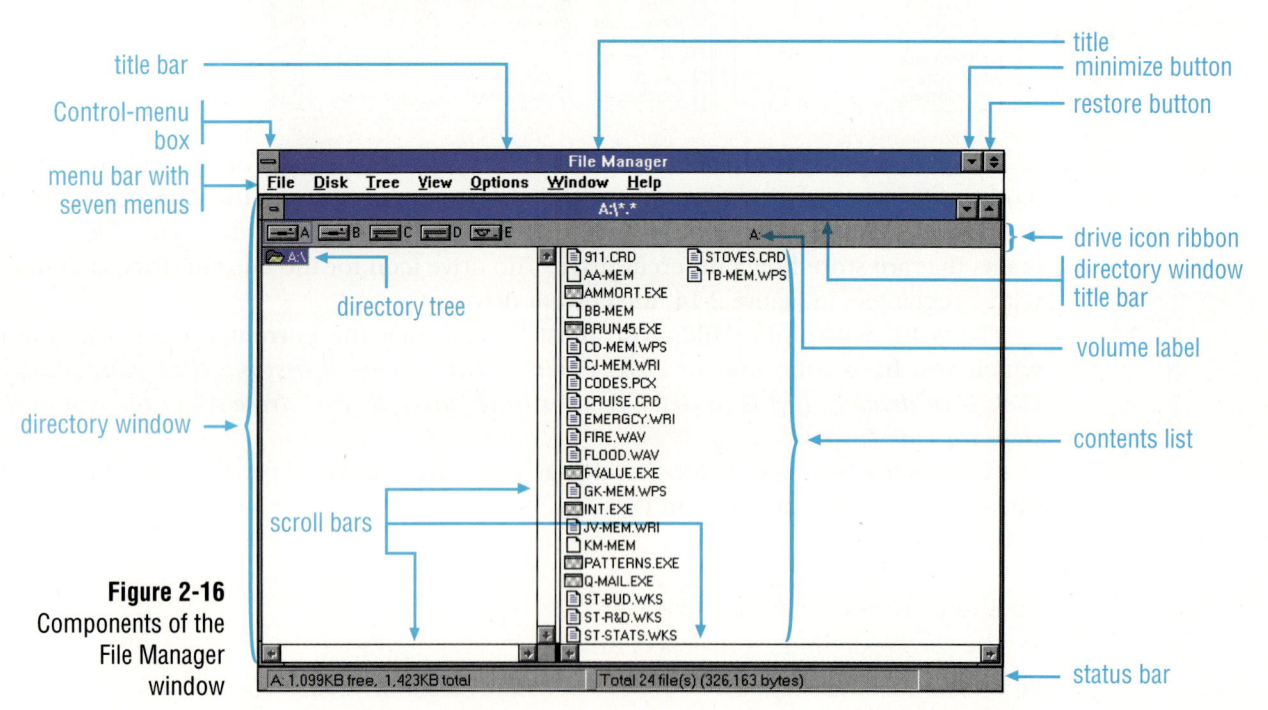

Figure 2-16
Components of the File Manager window

The top line of the File Manager window contains the Control-menu box, the title bar, the title, and the resizing buttons. The File Manager menu bar contains seven menus.

Inside the File Manager window is the **directory window**, which contains information about the current drive. The title bar for this window displays the current drive, in this case, A:*.*. This window has its own Control-menu box and resizing buttons.

Below the directory window title bar is the drive icon ribbon. On this line, the drive letter is followed by a volume label, if there is one. A **volume label** is a name you can assign to your disk during the format process to help you identify the contents of the disk. We did not assign a volume label, so the area after the A: is blank. Why is there a colon after the drive letter? Even though the colon is not displayed on the drive icons, when you type in a drive letter, you must always type a colon after it. The colon is a requirement of the DOS operating system that Windows uses behind the scenes to perform its file management tasks.

At the bottom of the screen, a status bar displays information about disk space. Remember that a byte is one character of data.

Notice that the directory window is split. The left half of the directory window displays the **directory tree**, which illustrates the organization of files on the current drive. The right half of the directory window displays the **contents list**, which lists the files on the current drive. Scroll bars on these windows let you view material that doesn't fit in the current window.

The Directory Tree

A list of files is called a **directory**. Because long lists of files are awkward to work with, directories can be subdivided into smaller lists called **subdirectories**. The organization of these directories and subdirectories is depicted in the directory tree.

Suppose you were using your computer for a small retail business. What information might you have on your disk, and how would it be organized? Figure 2-17 shows the directory tree for a hard disk (drive C) of a typical small business computer system.

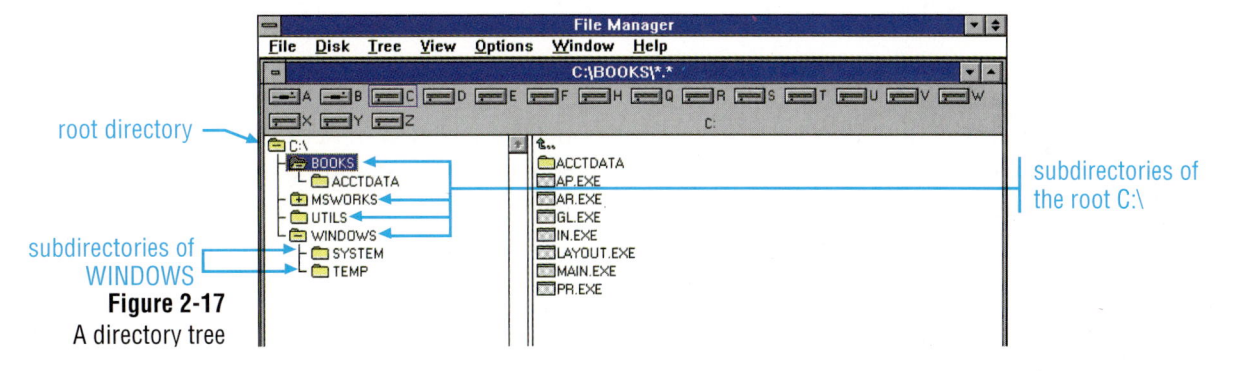

Figure 2-17
A directory tree

At the top of the directory tree is the **root directory**, called C:\ . The root directory is created when you format a disk and is indicated by a backslash after the drive letter and colon. Arranged under the root directory are the subdirectories BOOKS, MSWORKS, UTILS, and WINDOWS.

Directories other than the root directory can have subdirectories. In Figure 2-17 you can see that the BOOKS directory has a subdirectory called ACCTDATA. The WINDOWS directory contains two subdirectories, SYSTEM and TEMP. MSWORKS also has some subdirectories, but they are not listed. You'll find out how to expand the directory tree to display subdirectories later in the this tutorial.

Windows uses directory names to construct a path through the directory tree. For example, the path to ACCTDATA would be C:\BOOKS\ACCTDATA. To trace this path on Figure 2-17, begin at the root directory C:\, follow the line leading to the BOOKS directory, then follow the line leading to the ACCTDATA directory.

Each directory in the directory tree has a **file folder icon**, which can be either open or closed. An open file folder icon indicates the **active** or **current directory**. In Figure 2-17 the current directory is BOOKS. Only one directory can be current on a disk at a time.

Now look at the directory tree on your screen. The root directory of your Student Disk is called A:\. The file folder icon for this directory is open, indicating that this is the current directory. Are there any subdirectories on your disk?

The answer is no. A:\ has no subdirectories because its file folder icon does not contain a plus sign or a minus sign. A plus sign on a folder indicates that the directory can be expanded to show its subdirectories. A minus sign indicates that the subdirectories are currently being displayed. A file folder icon without a plus or a minus sign has no subdirectories.

Organizing Your Files

Ruth's disk, like your Student Disk, contains only one directory, and all her files are in that directory. As is typical of a poorly organized disk, files from different projects and programs are jumbled together. As Ruth's disk accumulates more files, she will have an increasingly difficult time finding the files she wants to use.

Ruth needs to organize her disk. First, she needs to make some new directories so she has a good basic structure for her files.

Creating Directories

When you create a directory, you indicate its location on the directory tree and specify the new directory name. The directory you create becomes a subdirectory of the current directory, which is designated by an open file folder. Directory names can be up to eight characters long.

Your Student Disk contains a collection of memos and spreadsheets that Ruth has created for a project code named "Stealth." Right now, all of these files are in the root directory. Ruth decides that to improve the organization of her disk, she should place her memos in one directory and the Stealth spreadsheets in another directory. To do this, she needs to make two new directories, MEMOS and STEALTH.

To make a new directory called MEMOS:

❶ Click the **file folder icon** representing the root directory of drive A. Figure 2-18 shows you where to click. This highlights the root directory A:\, making it the current directory.

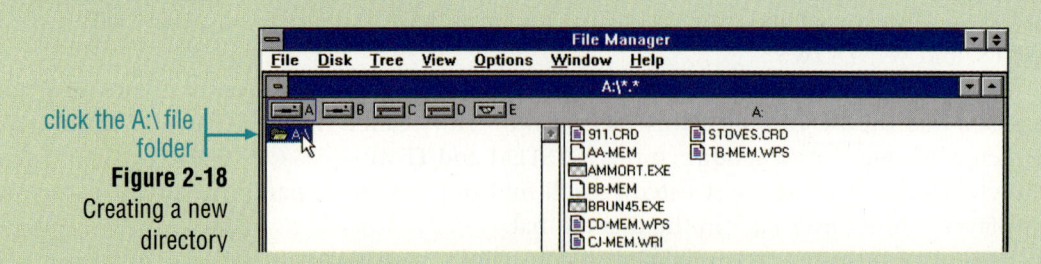

Figure 2-18
Creating a new directory

click the A:\ file folder

❷ Click **File**, then click **Create Directory...**. The Create Directory dialog box indicates that the current directory is A:\ and displays a text box for the name of the new directory.

❸ In the text box, type **MEMOS**, then click the **OK button**. It doesn't matter whether you type the directory name in uppercase or lowercase letters.

Organizing Your Files **WIN 49**

As a result, your screen should look like Figure 2-19. A new directory folder labeled MEMOS is now a subdirectory of A:\. The A:\ file folder now displays a minus sign to indicate that it has a subdirectory and that the subdirectory is displayed.

A:\ file folder displays minus sign

MEMOS subdirectory

Figure 2-19 The new subdirectory

TROUBLE? If you do not see the minus sign on the A:\ file folder, click Tree, then click Indicate Expandable branches.

Next Ruth will make a directory for the spreadsheets. She wants her directory tree to look like the one in Figure 2-20a, not the one in Figure 2-20b.

Figure 2-20a SHEETS is a subdirectory of A:\

Figure 2-20b SHEETS is a subdirectory of MEMOS

The spreadsheet directory should be a subdirectory of the root, *not* of MEMOS.

To make a directory for spreadsheets:
1. Click the **directory folder icon for A:**.
2. Click **File**, then click **Create Directory...**.
3. In the text box type **SHEETS**, then click the **OK button**.
4. Make sure that your newly updated directory tree resembles the one in Figure 2-20a. There should be two directories under A:\ — MEMOS and SHEETS.

   TROUBLE? If your directory tree is structured like the one in Figure 2-20b, use your mouse to drag the SHEETS directory icon to the A:\ file folder icon.

Now Ruth's disk has a structure she can use to organize her files. It contains three directories: the root A:\, MEMOS, and SHEETS. Each directory can contain a list of files. Ruth is happy with this new structure, but she is not sure what the directories contain. She decides to look in one of the new directories to see what's there.

Changing Directories

When you change directories, you open a different directory folder. If the directory contains files, they will be displayed in the contents list.

First, Ruth wants to look in the MEMOS directory.

To change to the MEMOS directory:
❶ Click the **MEMOS directory file folder icon**.

Notice that the A:\ file folder icon is closed and the MEMOS file folder icon is open, indicating that the MEMOS directory is now current.

Look at the status line at the bottom of your screen. The left side of the status line shows you how much space is left on your disk. The right side of the status line tells you that no files are in the current directory, that is, in the MEMOS directory. This makes sense. You just created the directory, and haven't put anything in it.

❷ Click the **A:\ file folder icon** to change back to the root directory.

Expanding and Collapsing Directories

Notice on your screen that the A:\ file folder icon has a minus sign on it. As you know, the minus sign indicates that A:\ has one or more subdirectories and that those subdirectories are displayed. To look at a simplified directory tree, you would **collapse** the A:\ directory. You would **expand** a directory to redisplay its subdirectories. Ruth wants to practice expanding and collapsing directories.

To expand and then collapse a directory:
❶ Double-click the **A:\ file folder icon** to collapse the directory. As a result the MEMOS and SHEETS branches of the directory tree are removed and a plus sign appears on the A:\ file folder icon.
❷ Double-click the **A:\ file folder icon** again. This time the directory expands, displaying the MEMOS and SHEETS branches. Notice the minus sign on the A:\ file folder icon.

The Contents List

The **contents list** on the right side of the desktop contains the list of files and subdirectories for the current directory. On your screen the directory tree shows that A:\ is the current directory. The status bar shows that this directory contains 26 files and subdirectories. These files are listed in the contents list. Ruth recalls that she had to follow a set of rules when she created the names for these files. Let's find out more about these rules, since you will soon need to create names for your own files.

Filenames and Extensions

A **filename** is a unique set of letters and numbers that identifies a program, document file, directory, or miscellaneous data file. A filename may be followed by an **extension**, which is separated from the filename by a period.

The rules for creating valid filenames are as follows:
- The filename can contain a maximum of eight characters.
- The extension cannot contain more than three characters.
- Use a period only between the filename and the extension.
- Neither the filename nor extension can include any spaces.
- Do not use the following characters: / [ ] ; = " \ : | ,
- Do not use the following names: AUX, COM1, COM2, COM3, COM4, CON, LPT1, LPT2, LPT3, PRN, or NUL.

Ruth used the letters ST at the beginning of her spreadsheet filenames so she could remember that these files contain information on project Stealth. Ruth used the rest of each filename to describe more about the file contents. For example, ST-BUD is the budget for project Stealth, ST-R&D is the research and development cost worksheet for the project, and ST-STATS contains the descriptive statistics for the project. Ruth's memos, on the other hand, begin with the initials of the person who received the memo. She used MEM as part of the filename for all her memos. For example, the file CJMEM.WRI contains a memo to Charles Jackson.

The file extension usually indicates the category of information a file contains. We can divide files into two broad categories, program files and data files. **Program files** contain the programming code for applications and systems software. For example, the computer program that makes your computer run the WordPerfect word processor would be classified as a program file. Program files are sometimes referred to as **executable files** because the computer executes, or performs, the instructions contained in the files. A common filename extension for this type of file is .EXE. Other extensions for program files include .BAT, .SYS, .PIF, and .COM. In the contents list, program files are shown with a **program file icon**, like the one you see next to the file PATTERNS.EXE on your screen and in Figure 2-21.

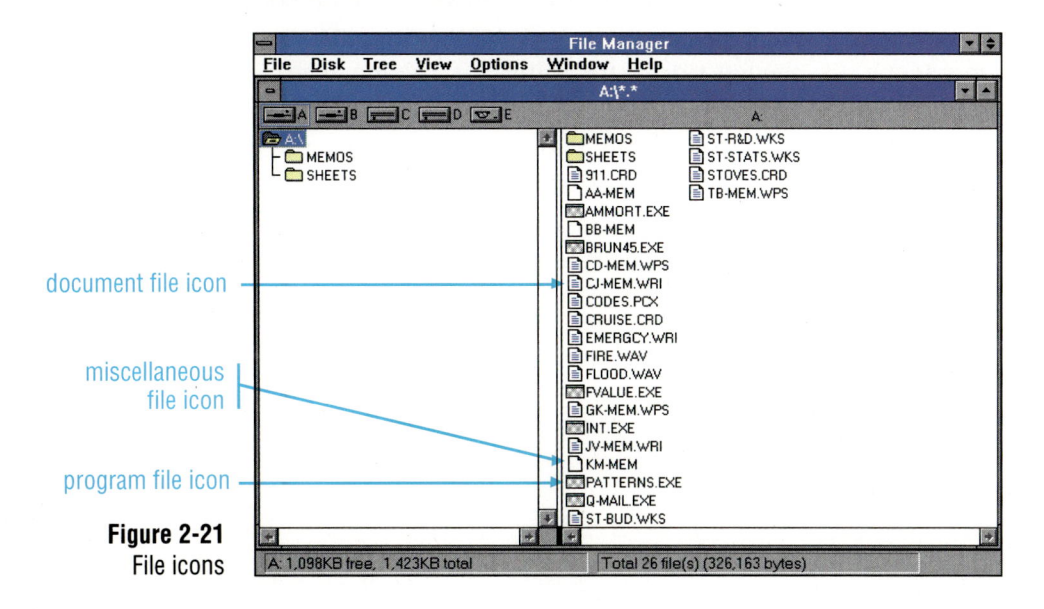

Figure 2-21 File icons

The second file category is data files. **Data files** contain the information with which you work: the memos, spreadsheets, reports, and graphs you create using applications such as word processors and spreadsheets. The filename extension for a data file usually indicates which application was used to create the file. For example, the file CD-MEM.WPS was created using the Microsoft Works word processor, which automatically puts the extension .WPS on any file you create with it. The use of .WPS as the standard extension for Works word processing documents creates an association between the application and the documents you create with it. Later, when you want to make modifications to your documents, Works can find them easily by looking for the .WPS extension.

Data files you create using a Windows application installed on your computer are shown in the contents list with a **document file icon** like the one you see next to CD-MEM.WPS on your screen. Data files you create using a non-Windows application or a Windows application that is not installed on your computer are shown in the contents list with a **miscellaneous file icon** like the one you see next to AA-MEM on your screen. AA-MEM was created using a non-Windows word processor.

Now that you have an idea of the contents for each of Ruth's files, you will be able to help her move them into the appropriate directory.

Moving Files

You can move files from one disk to another. You can also move files from one directory to another. When you move a file, the computer copies the file to its new location, then erases it from the original location. The File Manager lets you move files by dragging them on the screen or by using the File Manager menus.

Now that Ruth has created the MEMOS and SHEETS directories, the next step in organizing her disk is to put files in these directories. She begins by moving one of her memo files from the root directory A:\ to the MEMOS subdirectory. She decides to move JV-MEM.WRI first.

To move the file JV-MEM.WRI from A:\ to the MEMOS subdirectory:

❶ Position the pointer on the filename JV-MEM.WRI and click the mouse button to select it. On the left side of the status bar, the message "Selected 1 file(s) (1,408 bytes)" appears.

❷ Press the mouse button and hold it down while you drag the file icon to the MEMOS file folder in the directory tree.

❸ When the icon arrives at its target location, a box appears around the MEMOS file icon. Release the mouse button. Figure 2-22 on the following page illustrates this procedure.

Moving Files **WIN 53**

Figure 2-22
Moving a file

Step 3: release the mouse button when the destination is outlined with a rectangle

Step 2: hold the mouse button down while you drag the file outline to its new location

Step 1: position the pointer on the file you want to move

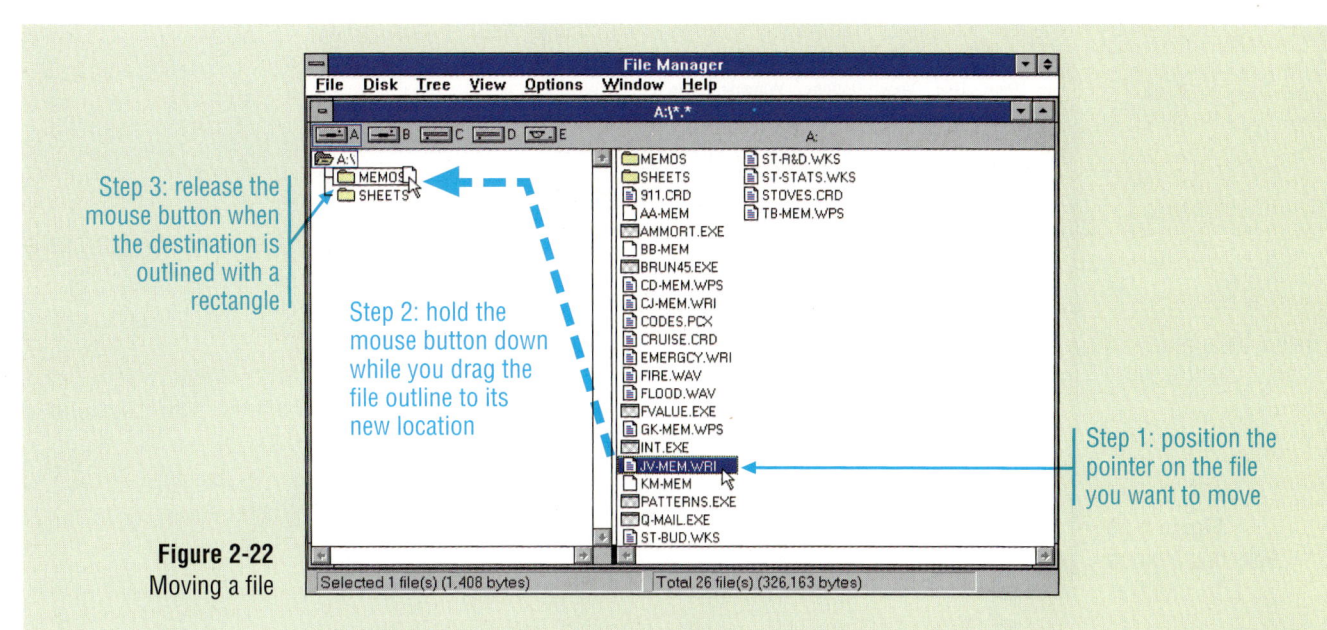

❹ Click the **Yes button** in response to the message "Are you sure you want to move the selected files or directories to A:\MEMOS?" A Moving... dialog box may flash briefly on your screen before the file is moved. Look at the contents list on the right side of the screen. The file JV-MEM.WRI is no longer there.

Ruth wants to confirm that the file was moved.

❺ Single click the **MEMOS file folder icon** in the directory tree on the left side of the screen. The file JV-MEM.WRI should be listed in the contents list on the right side of the screen.

   TROUBLE? If JV-MEM.WRI is not in the MEMOS subdirectory, you might have moved it inadvertently to the SHEETS directory. You can check this by clicking the SHEETS directory folder. If the file is in SHEETS, drag it to the MEMOS directory folder.

❻ Click the **A:\ file folder icon** to display the files in the root directory again.

Ruth sees that several memos are still in the root directory. She could move these memos one at a time to the MEMOS subdirectory, but she knows that it would be more efficient to move them as a group. To do this, she'll first select the files she wants to move. Then, she will drag them to the MEMOS directory.

To select a group of files:

❶ The directory A:\ should be selected on your screen and the files in this directory should be displayed in the right directory window. If this is not the case, click the directory icon for A:\.

❷ Click the filename **CD-MEM.WPS** to select it.

❸ Hold down [**Ctrl**] while you click the next filename you want to add to the group, **CJMEM.WRI**. Now two files should be selected. Ruth wants to select two more files.

❹ Hold down [**Ctrl**] while you click **GK-MEM.WPS**.

❺ Hold down [**Ctrl**] while you click **TB-MEM.WPS**. Release [**Ctrl**]. When you have finished selecting the files, your screen should look similar to Figure 2-23 on the following page. Notice the status bar message, "Selected 4 file(s) (4,590 bytes)."

WIN 54   TUTORIAL 2   Effective File Management

Figure 2-23
Selecting a group of files

status bar shows four files selected

hold down [Ctrl] as you click each file

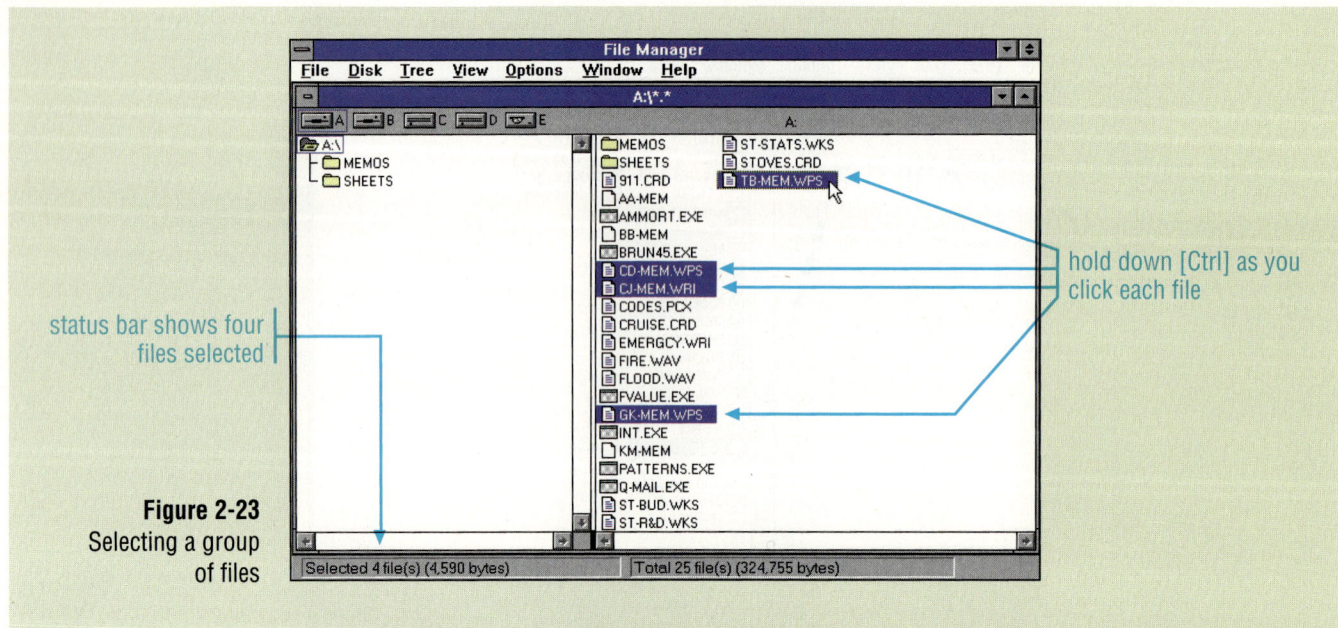

TROUBLE? If you click a file that you do not want to add to the group, hold down [Ctrl] and click that filename again. This will deselect that one file and remove the highlighting.

Now that Ruth has selected the files she wants to move, she can drag them to their new location.

To move a group of files:

❶ Position the pointer on any one of the highlighted filenames.

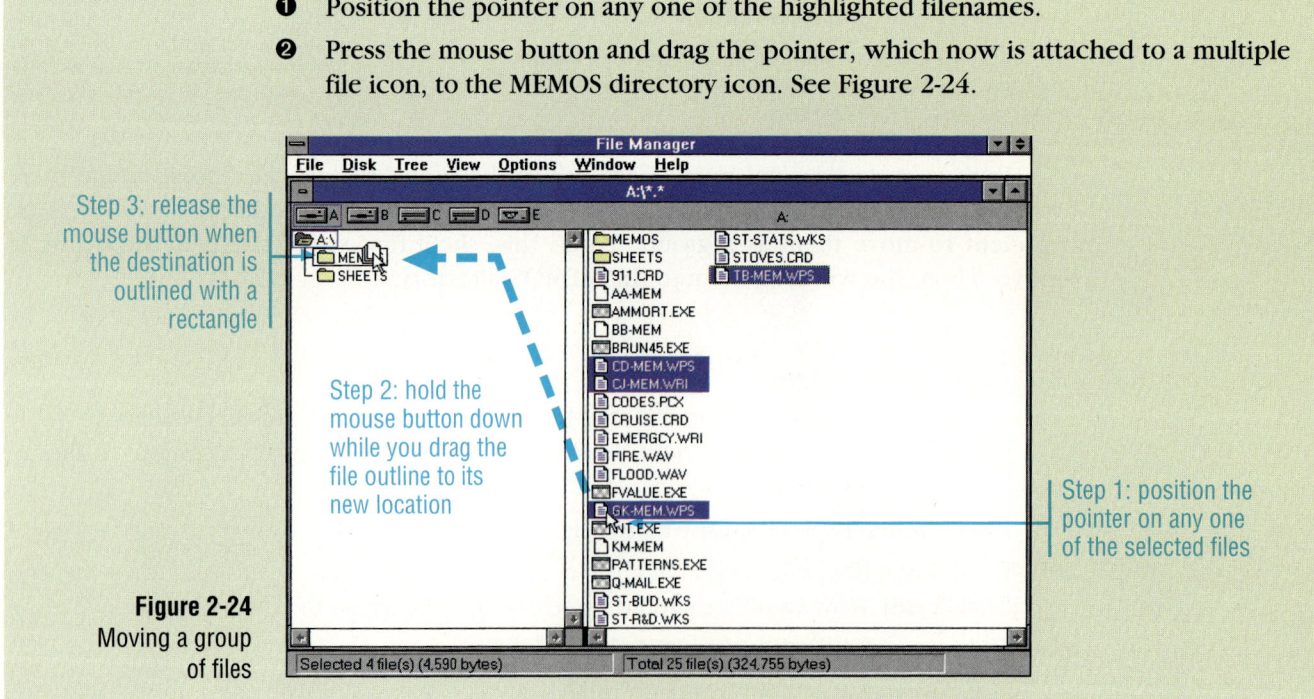

❷ Press the mouse button and drag the pointer, which now is attached to a multiple file icon, to the MEMOS directory icon. See Figure 2-24.

Figure 2-24
Moving a group of files

Step 3: release the mouse button when the destination is outlined with a rectangle

Step 2: hold the mouse button down while you drag the file outline to its new location

Step 1: position the pointer on any one of the selected files

❸ When the you move the file icon onto the MEMOS directory, a box will outline the directory icon. Release the mouse button. The Confirm Mouse Operation dialog box appears.

❹ Click the **Yes button** to confirm that you want to move the files. After a brief period of activity on your disk drive, the contents list for the A:\ directory is updated and should no longer include the files you moved.

❺ Click the **MEMOS directory icon** to verify that the group of files arrived in the MEMOS directory.

❻ Click the **A:\ directory icon** to once again display the contents of the root directory.

Renaming Files

You may find it useful to change the name of a file to make it more descriptive of the file contents. Remember that Windows uses file extensions to associate document files with applications and to identify executable programs, so when you rename a file you should not change the extension.

Ruth looks down the list of files and notices ST-BUD.WKS, which contains the 1994 budget for project Stealth. Ruth knows that next week she will begin work on the 1995 budget. She decides that while she is organizing her files, she will change the name of ST-BUD.WKS to ST-BUD94.WKS. When she creates the budget for 1995, she will call it ST-BUD95.WKS so it will be easy to distinguish between the two budget files.

To change the name of ST-BUD.WKS to ST-BUD94.WKS:
❶ Click the filename **ST-BUD.WKS**.
❷ Click **File**, then click **Rename**. See Figure 2-25. The Rename dialog box shows you the current directory and the name of the file you are going to rename. Verify that the dialog box on your screen indicates that the current directory is A:\ and that the file you are going to rename is ST-BUD.WKS.

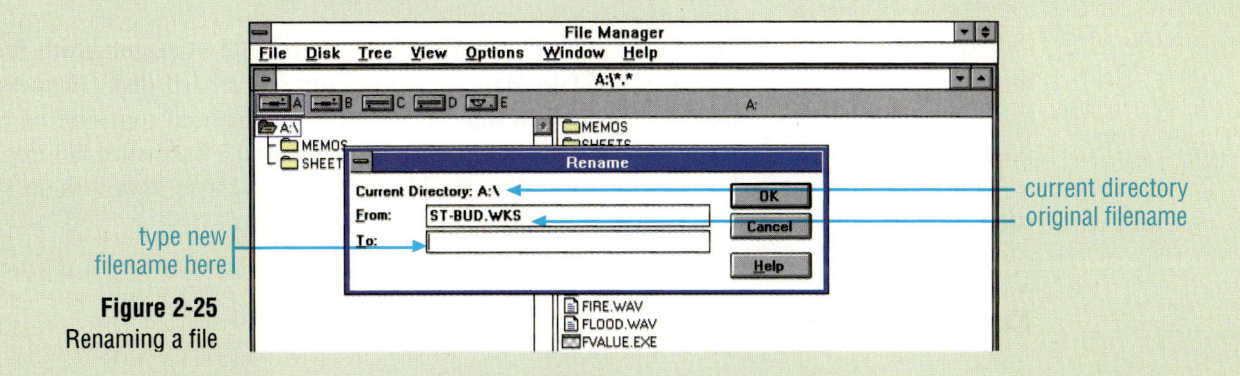

Figure 2-25
Renaming a file

TROUBLE? If the filename is not ST-BUD.WKS, click the Cancel button and go back to Step 1.

❸ In the To text box type **ST-BUD94.WKS** (using either uppercase or lowercase letters.
❹ Click the **OK button**.
❺ Check the file listing for ST-BUD94.WKS to verify that the rename procedure was successful.

Deleting Files

When you no longer need a file, it is good practice to delete it. Deleting a file frees up space on your disk and reduces the size of the directory listing you need to scroll through to find a file. A well-organized disk does not contain files you no longer need.

Ruth decides to delete the ST-STATS.WKS file. Although this file contains some statistics about the Stealth project, Ruth knows by looking at the file's date that those statistics are no longer current. She'll receive a new file from the Statistics department next week.

To delete the file ST-STATS.WKS:

❶ Click the filename **ST-STATS.WKS**.

❷ Click **File**, then click **Delete**. The Delete dialog box shows you that the file scheduled for deletion is in the A:\ directory and is called ST-STATS.WKS. See Figure 2-26.

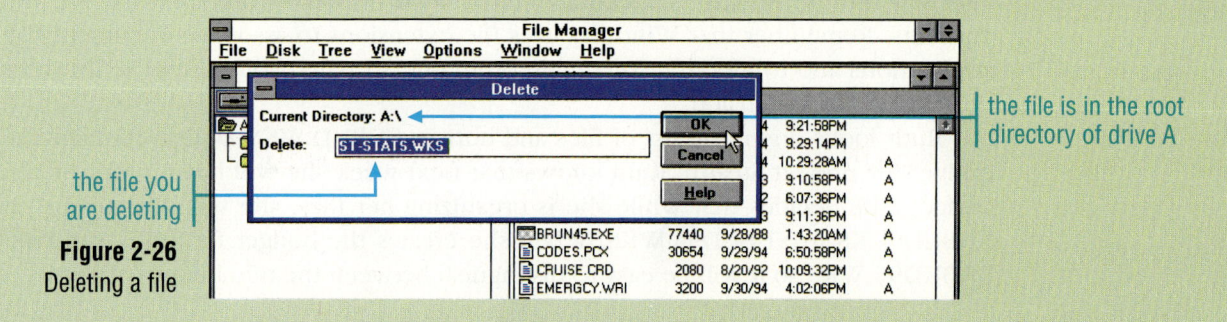

Figure 2-26
Deleting a file

- the file you are deleting
- the file is in the root directory of drive A

TROUBLE? If the filename ST-STATS.WKS is not displayed in the Delete dialog box, click the Cancel button and go back to Step 1.

❸ Click the **OK button**. The Confirm File Delete dialog box appears. This is your last chance to change your mind before the file is deleted.

❹ Click the **Yes button** to delete the file. Look at the contents list to verify that the file ST-STATS.WKS has been deleted.

After using a floppy disk in drive A to experiment with the File Manager, Ruth feels more confident that she can use the File Manager to organize her hard disk. However, she feels slightly uncomfortable about something else. Ruth just learned that one of her co-workers lost several days worth of work when his computer had a hardware failure.

Ruth resolves to find out more about the problems that can cause data loss so she can take appropriate steps to protect the data files on her computer.

Data Backup

Ruth's initial research on data loss reveals that there is no totally fail-safe method to protect data from hardware failures, human error, and natural disasters. She does discover, however, some ways to reduce the risk of losing data. Every article Ruth reads emphasizes the importance of regular backups.

A **backup** is a copy of one or more files, made in case the original files are destroyed or become unusable. Ruth learns that Windows provides a Copy command and a Copy Disk command that she can use for data backup. Ruth decides to find out how these commands work, so she refers to the *Microsoft Windows User's Guide* which came with the Microsoft Windows 3.1 software. She quickly discovers that the Copy and Copy Disk commands are in the Windows File Manager.

To prepare the File Manager for data backup:

❶ If you are returning from a break, launch Windows if it is not currently running. Be sure you see the Program Manager window.

❷ Relaunch the File Manager if necessary. Make sure your Student Disk is in drive A.

TROUBLE? If you want to use drive B instead of drive A, substitute "B" for "A" in any steps when drive A is specified.

❸ Click the File Manager **maximize button** if the File Manager is not already maximized.

❹ If necessary, click the **drive A icon** on the drive ribbon to make drive A the default drive.

❺ Click **View** and be sure that a check mark appears next to All File Details.

❻ Click **Window**, then click **Tile**. As a result, your desktop should look similar to Figure 2-27. Don't worry if your list of directories and files is different from the one shown in the figures.

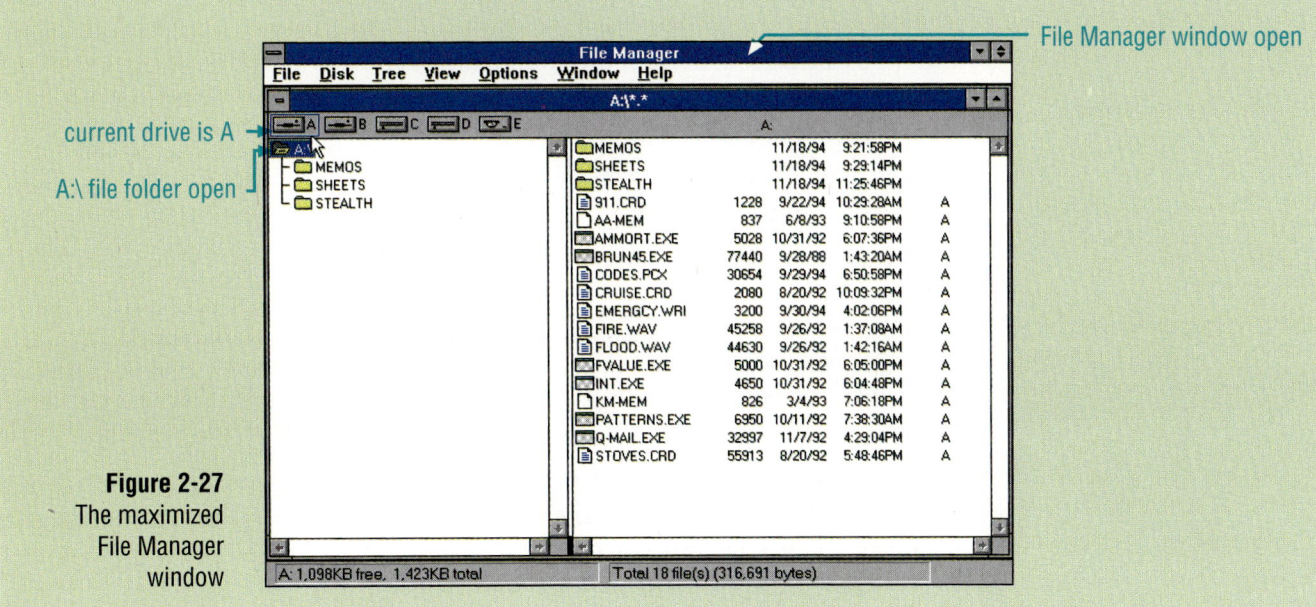

Figure 2-27
The maximized File Manager window

Now that Ruth has the File Manager window set-up, she decides to practice with the Copy command first.

The Copy Command

The Copy command duplicates a file in a new location. When the procedure has been completed, you have two files, your original and the copy. The additional copy of the file is useful for backup in case your original file develops a problem and becomes unusable.

The Copy command is different from the Move command, which you used earlier. The Move command deletes the file from its old location after moving it. When the move is completed, you have only one file.

If you understand the terminology associated with copying files, you will be able to achieve the results you want. The original location of a file is referred to as the **source**. The new location of the file is referred to as the **destination** or **target**.

You can copy one file or you can copy a group of files. In this Tutorial you will practice moving one file at a time. You can also copy files from one directory to another or from one disk to another. The disks you copy to and from do not need to be the same size. For backup purposes you would typically copy files from a hard disk to a disk.

Copying Files Using a Single Disk Drive

Ruth has been working on a spreadsheet called ST-BUD94.WKS for an entire week, and the data on this spreadsheet are critical for a presentation she is making tomorrow. The file is currently on a disk in drive A. Ruth will sleep much better tonight if she has an extra copy of this file. But Ruth has only one floppy disk drive. To make a copy of a file from one floppy disk to another, she must use her hard disk as a temporary storage location.

First, she will copy the file ST-BUD94.WKS to her hard disk. Then she will move the file to another floppy disk. Let's see how this procedure works.

To copy the file ST-BUD94.WKS from the source disk to the hard disk:

❶ Make sure your Student Disk is in drive A. Be sure you also have the backup disk you formatted earlier in the tutorial.

❷ Find the file ST-BUD94.WKS. It is in the root directory .

❸ Click the filename **ST-BUD94.WKS**.

❹ Click **File**, then click **Copy**.

TROUBLE? If you see a message that indicates you cannot copy a file to drive C, click the OK button. Your drive C has been write-protected, and you will not be able to copy ST-BUD94.WKS. Read through the copying procedure and resume doing the steps in the section entitled "Making a Disk Backup."

❺ Look at the ribbon of drive icons at the top of your screen. If you have an icon for drive C, type **C:** in the text box of the Copy dialog box. If you do not have an icon for drive C, ask your technical support person which drive you can use for a temporary destination in the file copy process, then type the drive letter.

❻ Confirm that the Copy dialog box settings are similar to those in Figure 2-28, then click the **OK button**. The file is copied to the root directory of drive C (or to the directory your technical support person told you to use).

Copying Files Using a Single Disk Drive **WIN 59**

name of the file you want to copy

the destination drive is C:

Figure 2-28
Copying
ST-BUD94.WKS
to drive C

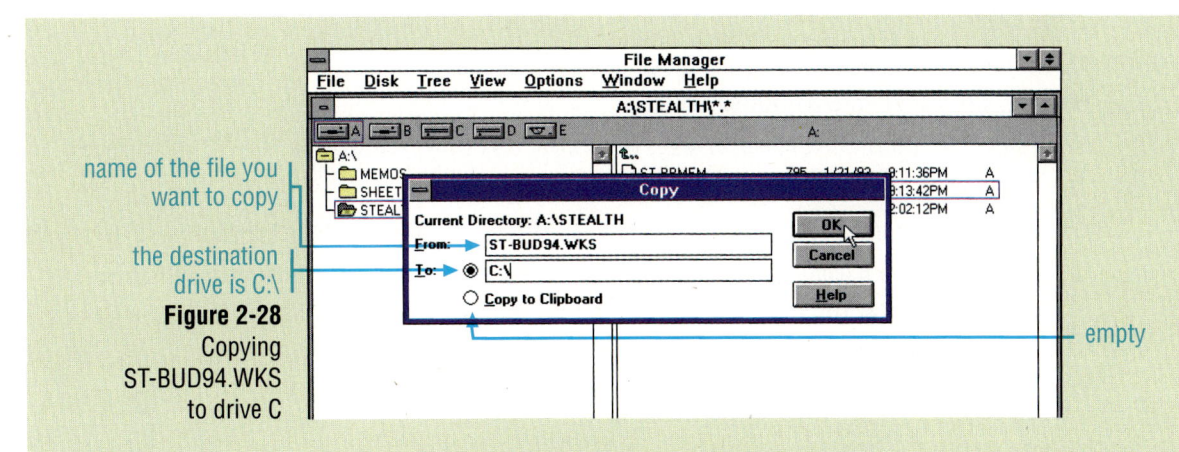

[File Manager dialog showing Copy window with Current Directory: A:\STEALTH, From: ST-BUD94.WKS, To: C:\, and OK, Cancel, Help buttons]

empty

> **TROUBLE?** If a dialog box appears and prompts you to verify that you want to replace the existing file, click the Yes button. This message appeared because another student left the ST-BUD94.WKS file on the hard disk.

After the file has been copied to the hard disk, Ruth needs to switch disks. She will take her original disk out of drive A and replace it with the disk that will receive the copy of the ST-BUD94.WKS file. After Ruth switches disks, she must tell the File Manager to **refresh** the directory tree and the contents list so they show the files and directories for the disk that is now in the drive.

> To switch disks and refresh the contents list:
>
> ❶ Remove your Student Disk from drive A.
>
> ❷ Put your Backup Disk in drive A.
>
> ❸ Click the **drive A icon** on the drive ribbon to refresh the contents list. The directory tree will contain only the A:\ folder, because your backup disk does not have the directories you created for your original Student Disk.

Now let's look for the copy of ST-BUD94.WKS that is on drive C.

> To locate the new copy of ST-BUD94.WKS:
>
> ❶ Click the **drive C icon** (or the drive your technical support person told you to use).
>
> ❷ Click the **C:\ file folder icon** (or the directory your technical support person told you to use).
>
> ❸ If necessary, use the scroll bar on the side of the content list to find the file ST-BUD94.WKS in the contents list.

Now you need to move the file from the hard disk to the backup disk in drive A. You must use Move instead of Copy so you don't leave the file on your hard disk.

To move the new file copy to drive A:

1. Click the filename **ST-BUD94.WKS**.
2. Click **File**, then click **Move**. (Don't use Copy this time.) A Move dialog box appears.
3. Type **A:** in the text box.
4. Click the **OK button**. As a result, ST-BUD94.WKS is moved to the disk in drive A.
5. Click the **drive A icon** on the drive ribbon to view the contents list for the Backup disk. Verify that the file ST-BUD94.WKS is listed.
6. Remove the Backup disk from drive A.
7. Insert the **Student Disk** in drive A and click the **drive A icon** in the drive ribbon to refresh the contents listing.

Now you and Ruth have completed the entire procedure for copying a file from one disk to another on a single floppy disk system. In her research, Ruth also has discovered a Windows command for copying an entire disk. She wants to practice this command next.

Making a Disk Backup

The Windows Copy Disk command makes an exact duplicate of an entire disk. All the files and all the blank sectors of the disk are copied. If you have files on your destination disk, the Copy Disk command will erase them as it makes the copy so that the destination disk will be an exact duplicate of the original disk.

When you use the Copy Disk command, both disks must have the same storage capacity. For example, if your original disk is a 3.5-inch high-density disk, your destination disk also must be 3.5-inch high-density disk. For this reason, you cannot use the Copy Disk command to copy an entire hard disk to a floppy disk. If your computer does not have two disk drives that are the same size and capacity, the Copy Disk command will work with only one disk drive. When you back up the contents of one disk to another disk using only one disk drive, files are copied from the source disk into the random access memory (RAM) of the computer.

RAM is a temporary storage area on your computer's mother board which usually holds data and instructions for the operating system, application programs, and documents you are using. After the files are copied into RAM, you remove the source disk and replace it with the destination disk. The files in RAM are then copied onto the destination disk. If you don't have enough RAM available to hold the entire contents of the disk, only a portion of the source disk contents are copied during the first stage of the process, and the computer must repeat the process for the remaining contents of the disk.

Ruth wants to practice using the Copy Disk command to make a backup of a disk. She is going to make the copy using only one disk drive because she can use this procedure on both her computer at home, which has one disk drive, and her computer at work, which has two different-sized disk drives.

While Ruth makes a copy of her disk, let's make a backup of your Student Disk. After you learn the procedure, you'll be responsible for making regular backups of the work you do for this course. You should back up your disks at least once a week. If you are working on a particularly critical project, such as a term paper or a thesis, you might want to make backups more often.

Making a Disk Backup **WIN 61**

To make a backup copy of your Student disk:

❶ Be sure your Student Disk is in drive A and that you have the disk you labeled Backup handy. If you want to be very safe, write-protect your source disk before continuing with this procedure. Remember, to write-protect a 5.25-inch disk, you place a tab over the write-protect notch. On a 3.5-inch disk you open the write-protect hole.

❷ Click **Disk**, then click **Copy Disk...**. Confirm that the Copy Disk dialog box on your screen looks like the one in Figure 2-29. The dialog box should indicate that "Source In" is A: and "Destination In" is A:. If this is not the case, click the appropriate down-arrow button and select A: from the list. When the dialog box display is correct, click the **OK button**.

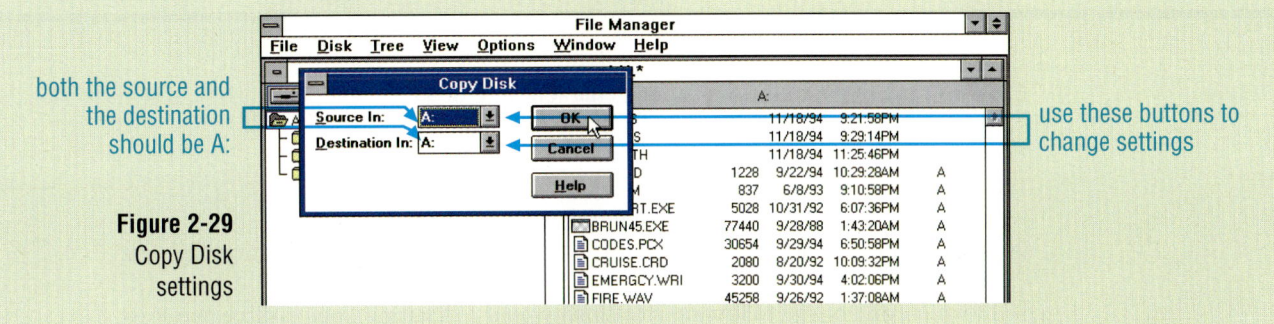

both the source and the destination should be A:

Figure 2-29 Copy Disk settings

use these buttons to change settings

❸ The Confirm Copy Disk dialog box reminds you that this operation will erase all data from the destination disk. It asks, "Are you sure you want to continue?"

❹ Click the **Yes button**. The next dialog box instructs you to "Insert source disk." Your source disk is the Student Disk and it is already in drive A.

❺ Click the **OK button**.

After a flurry of activity, the computer begins to copy the data from drive A into RAM. The Copying Disk dialog box keeps you posted on its progress.

❻ Eventually another message appears, telling you to "Insert destination disk." Take your Student Disk out of drive A and replace it with the disk you labeled Backup.

❼ Click the **OK button**. The computer copies the files from RAM to the destination disk.

Depending on how much internal memory your computer has, you might be prompted to switch disks twice more. Carefully follow the dialog box prompts, remembering that the *source* disk is your Student Disk and the *destination* disk is your Backup disk.

❽ When the Copy Disk operation is complete, the Copying Disk dialog box closes. If you write-protected your Student Disk in Step 1, you should unprotect it now; otherwise you won't be able to save data to the disk later.

As a result of the Copy Disk command, your Backup disk should be an exact duplicate of your Student Disk.

Ruth has completed her exploration of file management. Now, Ruth decides to finish for the day. If you are not going to proceed directly to the Tutorial Assignments, you should exit the File Manager.

> To exit the File Manager:
>
> ❶ Click the File Manager **Control-menu box**.
>
> ❷ Click **Close**.
>
> ❸ If you want to exit Windows, click the **Program Manager Control-menu box**, then click **Close**, and finally click the **OK button**.

Questions

1. Which one of the following is not a characteristic of a file?
   a. It has a name.
   b. It is a collection of data.
   c. It is the smallest unit of data.
   d. It is stored on a device such as a floppy disk or a hard disk.
2. What process arranges the magnetic particles on a disk in preparation for data storage?
3. In which one of the following situations would formatting your disk be the least desirable procedure?
   a. You have purchased a new disk.
   b. You have difficulty doing a spreadsheet assignment, and you want to start over again.
   c. You want to erase all the old files from a disk.
   d. You want to recycle an old disk that was used on a non-IBM-compatible computer.
4. If the label on your 3.5 inch diskette says HD, what is its capacity?
   a. 360K
   b. 720K
   c. 1.2MB
   d. 1.44MB
5. The disk drive that is indicated by a rectangle on the drive ribbon is called the _____ drive or the _____ drive.
6. Refer to the File Manager window in Figure 2-30 on the following page. What is the name of each numbered window component?

Figure 2-30

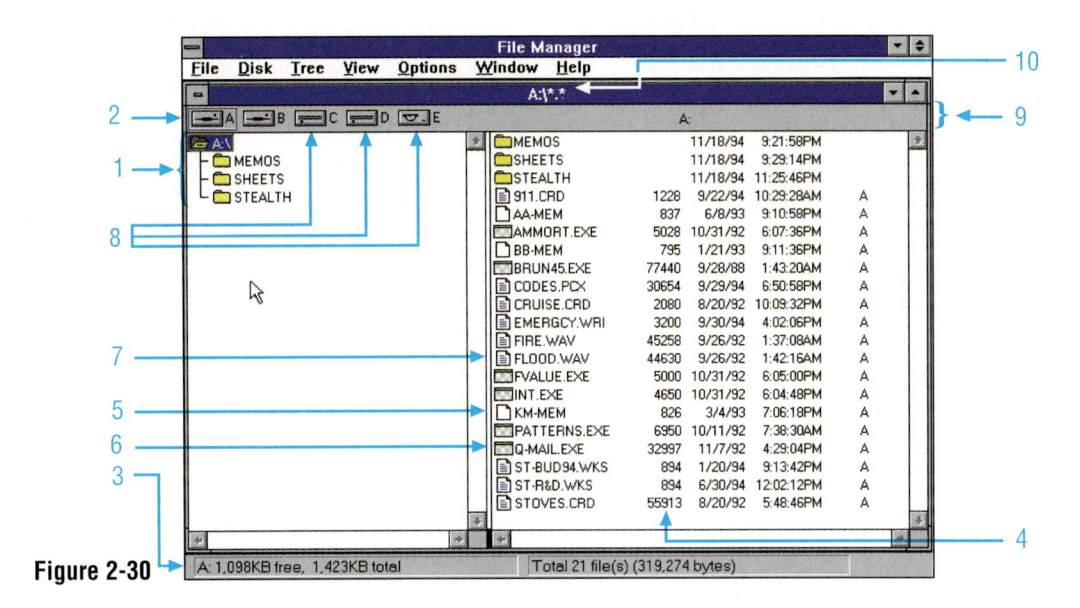

7. What is the directory that is automatically created when a disk is formatted?
8. What does a plus sign on a directory file folder icon indicate?
    a. The subdirectories are currently being displayed.
    b. The directory can be expanded.
    c. There are files in the directory.
    d. There are no subdirectories for this directory.
9. Indicate whether each of the following filenames is a valid or not valid Windows filename. If a filename is not valid, explain what is wrong.
    a. EOQ.WKS
    b. STATISTICS.WKS
    c. NUL.DOC
    d. VB-LET.DOC
    e. M
    f. M.M
    g. 92.BUD
    h. LET03/94
    i. CON.BMP
    d. Escape key

Tutorial Assignments

Launch Windows if necessary. Write your answers to Assignments 5, 6, 7, 8, 9, 11, 12, 13, and 14.
1. Move the two Microsoft Works spreadsheet files (.WKS extension) from the root directory to the SHEETS directory of your Student Disk.
2. You have a memo called BB-MEM that is about project Stealth. Now you need to change the filename to reflect the contents of the memo.
    a. Change the name to ST-BBMEM.
    b. Move ST-BBMEM into the MEMOS directory.
3. Create a directory called STEALTH under the root directory of your Student Disk. After you do this, your directory tree should look like Figure 2-30.
4. Now consolidate all the Stealth files.
    a. Move the file ST-BBMEM from the MEMOS directory to the STEALTH directory.

b. Move the files ST-BUD94.WKS and ST-R&D.WKS from the SHEETS directory to the STEALTH directory.
5. After doing Assignment 4, draw a diagram of your directory tree.
6. Make a list of the files that you now have in the MEMOS directory.
7. Make a list of the files that are in the SHEETS directory.
8. Make a list of the files that are in the STEALTH directory.
9. Describe what happens if you double-click the A:\ file folder icon.

E 10. Click to open the View menu and make sure the All File Details command has a check mark next to it.

E 11. Use the View menu to sort the files by date. What is the oldest file on your disk? (Be sure to look at all directories!)

E 12. Use the View menu to sort the files by type. Using this view, name the last file in your root directory contents list.

E 13. Use the View menu to sort the files by size. What is the name of the largest file on your Student Disk?

E 14. Change the current drive to C:, or, if you are on a network, to one of the network drives.
   a. Draw a diagram of the directory tree for this disk.
   b. List the filename of any files with .SYS, .COM, or .BAT extensions in the root directory of this disk.
   c. Look at the file icons in the contents list of the root directory. How many of the files are program files? Document files? Miscellaneous data files?
   d. Review the file organization tips that were in the article Ruth read. Write a short paragraph evaluating the organizational structure of your hard disk or network drive.

Windows Tutorials Index

A

Accessories icon, WIN 27
active directory, WIN 47
Alt key, WIN 22
application icon, WIN 15
applications
    filenames, WIN 52
    listing open, WIN 16
    switching, WIN 16-18
application window, WIN 12
    closing, WIN 14-15
    switching between, WIN 13

B

backup, WIN 56
Bold command, WIN 22, WIN 26
brush tool, WIN 28-29
buttons. *See* icons
byte, WIN 47

C

C:\, WIN 47
Cascade command, WIN 18
check box, WIN 24
check mark, WIN 20-21
child window, WIN 12. *See also* document window and window bar, WIN 13
Choose Picture command, WIN 21
Choose Slogan command, WIN 23-24
clicking, WIN 7
colon, WIN 47
colors, WIN 28
command buttons, WIN 24

commands, WIN 19
    availability, WIN 21
    grayed-out, WIN 21
computer, starting, WIN 4
contents list, WIN 47, WIN 50, WIN 59
Control menu, WIN 13
Copy command, WIN 56-60
Copy Disk command, WIN 56-57, WIN 60-61
copying files, WIN 56-60
Create Directory, WIN 48-49
CTI Win APPS, WIN 10-12
    system requirements, WIN 2
current directory, WIN 47

D

data files, WIN 52
    backup, WIN 56-57
Delete, WIN 56
desktop, WIN 3, WIN 5-6
destination, WIN 58, WIN 61
dialog box
    controls, WIN 24-26
directory, WIN 47-50
    changing, WIN 50
    collapsing, WIN 50
    creating, WIN 48-49
    expanding, WIN 50
    names, WIN 48
    tree, WIN 47-48, WIN 59
    window, WIN 46
disks
    backup, WIN 60-61
    capacities, WIN 42
    formatting, WIN 41-43
    naming, WIN 46-47

document window, WIN 12-13. *See also*
  child window
    organizing, WIN 18
double-clicking, WIN 8
dragging, WIN 9, WIN 52
drive icon, WIN 45
    ribbon, WIN 45
drives, WIN 45-46
    changing current, WIN 45-46

E

ellipsis (in menus), WIN 23-24
Enter key, WIN 25
.EXE, WIN 51. *See also* extensions
executable files, WIN 51
extensions, WIN 51-52, WIN 55

F

file folder icon, WIN 47
File Manager, WIN 37-41, WIN 57
    exiting, WIN 61-62
    moving files with, WIN 52-55
    settings, WIN 39-41
    window, WIN 46-47
filenames
    extensions, WIN 51-52
    invalid characters, WIN 51
files, WIN 38
    copying, WIN 56-60
    data, WIN 52
    deleting, WIN 56
    executable files, WIN 51
    listing, WIN 50
    moving, WIN 52-55
    moving a group, WIN 54-55
    naming, WIN 51
    organizing, WIN 48-50
    program, WIN 51
    renaming, WIN 55
    selecting a group, WIN 53-54
    transferring, WIN 43-44
Font, WIN 40-41
formatting, WIN 41-43

G

graphical user interface (GUI), WIN 3
group icons, WIN 6
GUI, see graphical user interface

H

Help facility, WIN 29-32
    Commands, WIN 31
    How To, WIN 31
    Tools, WIN 31
    tutorials, WIN 29

I

icons, WIN 6
    application, WIN 15
    group, WIN 6
insertion point, WIN 25
interface, WIN 3-4
Italic command, WIN 23, WIN 26

K

keyboard, WIN 9-11
    launching, WIN 9-12
    switching windows, WIN 17-18
    Tutorial, WIN 10
launching, WIN 4-5
linesize box, WIN 28
list box, WIN 24

M

maximizing windows, WIN 13-14
menu bar, WIN 13
Menu Practice program, WIN 19-26
menus, WIN 19-24
    and keyboard, WIN 22-23
    conventions, WIN 20-24
    opening and closing, WIN 20
minimizing windows, WIN 13, WIN 15
minus sign, WIN 48-49, WIN 50
mouse, WIN 6-9
    clicking, WIN 7
    double-clicking, WIN 8
    dragging, WIN 9
Move command, WIN 52-55, WIN 57
multi-tasking, WIN 4, WIN 12, WIN 18

O

OK button, WIN 25
option button, WIN 24
Options, WIN 40

P

Paintbrush, WIN 26-32
    help, 29-31
    launching, WIN 27
    tools, WIN 28-29
    window components, WIN 27-28
paint roller tool, WIN 29-32
palette, WIN 28
plus sign, WIN 48
pointer, WIN 6
    moving, WIN 7
    shapes, WIN 7, WIN 25, WIN 28
Position Picture command, WIN 21
program files, WIN 51
Program Manager, WIN 5-6

R

radio button. *See* option button
RAM (random access memory), WIN 60
Readme file, WIN 2
refresh, WIN 59
Rename, WIN 55
restore, WIN 13
root directory, WIN 47

S

selecting, WIN 7
shortcut keys, WIN 23
Show Picture command, WIN 20-21
source, WIN 58, WIN 61
spin bar, WIN 24
Student Disk
    preparing, WIN 2, WIN 43-44
subdirectory, WIN 47-48
    listing, WIN 50
    viewing, WIN 50
submenu, WIN 21

T

target, WIN 58
Task List, WIN 16
Text Attributes menu, WIN 22
text box, WIN 24
3-D effects, WIN 25
Tile command, WIN 18
title bar, WIN 13
toolbar, WIN 19
    description, WIN 26
toolbox, WIN 28
Tree, WIN 40

U

Underline command, WIN 22, WIN 26
underlined letter, WIN 22
Use Slogan, WIN 25

V

View, WIN 40
volume label, WIN 46-47

W

windows, WIN 6,
   active, WIN 13
   anatomy, WIN 12-13
   application, WIN 12
   child, WIN 12
   closing, WIN 18-19
   group, WIN 10
   resizing, WIN 13-16
Windows (Microsoft program)
   advantages, WIN 4
   basic controls, WIN 5-9
   exiting, WIN 33
   launching, WIN 4-5
   Users Guide, WIN 57
workspace, WIN 13
write protection, WIN 41

TASK REFERENCE
BRIEF MICROSOFT WINDOWS 3.1
Italicized page numbers indicate the first discussion of each task.

TASK	MOUSE	MENU	KEYBOARD
GENERAL / PROGRAM MANAGER			
Change dimensions of a window *WIN 15*	Drag border or corner	Click [■], Size	Alt spacebar, S
Click *WIN 7*	Press mouse button, then release it		
Close a window *WIN 18*	Double-click [■]	Click [■], Close	Alt spacebar, C or Alt F4
Double-click *WIN 8*	Click left mouse button twice		
Drag *WIN 9*	Hold left mouse button down while moving mouse		
Exit Windows *WIN 33*	Double-click Program Manager [■], click [OK]	Click Program Manager [■], Close, [OK]	Alt spacebar, C, Enter, or Alt F4, Enter
Help *WIN 30*		Click Help	F1 or Alt H
Launch Windows *WIN 4*			Type win and press Enter
Maximize a window *WIN 14*	Click [▲]	Click [■], Maximize	Alt spacebar, X
Minimize a window *WIN 14*	Click [▼]	Click [■], Minimize	Alt spacebar, N
Open a group window *WIN 10*	Double-click group icon	Click icon, click Restore	Ctrl F6 to group icon, Enter
Restore a window *WIN 14*	Click [⇅]	Click [■], Restore	Alt spacebar, R
Switch applications *WIN 16*		Click [■], Switch To...	Alt Tab or Ctrl Esc
Switch documents *WIN 28*	Click the document	Click Window, click name of document	Alt W, press number of document

TASK REFERENCE
BRIEF MICROSOFT WINDOWS 3.1
Italicized page numbers indicate the first discussion of each task.

TASK	MOUSE	MENU	KEYBOARD
FILE MANAGER			
Change current/default drive WIN 45	Click on drive icon ribbon	Click Disk, Select Drive...	Alt D, S or Ctrl [drive letter]
Change current/default directory WIN 50	Click		Press arrow key to directory
Collapse a directory WIN 50	Double-click	Click Tree, Collapse Branch	-
Copy a file WIN 58	Hold Ctrl down as you drag the file	Click the filename, click File, Copy	F8
Create a directory WIN 48		Click File, Create Directory	Alt F, E
Delete a file WIN 56		Click the filename, click File, Delete	Click the filename, press Del, Enter
Diskette copy/backup WIN 61		Click Disk, Copy Disk...	Alt D, C
Exit File Manager WIN 62	Double-click File Manager	Click, Close	Alt F4
Expand a directory WIN 50	Double-click	Click Tree, Expand Branch	*
Format a diskette WIN 41		Click Disk, Format Disk...	Alt D, F
Launch File Manager WIN 38	Double-click File Manager	Press arrow key to File Manager then click File, Open	Press arrow key to File Manager then press Enter
Make Student Diskette WIN 43	Double-click Make Win 3.1 Student Diskette	Press arrow key to Make Win 3.1 Student Diskette then click File, Open	Press arrow key to Make Win 3.1 Student Diskette then press Enter
Move a file WIN 52	Drag file to new directory	Click File, Move	F7
Rename a file WIN 55		Click File, Rename	Alt F, N
Select multiple files WIN 53	Hold Ctrl down and click filenames	Click File, Select Files...	Alt F, S

TASK REFERENCE
BRIEF MICROSOFT WINDOWS 3.1
Italicized page numbers indicate the first discussion of each task.

TASK	MOUSE	MENU	KEYBOARD
APPLICATIONS			
Exit application *WIN 33*	Double-click application ■	Click ■, **C**lose	`Alt` `F4`
Launch application *WIN 10*	Double-click application icon	Press arrow key to icon, click **F**ile, **O**pen	Press arrow key to icon, `Enter`